D1272412

12 POPULATION AND METROPOLIS

The Demography of London 1580–1650

CAMBRIDGE GEOGRAPHICAL STUDIES

Cambridge Geographical Studies is a series of monographs which presents new techniques of geographical analysis, publishes the results of new research work in all branches of the subject, and explores topics which unite disciplines that were formerly separate. In this way it helps to redefine the extent and concerns of geography. The series is of interdisciplinary interest to a wide range of natural and social scientists, as well as to planners.

POPULATION AND METROPOLIS

The Demography of London
1580–1650

ROGER FINLAY

Assistant Librarian
The John Rylands University Library of Manchester

CAMBRIDGE UNIVERSITY PRESS

CAMBRIDGE

LONDON   NEW YORK   NEW ROCHELLE

MELBOURNE   SYDNEY

Published by the Press Syndicate of the University of Cambridge
The Pitt Building, Trumpington Street, Cambridge CB2 1RP
32 East 57th Street, New York, NY 10022, USA
296 Beaconsfield Parade, Middle Park, Melbourne 3206, Australia

First published 1981

Printed in Great Britain at The Pitman Press, Bath

Library of Congress Cataloguing in Publication Data
Finlay, R. A. P.
Population and metropolis
(Cambridge geographical studies; 12)
Bibliography: p.
1. London–Population–History. I. Title.
II. Series.
HB3586.L6F56   301.32′9′421   78–20956
ISBN 0 521 22535 3

CONTENTS

TABLES

Tables

FIGURES

PREFACE

This is the first study of the population of London during the early modern period and it is also the first detailed book in English about the population of a European metropolitan city at this time. Villages have attracted a good deal of attention from historical demographers but very little is known about larger towns and cities. By the second half of the sixteenth century, London was firmly established as a metropolitan city. Reliable population estimates can first be made from around 1600, when the city numbered about 200,000 inhabitants, a figure which doubled during the first half of the seventeenth century. Because it contained more than 5 per cent of the population of England and was about twenty times the size of the largest provincial cities, London's importance is a recurring theme in the development of English society and economy. It is therefore difficult to study population trends in England without reference to the experience of London.

The analysis in this book is mainly concerned with the internal demography of London. It depends on the application of new techniques in historical demography, principally aggregative analysis and family reconstitution of parish registers, to the study of London population. It has always been thought the London parish registers are insufficiently reliable for this process because of the transient nature of London society and the ineffective compilation of parish registers in a metropolitan city. A good deal of the argument is therefore devoted to showing that claims such as these have been exaggerated, and that the London parish registers are worthy of serious study. The substantive results are concerned with establishing levels of fertility and mortality and with estimating the effect of the plague crises in sample parishes. These have been chosen from contrasting social areas to provide detailed estimates of demographic trends in London as a whole and to examine contrasts in population experience within the urban area. The results show that with high fertility, and very high mortality, population trends in a metropolitan city diverged sharply from the remainder of the country. There were also striking variations in demographic rates within the city.

Because of its size and the complexities of its social structure, a full study of the population of London cannot be undertaken within the compass of this book. It is hoped that this interpretation will point to some of the directions future research may take. Earlier versions of some of the arguments have been presented to seminars in the Universities of Cambridge, Lancaster, London and elsewhere, and have also appeared in journal articles listed in the references. I am grateful to the American National Council on Family Relations for permission to use copyright material here. Of course, I am fully responsible for the errors that remain.

Much of the research for this book was undertaken whilst I was a member of Peterhouse, Cambridge, and a preliminary version was awarded a Ph.D. by the University of Cambridge in 1977. I am very pleased to acknowledge the help of the SSRC Cambridge Group for the History of Population and Social Structure, especially from Mr P. Laslett and Dr R. S. Schofield. Dr Vivien Elliott, now of the University of Adelaide, South Australia, generously allowed me to use her unpublished thesis. I should particularly like to thank Professor E. A. Wrigley for excellent advice and encouragement at all stages of my research and for his continued interest over a number of years. Professor Emrys Jones of the London School of Economics was kind enough to send me the typescript of his article on the 1638 listing when it emerged that we were both working on the same material. My task in completing the typescript has been facilitated by several colleagues in the University of Lancaster. The Cambridge University Press has done much to improve the text. Most of all, I am very grateful to my parents for their support.

University of Lancaster   Roger Finlay
September 1980

xii

CHAPTER 1

INTRODUCTION: THE MAGNET OF THE METROPOLIS

The population history of London was the subject of the first major demographic treatise in English, John Graunt's *Natural and political observations and conclusions made upon the bills of mortality*, first published in 1662. Thus the London statistics have always been closely connected with the origins of historical demography in England. The bills of mortality consist of aggregate totals of baptisms and burials for the whole of London, compiled weekly from the individual Anglican parish registers by the Company of Parish Clerks to advise the city authorities of the onset of plague epidemics. The main series which now survives is of annual totals and these were used by Graunt. He explained that the object of his enquiry was:

to look out all the bills I could, . . . the which, when I had reduced into tables . . . so as to have a view of the whole together, in order to the more ready comparing of one year, season, parish, or other division of the city, with another, in respect of all the burials, and christenings, and of all the diseases, and casualties happening in each of them respectively.[1]

Graunt was a relatively ordinary London tradesman, and he tried in his book to convey his understanding of what was happening in his native city during the first half of the seventeenth century. The book was published only three years before the last plague epidemic, and so it appeared at the end of the period for which its conclusions were valid. However, it marked a new departure from the earlier commentators on London society such as John Stow and Thomas Dekker in that it was the first attempt at a statistical treatment of the subject; indeed, it was the first analysis of a statistical source. It was thus a pioneering book in the history of statistics, and influenced most of the classical demographers before the mid nineteenth century. The sources and methods of analysis adopted by Graunt formed the basis for many later advances in demography, in particular by Petty, King, Short and other leaders in political arithmetic.[2]

1. Graunt 1662: 2. Except where stated, all references to this work are to the facsimile of the first edition reprinted by Laslett 1973. The spelling and punctuation have been modernized in all the quotations.
2. Graunt's influence in early demography is discussed in Westergaard 1932: 25–43; Kuczynski 1938; Glass 1956; Glass 1973; and Cullen 1975: 1–8. It is interesting how the titles of books by the early demographers, and the subjects they considered, retain some similarity to Graunt's work. These include Petty, King, Short and Heberden as well as several contributors to the eighteenth-century population controversy.

1

Later writers on London population during the early modern period have used the bills of mortality; some of them have also used the work of their predecessors and reached many of the same conclusions.[3] It is therefore sensible to begin a study of the population of late Tudor and early Stuart London with a consideration of Graunt's interpretation.

Compared with other scientific pioneers of the seventeenth century, very little is known of Graunt's life.[4] Unlike many of the early Fellows of the Royal Society, Graunt was a Londoner and a working tradesman rather than a member of the 'Oxford Circle' or the 'Invisible College'. All Graunt shared with scientists such as Harvey and Wilkins was a commitment to the puritan cause and a desire to apply scientific methods to the study of human phenomena, but to social data rather than to medical research. In many ways, his life was very similar to that of the Londoners about whom he wrote. He was baptized on 24 April 1620 in the Parish of St Michael Cornhill, and apprenticed to his father Henry Graunt, described as a haberdasher of small wares. He was later admitted to the freedom of the Drapers' Company by patrimony. He must have become an important tradesman, for by 1671 he had risen to become Warden of the Drapers' Company. He also held office in local government, becoming a member of the Common Council of the City. During the Civil War, he was a leading puritan, and a captain in the militia. Graunt was married by licence in 1641, at the age of twenty, in the church of St Martin Ludgate, to Mary Stott, then aged seventeen, living in St Botolph Bishopsgate but from an Essex family.[5] The couple may have had four children, but their baptisms and subsequent careers have not been fully traced. Graunt was very friendly with that other scholar of demography and political arithmetic, Sir William Petty, but it is not known how they met. It has in fact been argued that Petty was the real author of the *Observations*, but modern opinion is against this viewpoint. After the Great Fire of 1666, Graunt found himself in financial difficulties, a situation not eased by his conversion to Roman Catholicism. He died on 18 April 1674 and was buried in the parish of St Dunstan in the West.

One of the main reasons that Graunt decided to investigate the bills of mortality with some precision was his wish to understand why so much social and economic dislocation was caused by high mortality, and especially the plague crises, in as important a city as London, which was among the most prosperous in the pre-industrial world. He thought that London was

3. See, for example, Creighton 1891a; George 1965; and Sutherland 1972.
4. The best accounts of Graunt's life and work are Glass 1963 and Sutherland 1963. The summary here is based on these two sources. Other useful accounts of Graunt's importance in early statistics and demography include: Bonar 1931: 67–105; Westergaard 1932: 16–25; Willcox 1940: 455–66; Greenwood 1948: 1–39; and Cullen 1975: 1–8.
5. Londoners often married at a young age, and in parishes in which neither partner was resident.

too large, 'a head too big for the body, and possibly too strong',[6] and 'that the troublesome seclusions in the plague time is not a remedy to be purchased at great inconveniences'.[7] At this time, London's importance was reflected both in its size and extent and also in its range of services and trading connections. Graunt attempted to calculate the number of London inhabitants, and at one point estimated a population of 384,000 (1662: 59–61), but elsewhere he gives 460,000 (*ibid.*: 42). The latter is a more accurate figure for the early 1660s, and the large discrepancy may be accounted for by different areas of the city being examined for each estimate. It is surprising that Graunt came so close to the modern estimates of the population of London.

Graunt understood one of the central points about London population trends which was that the city was increasing in population size at a faster rate than the remainder of the country (*ibid.*: 53–6), and that it 'grows three times as fast as the body unto which it belongs'.[8] He also calculated that the number of burials recorded in the bills of mortality was greater than the number of christenings, suggesting that the population would actually have fallen but for migration from the countryside, which accounted for all the growth that occurred.

The next observation is, that in the said bills there are far more burials than christenings. This is plain, depending only upon arithmetical computation; for in 40 years, from the year 1603, to the year 1644, exclusive of both years, there have been set down (as happening within the same ground, space, or parishes) although differently numbered, and divided, 363,935 burials, and but 330,747 christenings within the 97, 16 and 10 out-parishes, those of Westminster, Lambeth, Newington, Redriff [Rotherhithe], Stepney, Hackney, and Islington, not being included.

From this single observation it will follow, that London hath decreased in its people, the contrary thereof we see by its daily increase of building upon new foundations, and by the turning of great palacious houses into small tenements. It is therefore certain, that London is supplied with people from out of the country, whereby not only to repair the overplus difference of burials above mentioned, but likewise to increase its inhabitants according to the said increase of housing.[9]

Graunt estimated the extent to which London was dependent upon the countryside for migrants. He suggested that 'if about 250,000 be sent up to London in the said 40 years, Viz. about 6,000 per annum, the said

6. Graunt, *Observations on the bills of mortality*, Epistle Dedicatory to Lord Roberts.
7. *Ibid.*
8. *Ibid.*, Epistle Dedicatory to Lord Roberts.
9. *Ibid.*: 41–2. Using the figures in Appendix 1, there were 437,495 burials and 329,867 christenings in London during the period mentioned by Graunt. Of the burials, 73,119 were attributed to plague in the bills. Other causes therefore accounted for 364,376 burials, giving figures which are very close to Graunt's.

admission will make good the alterations, which we find to have been in and about London, between the years 1603 and 1644 above mentioned.[10]

As well as outlining the main features of London population trends, Graunt also examined patterns of fertility and mortality in greater detail. He discussed causes of death in an elementary way (1662: 15–32), and he analysed the severity of the main plague years by calculating the extent to which the number of burials exceeded the number of christenings. Thus, he argued that the intensities of the 1603 and 1625 crises were of about equal magnitude, although he felt that in 1625 more died than were recorded as having done so (*ibid.*: 35–6). In optimistic fashion, he calculated that these plague outbreaks did not have much effect on London population growth, despite their severity. 'Let the mortality be what it will', he argued, 'the city repairs its loss of inhabitants within two years' (*ibid.*: 39). Graunt also devised the idea of the life table which is of fundamental importance in demographic analysis.

Graunt's analysis of fertility was not as sophisticated as his studies of mortality, partly because less information was available to him in the bills of mortality. Other sources are required to study the London marriage pattern and household structures. All that the bills contain are lists of the total number of christenings in each year, so that it is very difficult to analyse strategies of family formation. Graunt's conclusions about London fertility were ambiguous and he partly misread the evidence, although in one place he suggested that 'the number of child-bearing women might be about double to the births; forasmuch as such women, one with another, have scarce more than one child in two years' (*ibid.*: 60). This was probably about right with respect to marital fertility, for it implies mean birth intervals of about twenty-four months. However, the main conclusion of Graunt's discussion about London fertility was that it was lower in London than in the countryside, a mistake duplicated by most of the classical demographers.

As to the cause of barrenness in London, I say, that although there should be none extraordinary in the native air of the place, yet the intemperance in feeding, and especially the adulteries and fornications, supposed more frequent in London than elsewhere, do certainly hinder breeding. For a woman admitting ten men, is so far from having ten times as many children, that she hath none at all.

Add to this, that the minds of men in London are more thoughtful and full of business than in the country, where their work is corporal labour, and exercises. All which promote breedings, whereas anxieties of the mind hinder it.[11]

10. Graunt 1662: 43. According to Appendix 1, the deficit of baptisms from 1604 to 1643 was about 108,000. During this period, the population grew from 178,000 to 307,000, or by 129,000 individuals. Therefore, a net total of 237,000 migrants was required over these forty years, an average of 5,925 per year, to account for the growth of London, which is very close to Graunt's calculations.
11. Graunt 1662: 46. Graunt's conflicting views on London fertility are mentioned by Kuczynski 1938.

Although Graunt's analysis of the causes of low fertility in London is not very convincing, he should at least be credited with drawing the distinction between rural and urban demographic experience. In fact, marital fertility was probably higher in London than elsewhere, but rates of non-marital fertility were low and similar to other places. Overall fertility may have been more moderate because of late marriage, a point which the bills of mortality did not permit Graunt to consider.

The clarity of Graunt's study of population trends in London obscures the complex social geography of the metropolis on the eve of the Great Fire which destroyed large portions of the city, and this is why many contemporaries did not fully understand the social and economic developments occurring in the capital during the seventeenth century. The physical appearance of the townscape just before the Fire did not differ greatly from that at the beginning of the century, except that the area it covered had increased considerably, as is shown in Figure 3.4, and even the broad outlines of its social pattern were not greatly altered by the rebuilding. London remained a walled city, with narrow streets, many churches, and timber-framed houses, although a few were constructed of brick and stone. It was much overcrowded, especially in the suburban tenements and in the lanes and alleyways immediately behind the substantial houses of the main streets.

During the seventeenth century, the metropolis was in a state of transition due to its rapidly growing population even though, as Graunt observed, its principal demographic features did not alter very greatly during his lifetime. In 1660, the chief contrast was between the wealthy central city and its peripheral suburbs and this had persisted throughout the period. However, much of the physical growth of the city was occurring westwards, as the dual centres of London and Westminster were merged by building developments. Other suburban nuclei in the East End and in Southwark, across the river, were also much enlarged.

This book will concentrate on the demography of the city itself although the growth of population in the suburbs deserves a full analysis. The chief aim of this brief description of Graunt's work and background has been to indicate what may have been known to him and his contemporaries about the population of seventeenth-century London. As we have seen, Graunt's sources and methods, and many of his conclusions, were adopted by later writers. This book will discuss how far new sources and methods of analysis confirm Graunt's viewpoint, and it will cover new topics which cannot be studied from the bills of mortality. An examination of the internal demography of London will show how the population of an early modern metropolitan city differed from that of the country areas of England. The demographic structure of London will be investigated by detailed studies of fertility and mortality.

There are three main reasons why a re-examination of London population trends in the seventeenth century is important: the size of the capital, the significance of its connections with the remainder of the country, and the discovery of new sources and methods of analysis. However large London had become by the beginning of the seventeenth century, Graunt's view that it was too large was the opinion of both the authorities and also of many inhabitants. From as early as 1580 the Crown and the city government had tried, but largely failed, to regulate the size of the city. They were concerned both with the difficulties of feeding its expanded population and with the threat to public order such a concentration of people could make. One of the main problems was that the city's jurisdiction did not spread into the Liberties and suburbs, in whose large parishes problems of local government were most severe (Brett-James 1935: 67–126, 296–308; Pearl 1961: 9–44). The widespread concern about the size of London is indicated by the nine separate proclamations issued by James I between 1605 and 1624 in attempts to regulate it.[12] The proclamation dated 16 July 1615 commented that:

Our city of London is become the greatest or next the greatest cities of the Christian world. It is more than time that there be an utter cessation of further new buildings, lest the surcharge and overflow of people do bring upon our said city infinite inconveniences, which have been so often mentioned.[13]

However, the repetition of these proclamations throughout James I's reign indicates that neither the Crown nor the city were able to stop the flow of migrants to London.

Several problems are involved in estimating the actual size of London during this period. There are no listings of inhabitants for the whole city, so calculations have to be made from the series of christenings in the bills of mortality, after having made an allowance for possible omissions and having found a suitable birth rate. At present, the best estimates suggest that the population increased from just over 100,000 in 1580 to about 200,000 in 1600 and 400,000 by 1650. These figures are a little lower than earlier calculations, but they suggest that this was the period when the rate of demographic growth was highest. Although much depends on what area of London is included, and whilst these estimates could be refined in the light of further research, they provide a good idea of the size of London's population at this time. Indeed, the problem of making estimates illustrates how little work has been undertaken in urban population history: a good deal is now becoming known about the historical demography of rural areas, but very little is understood about the towns.[14] Table 1.1 demonstrates the usefulness of a study of the proportion of the population

12. These are printed in Larkin and Hughes 1973: 111–12, 171–5, 193–5, 267–9, 345–7, 398–400, 485–8, 597–8.
13. 'A proclamation for buildings', 16 July 1615, in Larkin and Hughes 1973: 345–6.
14. Good surveys of recent findings include Schofield and Wrigley 1979; and Smith 1978.

Table 1.1. *Estimates of the population of England by urban and rural residence, 1600–1700*

	1600			1700		
	No. of centres	Approx. pop.	% of total pop.	No. of centres	Approx. pop.	% of total pop.
Metropolitan London	1	200,000	4.9	1	575,000	10.4
Other centres of 10,000+	3	35,000	0.9	6	103,000	1.9
Other centres of 5,000+	14	88,000	2.1	24	165,000	3.0
Total urban population	18	323,000	7.9	31	843,000	15.3
Total population of England		4,100,000			5,500,000	

Sources: Corfield 1970: 40 table 1, 42 table 2; 1976; Smith 1978: 207 figure 8.3.

of England that inhabited urban centres of over 5,000 inhabitants. Towns of less than this size are excluded because many were hardly distinguishable from villages. The populations of these larger urban centres have been estimated from a variety of studies of their local histories, and so the totals given here are approximate, but they are sufficiently accurate to allow conclusions about the importance of London to be drawn. The urban population of England was quite small in 1600, accounting for only 8 per cent of the national total, but this proportion almost doubled during the seventeenth century as English society became more urbanized. However, more than half the urban population lived in London, and by 1700, London was more than twice the size of all the other urban centres combined. Thus, during the seventeenth century, London was growing much faster than the country as a whole and also faster than the other urban centres. In 1600, one Englishman in twenty was a Londoner, and by 1700 one in ten.

London was thus of great importance in English society and economy, not only because such a high proportion of the total population lived in the metropolis, but also because the high mortality rate meant that the population of London was unable to replace itself. This was argued very clearly by J. Patten (1978: 125):

The consistent picture was, however, that burials exceeded baptisms in every English town in the pre-industrial period. A few places by 1700 may have been able to replace themselves, but for most this was not the case; they were experiencing natural decrease. Yet . . . they grew, London enormously, some others quite quickly, and migration is clearly the key to an explanation of their growth.[15]

15. Also see Patten 1978: 17, 98, 236.

London was certainly able to attract migrants during the seventeenth century; indeed, people travelled to the capital from all over the country during the period before the Civil War. This was partly related to national demographic trends; according to the most recent estimates, the national population increased from 3 million in 1550 to 5½ million by 1650. During the succeeding century, the rate of growth slowed considerably and the total reached 6 million by 1750, after a period of temporary decline in the second half of the seventeenth century.[16] Much of the history of pre-industrial England may be explained in terms of how the economy adapted itself to absorb increasing numbers, and through its own demand for goods London played a large part in improving the economy.

The internal demography of cities must be looked at in the context of the whole country. Urban death rates consistently exceeded birth rates, and in large metropolitan cities the death rate was very high compared with other areas. The greatest of the nineteenth-century English demographers, William Farr, was correct in believing that mortality rates were closely related to settlement size. He commented that 'the mortality of districts is nearly as the 12th root of their densities' (1885: 175). Even in small towns such as Banbury and Gainsborough, infant and child mortality rates were noticeably greater than in villages (Smith 1978: 210–11 table 8.3). The close residential proximity of urban inhabitants allowed diseases to spread relatively easily within the city, and high mortality was not completely offset by high fertility. In contrast, the birth rate was usually greater than the death rate in many country districts; rural populations were therefore growing. Thus the rate of natural increase was frequently positive in the countryside and negative in the cities. Migration to cities was the equilibrating mechanism which balanced the rural surplus with the urban deficit. The whole of the growth of population which occurred in metropolitan cities was due to migration from the countryside. The demographic history of many European towns follows this pattern (Hélin 1963; Deyon 1967; Bennassar 1969; Perrot 1970; Soliday 1974; Petraconne 1974; De Vries 1974; François 1975).

Cities affected the growth of national populations in three important ways. First, the rate of natural decrease in a city determined how many migrants were required to maintain its population. Secondly, and of equal significance, disregarding overseas migration, the proportion of the national population that was urbanized gives an indication of how much of the surplus population in the countryside could be absorbed by the towns. Thirdly, the relative gap in economic performance between town and countryside influenced the number of migrants from rural to urban areas. Thus, an expanding urban economy attracted migrants, and several

16. These estimates were made at the S.S.R.C. Cambridge Group for the History of Population and Social Structure and are reported by Smith 1978: 207 fig. 8.3.

successive poor years in the countryside encouraged people to travel great distances to seek work in towns.

London's influence may be outlined as follows. It may be assumed that the death rate exceeded the birth rate by 10 per thousand in the city, whilst the birth rate was greater than the death rate by 5 per thousand in the remainder of the country, and the birth rate was 34 per thousand in town and country. Recurrent plague crises during the period suggest that the differences in vital rates may not be unrealistic for the purposes of these estimates; the actual levels of vital rates do not matter too much, for the connections between city and countryside were important whether 2,000 or 12,000 net migrants travelled to London each year. The population of the capital increased from about 70,000 to about 400,000 between 1550 and 1650, or by 3,300 inhabitants per year on average. When the population was 250,000, for example, the shortfall of births each year was 2,500, so that a net annual immigration of around 6,000 persons was required to maintain London's growth. If these were survivors from a cohort half as large again at birth, then 9,000 births were necessary each year for London's increase in population to be continued. The population of England in 1600 was about 4 million, so the total birth surplus would be 20,000 (the birth rate exceeds the death rate by 5 per thousand). London was therefore absorbing the natural increase of a population of almost 2 million, or about half the English national population. Similarly, if 200,000 people lived in London, and 4 million in England, and the birth rate was 34 per thousand throughout the country, then 6,800 births occurred each year in London and 136,000 in the rest of England. From the calculations above, 9,000 births were necessary to maintain London's rate of growth, and there were 6,800 new births in the capital each year making a total of 16,000 births. Therefore, the survivors of about an eighth of the country's births eventually became Londoners at some stage of their lives. London's impact deepened still further during the century after 1650; Wrigley (1967) has shown from similar calculations, on which these are based, that the survivors of a sixth of all English births were destined to become Londoners.[17]

17. Recent work on the demography of Holland demonstrates even more clearly the importance of cities for population trends in the whole country. Over half the population was urbanized. One of the reasons for the failure of numbers to increase in the eighteenth century was that the growth of population in the countryside was completely absorbed by the deficit in the cities. Declining population in the early eighteenth century was connected with a decrease in economic activity, but the importance of Amsterdam itself was enhanced as the 'Randstad' system of cities was dissolved into city-regions based on Amsterdam and Rotterdam. See De Vries 1974 and 1978. A recent article by A. Sharlin has questioned the interpretation that metropolitan cities would have declined in population in the absence of rural-urban migration. He argued that most cities consisted of two kinds of people: permanent residents and temporary migrants. The permanent residents replaced themselves whilst the temporary migrants did not so that aggregate series of births and deaths which show a natural deficit obscure the fact that some groups

It ought perhaps to be stressed that the reasons for London's growth are not just to be found within the context of its demographic experience, because population trends both affected and were influenced by the associated societal changes which occurred in London during the period preceding the revolutionary years of the mid seventeenth century. The general importance of London for the political events of the period is now well recognized,[18] but London's role in the national economy and society, around which the political significance of the capital hinged, is neither well researched nor fully understood. This is clearly not the place for a full examination of the complex changes associated with the transformation of London from an important, but compact, medieval city to a sprawling metropolis which essentially took place during the period covered in this book, but it should be evident that migration, which ensured the continued pre-eminence of London, occurred in the context of social and economic changes.

A central point to bear in mind is that the growth of London was completely uncontrolled and the authorities were unable to regulate the size of the capital. It is therefore important to consider why so many migrants travelled to London, often from long distances, rather than to other cities which must have been much closer. London was growing at the expense of the main provincial capitals and other centres. As we saw in Table 1.1, the population of London almost trebled during the course of the seventeenth century whereas the other cities only doubled in size. Another important question is why London's rate of increase quickened during the third quarter of the sixteenth century. Given that the changes were unplanned, they must have operated through the market mechanism which connected the urban economy's demand for labour with migration patterns. The links between population and the economy therefore flowed in both directions, with a natural deficit creating a need for migrants to maintain the size of the city, and a flourishing metropolitan economy encouraging new migrants from the remainder of the country. It should be added that the enhanced importance of London was facilitated by a number of institutional changes. A good deal of weight has been attributed to the dissolution of the monasteries as a cause for change because they provided land within the city on which part of the expansion occurred

---

in the population did not rely on migrants. However, life table death rates demonstrate that in London natives were unable to replace themselves, as is reported in Chapter 5. This was also true of Geneva in the seventeenth century. Nevertheless, what Sharlin argued is at least partly true as the experience of natives and migrants differed in cities, and natives came closer to replacing themselves than migrants. In London, the migrants were more susceptible to plague, and they also married later which is indicative of lower fertility. Sharlin 1978.

18. This is explained in Pearl 1961; Brenner 1973; Ashton 1979.

(Davis 1924; Pearl 1961: 10–11), but this was only one of several new developments. Economic changes were facilitated by the guilds as the 'custom of London' conferred the right to exercise any trade, not just that from which a particular company took its name. The legal profession was expanding, as indicated by the growing number of recruits to the Inns of Court. The level of education, measured by the extent of illiteracy, was much higher in London than elsewhere, which also encouraged the free expression of religious and political beliefs.[19]

During the sixteenth and seventeenth centuries, the English space-economy was gradually restructured to enable it to adapt to the secular rise in population from the early Tudor period. Such institutional changes were essential to increase the efficiency of a relatively poor economy to enable the additional people to be fed and employed. When it is realized that many of the changes occurred in London earlier than elsewhere, and that the national economy was increasingly centred on London, the capital's insatiable demand for migrants and its growing numerical importance from the later Tudor period may be appreciated. Although London, being the largest city, was probably also the largest manufacturing centre in the country, it was predominantly a trading city. Analyses of urban occupations from parish register entries confirm this viewpoint (Beier 1978). F. J. Fisher has provided the most persuasive reasons why the English economy came to favour the London market towards the end of the sixteenth century. He argued that the pattern of international trade shifted from one which was predominantly concerned with exporting wool and cloth manufactured in the provinces, chiefly through the Antwerp market, to a centre importing goods from the continent. This change caused many of the problems associated with the balance of payments crises of the early seventeenth century which were primarily due to the increasing difficulty of finding overseas markets for English exports, leading to the growing importance of re-exports by the London merchants. This not only made London the focus for internal trade, with other developments like the growth of the capital's food market doing much to stimulate the agricultural sector, but the metropolis also became a centre for 'conspicuous consumption' so that incomes earned in the provinces were spent in London (Fisher 1935; 1962; 1968; 1976). All these changes drew migrants to London, reinforcing the city's place in all levels of society, and made its importance in seventeenth-century history inevitable. Once set in train, the growth of London was cumulative so that new patterns of trade were associated with new attitudes and beliefs which helped fashion London as a further force for modernizing English society from the second half of the seventeenth century (Wrigley 1967).

19. Some of these developments are discussed in Ashton 1979: 48–70; Prest 1972; Cressy 1980; Seaver 1970.

Little work has been undertaken that analyses the population of London in detail, and much of the discussion has lacked precision and has been based on a number of estimates and assumptions. Both Graunt and more recent scholars have demonstrated the central role of London's demographic history. It would thus be especially helpful if accurate estimates of its demographic rates could be made. Such studies are undertaken in this book by applying new techniques in historical demography, principally aggregative analysis and family reconstitution, to the London registers.

The reconstitution methods adopted here are almost the same as for those rural areas where successful studies have been undertaken, so as to ensure comparability between city and country parishes. The main sources are the nominative listings of baptisms, weddings and burials contained in the Anglican parish registers from which the bills of mortality, as analysed by Graunt, were compiled.[20] Family reconstitution is a relatively simple process, and consists of gathering together the records of all the baptisms, burials and weddings in each family on to a printed family reconstitution form (FRF). This is essentially a genealogical method, but it is concerned with assembling the histories of all families, not just the rich and the well-born. It is necessary to do this because the size of the population at risk is not known from parish register entries alone; it is impossible to measure rates of fertility and mortality from the kind of data used by Graunt. A rate, or a probability of a demographic event, is calculated by comparing the number of persons to whom the event actually happens with the number of persons to whom it could happen, that is the number 'at risk'. The population at risk is usually obtained from censuses; before the first census of 1801 historical demographers have to devise techniques to calculate vital rates from registration data alone. The value of genealogical methods in historical demography is that they allow the number of people at risk to be calculated by following a set of rules which enables the number of individuals in observation to be determined independently of the actual events (births, marriages, deaths) being measured. Once the number of events and the population at risk are known, fertility and mortality can be measured as well as the age at marriage. Because it is time-consuming to work at the level of the individual, reconstitution studies must be restricted to single parishes. This can be advantageous because it allows information to be assembled for small areas and so enables contrasts in the demographic performance of different areas of the city to be investigated.

It is often thought that reconstitution methods are not well suited to the analysis of large urban areas because they work best where families were stable and did not migrate. The effect of a very mobile population is to reduce the representativeness of the results, although relatively few people

---

20. The most useful references to family reconstitution methods are: Fleury and Henry 1956; Wrigley 1966c; Henry 1967; and Wrigley 1972b.

in any part of England stayed within the same parish for the whole of their lives. The restricted geographical area of many urban parishes increases the probability of migration across their boundaries. However, it was found that once couples had married and set up home in a particular parish they often remained there for long periods and had their children christened and buried in the parish church. Thus family reconstitution studies can be usefully pursued in urban areas. In this research, partial reconstitutions were undertaken by eliminating the process of making links from one generation to another, because most couples who started families in London had themselves been migrants from outside the capital. This shortens the time necessary to complete reconstitutions but it also means that it is only possible to calculate a more restricted range of measures. Further evidence that stability as well as migration was a characteristic of many parishes was demonstrated by the effectiveness of the system of parochial administration, especially the relief of the poor (Pearl 1979: 4–5).

Family reconstitution has also been criticized because the results may not be representative of all individuals inhabiting a particular parish. However, all the baptisms and marriages and most of the burials appearing in a particular register are transferred to FRFs, and demographic measures are calculated from those FRFs which satisfy particular observational requirements. Therefore, different numbers of FRFs are used in different calculations, and the representativeness of the results depends on the demographic measure being calculated. For example, families have to be in observation for only a year to be of some use in the construction of life tables, whereas mean birth intervals by birth order of children may be calculated only from those FRFs where the date of marriage is known. A much higher proportion of the population will enter into the construction of life tables than into the calculation of birth intervals. However, criticisms of the representativeness of family reconstitutions must be kept in mind when evaluating the results.

Another general problem which complicates urban historical demography in England relates to the experience of nurse-children. It is difficult to estimate the proportion of infants sent to nurses both within London itself and also in the countryside. The age at which children were boarded out, the length of time spent at nurse, and the probability of children surviving away from home have also to be estimated. Few records of nursing have been found apart from parish register entries and literary sources concerning the experience of wealthier families. It is therefore difficult to estimate the effect of nursing on both mortality and fertility.[21]

This study of the population of London focuses on the period between 1580 and 1650. For successful reconstitution, it is important that the

21. For comparative studies in France, see Van de Walle and Preston 1974; Galliano 1966; and Ganiage 1973.

numbers of baptisms, weddings and burials recorded in the registers approximate to the actual numbers of births, weddings and deaths that occurred, and parish registers seem likely to be most accurate at this time because everyone was at least nominally within the framework of the Anglican church. It has been argued that the accuracy of the London parish registers had deteriorated sharply by the 1690s (Glass 1972: 283 table 5), which suggests again that the period before the Civil War would be a good one to begin studies of London population history. Much of the discussion will be concerned with establishing that the data are reliable, because the opposite point of view has frequently been taken (e.g. Glass 1973: 16). It is difficult to make independent checks of the bills of mortality, because they are only aggregate listings, although it is clear that they deteriorated during the Civil War period (Graunt 1662: 31). This means that attention must be concentrated on the parish registers from which the bills themselves were compiled, and detailed analysis of their accuracy is thus essential to the argument. The technical aspects of this book are therefore important because they show, for the first time, that parish register demography is an effective analytical method in an urban context.

The London parish registers were generally well-kept before the commencement of the civil registration experiment in 1653, and as trends in baptism and burial in the registers and the bills moved in step with each other, it seems very likely that both sources are sufficiently good for demographic work to be undertaken. Assuming that a particular register appears to have been conscientiously compiled without any obvious gaps, the main source of omission will probably be of infants who died before they could be baptized. It is far more likely that births would be under-registered than deaths, because the problem of disposing of a decomposing body meant that burials had to take place shortly after death. It would thus be unlikely for burials not to take place in the parish graveyard and not to be recorded in the parish registers (the number of parishes which kept registers was only exceeded by the number of burial grounds at the beginning of the eighteenth century). Therefore, any study of the effectiveness of the parish registration system in recording the number of vital events that actually occurred should concentrate on the length of the interval between birth and baptism. If this interval were short, it is unlikely that many infants would have died before baptism and been omitted from the registers, and in fact the birth–baptism interval was generally found to be short in the few parishes where it could be calculated from the information contained in the registers. A more effective way of tackling the problem of estimating the extent of registration deficiencies, which can be applied to all parish registers, is to calculate endogenous and exogenous components of infant mortality. Very low endogenous infant mortality rates are indicative of defective registration of births because

14

virtually all infant deaths due to endogenous causes occur within the first month of life. Low endogenous rates were not found in an analysis of a wide range of London parish registers.

The making of links from one generation to another was not undertaken as several registers were reconstituted for short periods between about 1580, when many of the London registers first meet the requirements for successful reconstitution, and the establishment of civil registration in 1653. An example of this kind of link consists of matching the partners of a marriage with their own baptisms. The majority of adults resident in the capital had not actually been born in London, and it would be very difficult to trace places of birth outside London for so many individuals. This means that it is almost impossible to calculate demographic measures which require the date of baptism of adults to be known, in particular the age at marriage for individuals born in a different parish from which they were married, age-specific fertility rates, and adult life tables.

The fact that the bills of mortality were compiled from the parish registers, which were themselves reliable, can be used to show that the bills were a better record than is often thought. The course of population increase in London may be charted if the assumption of a constant birth rate is made (see Appendix 1), since an index of the number of christenings is also an index of population change. The estimation of actual population totals for London is more difficult because a realistic birth rate to fit the data is not known, and the assumption of a fixed birth rate means that such estimates can only be very general. More exact population estimates also depend on the area of London being considered as the city was growing quickly during this period. However, demographic trends in a sample of ten parish registers typical of contrasting areas were found to be similar to the pattern revealed by the bills of mortality, giving confidence in both sets of data. Broad population movements in the individual parishes were similar to the overall pattern. Whatever the actual population total, and despite the serious setbacks of plague crises in 1593, 1603 and 1625, and a minor outbreak in 1636, London was growing at a faster rate in this period than towards the end of the seventeenth century, and at a faster rate than the country as a whole. Migrants were travelling to London from throughout the country, and especially from midland and northern counties. At the end of the sixteenth century, mass immigration from the Low Countries and France added to the population of London, but this alien community soon lost its distinctiveness in the absence of a continuous flow of migrants. The history of this group of newcomers provides an excellent illustration of the effect of high urban mortality in progressively reducing the size of a pre-industrial urban population without a continuous stream of new migrants.

The population of London was strongly differentiated by the wealth of its inhabitants, rather than on the basis of the distribution of its guilds and trades. Although the social structure of London was complicated, with no simple connections between it and the spatial form of the city, people of similar means lived close to each other. From as early as 1638, social areas in London may be distinguished by the value of property inhabited by residents. The wealthier Londoners tended to live in the centre of the city whilst the poor were more likely to occupy the peripheral areas around the walls and along the riverside. The residence of the majority of Londoners of intermediate means was less well defined. At this time, the family was the basic unit in urban society, just as it was in the countryside. Home and workplace were not physically separated. Residential differentiation is therefore of some importance to an understanding of the structure of London society. How the demography of these social areas varied can be examined by selecting parishes for detailed study which were typical of each, thus bringing out the contrasts in society. There were striking variations in both fertility and mortality between parishes located in wealthy and poor areas. The distinctive demography of these social areas reinforces their distinctive identities as the wealthier central parishes were characterized by higher fertility and lower mortality than the poorer suburban parishes.

Having studied the overall historical demography of the capital, the remainder of the book will concentrate on showing in greater depth its connection with trends in fertility and mortality, and how demographic rates varied between social areas. Since the level of mortality was the chief influence on the demography of London in its determination of how many migrants were required to prevent the population from falling, it is necessary to establish how high the death rate actually was. This may be done for children by constructing life tables from family reconstitutions. These tables allow the expectation of life at birth to be estimated by comparison with model life tables, as the expectation of life is an independent measure of mortality which does not require the age-structure of the population to be known. This procedure enables the background level of mortality to be studied with much greater precision than from simple aggregative analyses of the data. There were very marked differences in the mortality experience of wealthy and poor parishes. In the poorer parishes, only about 500 children per thousand survived until their fifteenth birthday compared with about 600 in the parishes of their wealthier counterparts. Since these parishes represented extremes at each end of the socio-economic spectrum, it may be suggested that on average about 550 children survived till age fifteen. It is therefore unlikely that half the London-born children survived to a marriageable age. This leads yet again to the suggestion that since the London death rate exceeded the birth rate, migration was the cause of the city's growth. The case is further reinforced by the suggestion that mortality in England at this time was generally more severe for adults than for children (Schofield and Wrigley

1979: 93–5), an assumption that must be built into estimates of the expectation of life at birth.

It is not certain why mortality rates were higher in some parishes than in others. The socio-economic characteristics of the parishes were obviously one determinant of differential mortality. Another factor was water supply. Riverside parishes had much higher mortality rates than inland parishes, irrespective of their social status. There is some evidence, but insufficient to be conclusive, that the riverside parishes drew their water supply from the Thames and the inland parishes from conduits and pipes fed by wells and springs, purer than the river water. This might be a partial explanation of higher mortality and a different age-structure of mortality in the riverside parish studied in detail.

Plague was the single most important cause of death, although by no means the only infectious disease in the capital. Whilst it is well known that a high death rate from infrequent epidemics has less effect on the general level of mortality than a consistently high death rate from endemic infection (McKeown 1976: 69), life tables measuring the background level of mortality overestimate the number of surviving children. This is because of the serious plague crises of 1563, 1593, 1603, 1625 and 1665. There was a lesser outbreak of plague in 1636. About 15 per cent of all London deaths during the period between 1580 and 1650 occurred during these epidemics. Children and young adults, who could not have gained any immunity from having survived previous exposure to the plague, were the most frequent casualties. Another important point about the disease is that its impact declined in successive major epidemics between 1563 and its disappearance after 1665, but that the decrease in the proportion of excess deaths occurred first in the wealthier parishes and last in the poorest parishes. No London parishes entirely escaped the plague, but its effect was always greatest in the poorest parishes and least in the wealthiest parishes. The pattern of diffusion of plague was far from simple, and there were clear differences in mortality rates from plague in various parts of London, but the disease made certain that before 1650 the population of London could not replace itself.

The dramatic nature of the occurrence of plague attracts attention which is out of proportion to its importance. There were far more deaths from endemic diseases which are much less easily distinguishable in the parish registers, if it is possible to identify them at all, than from epidemics such as plague. It is unlikely that the background level of mortality would have fallen very markedly in the absence of plague. The death rate from other infectious diseases such as tuberculosis and smallpox increased after plague disappeared in the 1660s. Nevertheless, the short-term effects of plague were catastrophic because mortality rates were so high during the crises, and also because of the dislocation of the London economy and the daily life of the capital that it caused. Younger people were more likely to die

17

from plague (a fact which supports the hypothesis that survival from previous exposure guaranteed at least some immunity to the disease), and were also the most easily replaced, as migrants tended to be young adults.

The argument that migration was important for the early modern city necessitates demonstrating that there was a gap between the birth rate and the death rate. The level of the birth rate must therefore be estimated to indicate the dimensions of the shortfall of births. The study of London fertility is complicated, but it can be shown that the birth rate was lower than the death rate. The birth rate may have been a little higher than in the countryside – it is difficult to substantiate this point – but it did not reach the exceptionally high level necessary to match the death rate. Marital fertility was high. In the wealthier parishes, the mean interval between successive births was as short as twenty-three months, suggesting exceptionally high fertility and equivalent to a fertility rate of at least 500 live births per 1,000 woman-years lived, for women in their twenties. A recent survey of marital fertility rates in the early modern period covering twenty-eight places in Europe and North America has indicated that very few areas had rates of fertility this high, French Canada, parts of the southern Netherlands (Belgium), and areas of northern France being important exceptions (Andorka 1978: 48–64). Such high fertility in London was connected with the practice of sending infants to wet-nurses in the countryside, as women who do not care for their own infant children can conceive again more quickly after a birth. Examination of registers of parishes within about thirty-five miles of London showed that many places were accepting children for nursing. But fertility was also high in the poorer parishes of London, with birth intervals of around twenty-seven months, probably explained by high infant mortality in these areas. In contrast, marital fertility was much lower in rural areas. Birth intervals were at least thirty months in country parishes, and were frequently much longer. Short birth intervals reflect high marital fertility. The city was not associated with high rates of illegitimacy at this time and fertility outside marriage was not high in London. Fewer than 5 per cent of births were illegitimate, and this figure is the same as that for the country as a whole.

Because the vast majority of children were born within marriage, much of the argument about the London birth rate hinges around the age at marriage. If the average age of first marriage for women were young, there would be good cause to argue that the birth rate was high, whilst a high age at marriage would indicate that the birth rate was more moderate. It is difficult to be precise about the London marriage pattern at this time. London-born girls married young in the capital, and a recent analysis of marriage licences found that native-born single women married at 20.5 years between 1598 and 1618. However, it has already been shown that the majority of women marrying for the first time in London would have been migrants, and their mean age at marriage was 24.2 years (Elliott 1978: 325

table 18). Thus, migration delayed marriage and contributed to a reduction in fertility. Another point which is highly relevant to a study of the London birth rate is the nature of the age–sex structure of the population. During the first half of the seventeenth century, there was a marked surplus of men in the city's population, which had disappeared by 1700 but which contributed to relatively early marriage for women. One of the reasons for the surplus of men is that there were so many apprentices in London during that period. The proportion of apprentices fell from about 15 per cent of the city's population to just over 4 per cent during the course of the seventeenth century, and as all apprentices were male, this decline would account for much of the reduction of the sex ratio. Men married quite late, the mean age for first marriages being 28.4 years. This was in part due to the lengthy apprenticeships served, averaging eight years and delaying marriage by an equivalent period. There was a substantial difference in ages between husbands and wives. The main point of interest about the age at marriage for the present discussion is that whilst levels of marital fertility, and relatively early marriage for women, suggest that the birth rate may have been quite high, in reality this would have been reduced by a shortage of women in the population and a relatively large number of people, especially apprentices, who were unmarried. The age–sex structure of the population of London suggests that although marital fertility was high, the proportion of married women of childbearing age may have been fairly low. Thus it is difficult to estimate a figure for the actual birth rate, but the evidence about fertility and marriage in the first half of the seventeenth century supports our proposition that the birth rate was lower than the death rate.

The main themes of this book have now been outlined. It has been shown that Graunt's investigation of London population trends provides a good basis for further research using new techniques of parish register analysis. The demographic implications of the growth of London may now be examined in greater detail and the evidence presented more fully. By concentrating on detailed studies of individual parishes, both the overall demography and the range of variations that existed will be examined. This discussion of the population of London between 1580 and 1650 should be viewed as a case-study of the impact of a metropolitan city in early modern historical demography.

CHAPTER 2

THE ACCURACY OF THE LONDON PARISH REGISTERS

Graunt's analysis of the London bills of mortality showed that the population of London would merit further study. However, conclusions based on the bills of mortality will always be open to question because it is not possible to verify the aggregate totals of baptisms and burials which are not subdivided by parish. A serious reconsideration of the parish registers in association with which the bills were compiled is thus called for. In a recent review of urban history during the early modern period, J. Patten (1978: 18) wrote that 'until far more work is done on the direct evidence of parish registers, it will be hard to consider actual population dynamics and growth in detail and on any scale'. But it is often thought that the reliability of the London parish registers is doubtful. For example, I. Sutherland commented that 'family reconstitution studies on the London parish registers do not appear to be a practical proposition'. He went on to explain his reasons for this view (1972: 310–11).

It seems unlikely that during the period under review all the burials came to the notice of the parish authorities, and that deficiencies, perhaps of the order of 10 per cent, will have occurred by omissions either from parish registers or the bills of mortality. The deficiencies in christenings before the Civil War will certainly have been greater than those in burials.

It is evident that if the London parish registers are to be used for population studies, their reliability must be assessed.

An important paper by M. F. and T. H. Hollingsworth (1971) first showed that it is possible to use parish registers directly for demographic work in London. The subject of their article was the calculation of plague mortality rates for one large parish, St Botolph without Bishopsgate, in 1603, from the burial register, which was unusual in giving ages at death. Although they did take account of the inaccuracy of the data, the completeness of the register was not the principal objective of their research. Indeed, they may have overcompensated for omissions. The real value of the paper is that it shows how parish register studies of London population trends could be taken further, provided that the reliability of the data could be demonstrated.

A sample of eight London parishes have been chosen here to test the accuracy of the registers. Four of these, Allhallows Bread Street (2), St Peter Cornhill (90), St Christopher le Stocks (26), and St Michael Cornhill

(74) were situated in the richer central part of the city.[1] St Dunstan in the East (29) was of intermediate wealth and situated along the river near to the Tower. The remaining three parishes were very poor. St Mary Somerset (68) was located by the riverside towards the western sector of the city. Allhallows London Wall (7) was just inside the wall in the north-eastern suburbs of the city, and St Botolph Bishopsgate (103) was adjacent but outside the wall (their locations are shown on the map in Appendix 3).[2] The registers of all these parishes were complete and without serious gaps for long periods. Each of them also contained sufficient information to identify every individual exactly, which enables the baptisms of individuals to be matched to their burials with reasonable confidence. In practice, the necessary conditions for this are either that the relationship of the person baptized or buried to the head of the household in which he lived should be stated, or alternatively that the age at burial is given. This latter form of entry is rare nationally, but occurs in St Botolph's throughout the period, and for part of the time in St Peter's and Allhallows London Wall. Because many parish registers do not satisfy these conditions for long periods, and because cross-matching data is very time consuming, the study of a sample of parishes is inevitable. All the registers before 1598 consist of parchment transcripts from original registers, made as part of an attempt to provide a more accurate and a more permanent record.[3] Although in many parishes the transcripts date back either to the commencement of the registers in 1538 or to the accession of Queen Elizabeth in 1558, the information they contain is generally good enough only from about 1580, although there are exceptions. Many London registers are in print, mainly through the work of the Harleian Society.[4]

The most likely defect in the burial register is for the relationship of the person buried to the head of the household in which he lived not to be given consistently. The defect excludes a register from analysis because it means that insufficient information is available to make links with confidence. However, the number of unrecorded deaths is likely to be much

1. The number following the name of each parish corresponds to its location on the map (Figure A3.1).
2. In all tables, parishes will be arranged in descending order of socio-economic status in 1638. See Chapter 4 for a full discussion of how London parishes may be subdivided into geographical areas based on their social distribution of wealth.
3. The history of the registers is well related in Cox 1910; Tate 1969: 43–83; Steel 1968/73: I, 9, 25–9. Genuine pre-1598 registers exist for at least two London parishes and they show the amount of information missing from each parchment transcript. One was the particularly full set of books which form the basis for a parish history from the point of view of the medical historian in Forbes 1971. Similarly, there is a paper book for Allhallows London Wall from 1575 to 1598 containing very full entries for most of this period. Paper rough books exist for some of the other parishes but do not contain this detail.
4. There is a comprehensive guide to London parish registers published by the Guildhall Library entitled *Parish registers*.

21

smaller than the number of births not leading to recorded baptisms, for two reasons. First, the problem of disposing of the body occurs very soon after death. Burials would therefore stand a greater chance of being registered than births, since the birth–baptism interval is longer than the death–burial one.[5] Secondly, although it is often argued that the recording of burials in the bills of mortality is defective in the eighteenth century because of the existence of many burial grounds outside London (Maitland 1756: II, 740–2), this problem did not arise before the Civil War. So the information contained in the burial register is adequate for record linkage for a sufficiently large number of London parishes, and there are few grounds to suspect that burials were under-registered. It is therefore necessary to concentrate on baptisms in the discussion of data accuracy.

The accuracy of the baptism registers depends on how many more births there were in a parish than baptisms recorded in the register. This discrepancy was most marked nationally in the period from 1750 to 1850, during the growth of non-conformity and the transition from ecclesiastical to civil registration. Before the Civil War, however, there was basically only one church. There were a few immigrant communities which maintained their own places of worship and kept separate registers, but events in those communities were often recorded in the parish registers too. Although this period saw the rise of puritanism, both in London and nationally, it is unlikely that it would have had much effect on the quality of registration. Most of the godly people were concerned to stress the importance of infant baptism,[6] despite problems of a liturgical nature such as the continued use of the sign of the cross at baptism (Kennedy 1924: cxi; Foster 1926: lxiv). Before the political breakdown, most puritans remained within the context of the established church, and parents would probably have wanted to have their children properly christened. Even if the characteristics of urban life reduced the significance of religion in the minds of many people, baptism and burial in church may well have been forced on the ordinary inhabitants of the capital by the Laudian faction in the church. As M. Tolmie (1977: 14) commented: 'Weekly attendance at the parish church was probably of little consequence in the teeming parishes of London, but the failure to produce newly-born children before the parish minister for baptism may have been a source of serious trouble in the parish.' He also suggested that 'parochial baptisms were performed in the parish where the parents lived, whether godly or not'. These remarks

5. The only parish where the registers contain the dates of both death and burial before 1653 is St Thomas the Apostle (96). For 216 cases between 22 March 1646 and 23 August 1653, the cumulative distribution of death–burial intervals was:

0	1	2	3	4	5	6	7	8	9
20%	76%	94%	98%	99%	99%	99%	99%	100%	100%

6. New 1964: 67; Macfarlane 1970: 88; and Thomas 1971: 36–57. For London in particular, see Tolmie 1977.

imply that the baptism register mainly included children actually resident in the parish and that parents did not usually take their children for baptism and burial to churches in parishes where they did not live.

Although the bills of mortality deteriorated after the beginning of the open, armed conflict, the quality of some parish registers hardly seems to have been affected. The transition from Anglicanism to Presbyterianism was at times very complicated, but the real problem concerning the accuracy of the parish registers came only once the puritans had succeeded in their attempts to root out Laudianism, and fragmentation and sectarianism occurred in the general confusion surrounding the later Civil War years. This was particularly true once individual ministers began to gather churches around them. Most of the separate churches were not formed until the 1640s and would not have affected registration before then.[7] The growth of Independency had an impact on parochial registration in two ways. First, many congregations were drawn from a wide area of London; for example, William Greenhill's meeting at Stepney in the eastern suburbs contained members who lived in parishes within the walls (Jones 1887: 15–16; Marsh 1871: 23). Secondly, the incumbent administered the sacraments including baptism only to the covenanted members of his church.[8] In some places where the Independent minister was also the parish priest, he performed his functions for the benefit of the laity of the parish as well as for the gathered church (Jones 1887: 35–6). The growth of religious toleration influenced the quality of the parish registers as is shown by the situation in the northern Netherlands where historical demography is not well advanced, mainly because there was no single registration authority. For example, an important article by A. M. van der Woude and G. J. Mentink (1966) on the demography of Rotterdam considers the registers of ten separate religious groups as well as civil records. In London, however, the rise of puritanism did not affect the quality of parochial registration until episcopacy had been overthrown and the growth of the gathered churches occurred. This happened only at the extreme end of our period.

It would thus appear that registration problems should be less of an impediment to demographic studies in this period than later. The major cause of omissions was the length of the customary interval between birth and baptism, because some children died before they would have been baptized. Children were normally christened on the Sunday after they were born, and weekday baptisms were usually reserved for children who were very weak at birth.[9] It is hard to obtain evidence for the interval between

7. Lists of separate churches are contained in Tolmie 1977: 245; and Nuttall 1957: 40.
8. Nuttall 1957: 136; Freshfield 1887a: 8; 1890: II, 26, entry for 27 August 1649; and Shaw 1900: II, 132–6.
9. The form of words first used in 1548 was repeated several times. 'Wherefore the people are to be admonished, that it is most convenient, that baptism should not be administered but upon Sundays and other Holy Days when the most number of people may come together.

cont'd

Table 2.1. *Interval in days* (± 0.5) *by which the stated percentile of 80 sample births had been baptized before 1653*

Parish and dates	25%	50%	75%	Semi-inter-quartile range	% of incomplete entries
St Peter Cornhill, 1574–8	2	3	5	2	2
St Vedast Foster Lane, 1645–8	2	6	10	4	8
St Thomas the Apostle, 1645–8	4	7	11	4	0

Source: Berry and Schofield 1971: 456 table 1.

birth and baptism, but it was generally short, especially when compared with eighteenth-century practice. Table 2.1 shows birth–baptism intervals in the only three London parishes for which these data may be calculated, and it confirms that most children were christened within a fortnight of birth. The semi-interquartile range given in this table provides a measure of the spread of the birth–baptism interval and gives the period in days over which the middle quarter of the population were being baptized. A small range implies a relatively consistent baptism practice (obviously the case in these three parishes), whilst a broader range would indicate a much greater variation in the individual birth–baptism intervals.

The available information from which the birth–baptism interval may be calculated is inadequate to show that the interval was short throughout most of the period in all the parishes studied. Therefore, it is necessary to find an alternative way to measure the birth–baptism shortfall. It is known that infants have a high risk of dying very close to birth and that this risk declines with increasing age. For example, it is a fair generalization to suggest that in many pre-industrial communities the infant mortality rate would be of the order of 200 per thousand, and half the deaths would occur within the first month of life. Therefore if the interval between birth and baptism were a month, the infant mortality rate would in effect be reduced by half, and 10 per cent of all births would not be recorded as baptisms. Thus the problem of the accuracy of the parish registers is one which may be tackled statistically by demonstrating that observed distributions over time of infant deaths do in fact match up with expected distributions. If the infant mortality rate were too low, or too small a proportion of infant deaths occurred within the first month after christening, it would be necessary to suspect that baptisms were not being completely registered.

... Nevertheless (if necessity so require) children may be baptised upon any other day.' Gibson 1713: 362, 369, quoted in Wrigley 1977: 282, n. 7. The intention of the church for early baptism is discussed more fully in Berry and Schofield 1971: 454. Parish registers occasionally record the baptism of infants at home. On 17 December 1564, the register of St Michael Cornhill states: 'Christened by ye mydwyfe, Jone Gybbyns the daughter of Randall Gybbyns: in his house.'

A method by which the birth–baptism shortfall may be calculated has been developed in an important article by E. A. Wrigley (1977), and this technique will be applied to the London registers. Although he stresses that his results are only preliminary and that the number of parishes he was able to investigate is too small to approximate to a national survey, it is instructive to compare the results for London with the figures which he obtained (which did include data from two London parishes, St Michael Cornhill and St Vedast Foster Lane). Wrigley writes (1977: 310):

in round figures, my estimates suggest that in the five successive half centuries from 1550–99 to 1750–99 the number of baptisms registered should be increased by 2, $3\frac{1}{2}$, 4, 5 and $7\frac{1}{2}$ per cent to offset the combined effect of the increasing delay before baptising a child and the impact of infant mortality. They also suggest that at any time before the end of the seventeenth century there were very few infant deaths not recorded in the burial register, whether or not there was a corresponding baptism in the register.

The basis of this work is a biometric method devised by J. Bourgeois-Pichat (1952: 1; 1951) to divide infant mortality into two components:

The first comprises those cases in which the child bears within itself, from birth, the cause resulting in its death, whether that cause was inherited from its parents at conception or acquired from its mother during gestation or delivery. These deaths constitute as a class what is here called endogenous infant mortality. The second category comprises those cases in which the infant picks up the factor which causes its death in the environment in which it lives. This is exogenous infant mortality, which may be regarded as accidental, in the broadest sense of the term; and clearly it is particularly for the second type of mortality that society must hold itself responsible.

He also showed that the probability of dying with a certain number of days from birth (Pn) is represented by the sum of the endogenous and exogenous rates (a and b) such that $Pn = a + bTn$, where Tn approximates to the function $\log^3 (n + 1)$. The plot of the cumulative number of infant deaths against time from birth (Tn) measured in days is a straight line after the first month. The slope of the line gives an estimate of the exogenous rate and the intercept on the vertical axis of the graph gives a best estimate of the endogenous rate (Figure 2.1). It is a characteristic of infant mortality that deaths from endogenous causes hardly ever occur after the first month from birth. When this line cuts either the vertical axis close to the origin as in Figure 2.2, or even the horizontal axis, it implies that there were few endogenous infant deaths. In other words the expected proportion of infants were not dying within the first month of life and so births must have been under-registered.[10] Most French demographic studies for the eighteenth century have shown that infant mortality may be

10. Wrigley 1977; 285. Examples of the way by which postponement of baptisms affects infant mortality rates are also given by Krause 1965: 390–1; and Jones 1976.

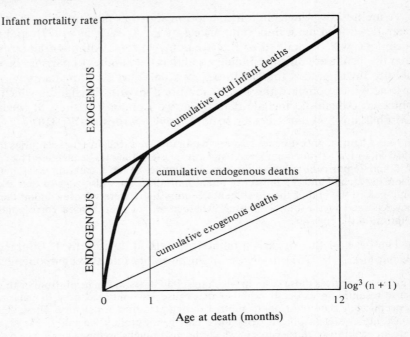

Figure 2.1 Biometric analysis of infant mortality.

analysed in this way, and Wrigley has demonstrated how the method may successfully be applied to many English parish registers also.

In another important study, J. Knodel and H. Kintner (1977) have argued that the cumulative distribution of infant deaths is strongly affected by child rearing practices. With special reference to Germany at the end of the nineteenth century, they suggested that the slope of the line is influenced by breast feeding customs. In particular, they found an upturn in infant mortality rates at weaning. The implication of their research is that the biometric method of calculating endogenous and exogenous components of infant mortality rates will provide only a range of estimates of these components which may depend on the way the graphs are drawn. The object of the work reported in this chapter is to show that endogenous infant mortality rates calculated from the parish register data are plausible despite the important issues raised by Knodel and Kintner about the reliability of the biometric method. The method remains more than satisfactory for showing that the London parish registers merit serious consideration.

The data with which this kind of analysis may be pursued have been set out for the eight sample parishes in Table 2.2, which also demonstrates the pattern of infant deaths in each of the parishes throughout the first year of

26

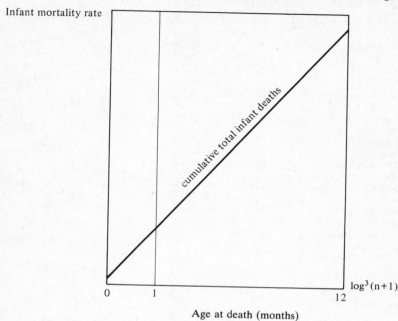

Figure 2.2 Biometric analysis of infant mortality if births are under-registered.

life. The fact that most deaths occured close to birth gives confidence in the data. In Table 2.3, infant mortality rates have been calculated as the number of infant deaths per thousand baptisms. This simpler method of calculation has been used rather than family reconstitution methods so that the rates may be compared with those for the 1690s, when the extent of under-registration means that family reconstitution may not be a practical proposition. The method also allows a greater number of parishes to be considered. However, the rates derived in this way are close to rates derived by family reconstitution methods (Table 2.21) and they have the advantage of including all infants dying in the parish who had been born there (figures have been omitted for children born in the parish but whose deaths are recorded elsewhere owing to migration). This is because the data do not have to satisfy the strict observational rules that family reconstitution methods impose.

Endogenous and exogenous components have been estimated by the graphical method outlined by Bourgeois-Pichat. The proportion of endogenous infant deaths is not so low as to mean that the under-registration of births was widespread in any of the parishes for which a special study has been made. Perhaps the most striking point which emerges is that although the proportion of endogenous deaths was high, the total infant mortality

27

Table 2.2. *Distribution of infant deaths within the first year of life*

Parish and dates	Days								Weeks		
	0*	0	1	2	3	4	5	6	1	2	3
Allhallows Bread Street, 1538–1653	49	5	13	8	6	6	3	3	13	9	6
		54	67	75	81	87	90	93	106	115	121
St Peter Cornhill, 1580–1650	43	6	17	10	9	9	2	4	17	9	8
		49	66	76	85	94	96	100	117	126	134
St Christopher le Stocks, 1580–1653	39	5	5	5	1	2	1	1	8	3	1
		44	49	54	55	57	58	59	67	70	71
St Michael Cornhill, 1580–1650	62	7	17	14	9	11	3	3	39	17	12
		69	86	100	109	120	123	126	165	182	194
St Dunstan in the East, 1605–53	85	8	59	72	59	37	43	32	152	48	30
		93	152	224	283	320	363	395	547	595	625
St Mary Somerset, 1605–53	46	10	34	46	26	19	29	22	108	28	19
		56	90	136	162	181	210	232	340	368	387
Allhallows London Wall, 1570–1636	129	20	20	17	17	10	7	10	35	11	12
		149	169	186	203	213	220	230	265	276	288
St Botolph Bishopsgate, 1600–50	191	4	29	19	12	6	10	5	45	26	15
		195	224	243	255	261	271	276	321	347	362
Indexed to base 100											
Allhallows Bread Street		31	39	43	47	50	52	53	61	66	70
St Peter Cornhill		21	29	33	37	41	42	44	51	55	59
St Christopher le Stocks		45	50	55	56	58	59	60	68	71	72
St Michael Cornhill		23	29	33	36	40	41	42	55	60	64
St Dunstan in the East		12	19	28	36	36	40	46	50	69	79
St Mary Somerset		10	16	24	29	32	37	41	60	65	68
Allhallows London Wall		36	41	45	49	52	53	56	64	67	70
St Botolph Bishopsgate		33	38	41	43	44	46	47	54	59	61

*Dummy births

rates were low in the four richest parishes. Despite the fact that, as Wrigley points out, the main problem in analysing infant mortality rates is that it is not known how high and how stable these rates would have been in pre-industrial England, particularly the endogenous component, and although English historical demography before the period of the industrial revolution is characterized by its variety, these rates for London appear to be much lower than might be expected in an urban environment. For example, the infant mortality rate for Stockholm was as high as 293 per thousand as late as 1861. In Berlin in 1879–81, the average of the male and female rates combined was also 293 per thousand. The overall infant mortality rate for London between 1580 and 1650 was much lower than this. Even in the poorer parishes the rate did not reach the proportions of some nineteenth-century metropolitan cities. In small areas of such cities,

				Months							Total births
1	2	3	4	5	6	7	8	9	10	11	
9	12	7	2	3	2	4	1	8	1	4	
130	142	149	151	154	156	160	161	169	170	174	1,562
16	10	6	10	13	6	3	11	5	8	6	
150	160	166	176	189	195	198	209	214	222	228	1,769
4	4	2	1	2	4	1	3	1	1	4	
75	79	81	82	84	88	89	92	93	94	98	1,115
25	7	11	12	9	7	7	4	11	8	6	
219	226	237	249	258	265	272	276	287	295	301	2,261
41	22	12	14	10	4	15	10	15	9	15	
666	688	700	714	724	728	743	753	768	777	792	3,103
25	15	17	14	15	14	23	9	20	13	14	
412	427	444	458	473	487	510	519	539	552	566	2,079
25	12	12	16	11	12	9	7	5	8	8	
313	325	337	353	364	376	385	392	397	405	413	1,839
34	44	26	19	21	21	15	12	13	12	13	
396	440	466	485	506	527	542	554	567	579	592	2,809
75	82	86	87	89	90	92	93	97	98	100	
66	70	73	77	83	86	87	92	94	97	100	
77	81	83	84	86	90	91	94	95	96	100	
73	75	79	83	86	88	90	92	95	98	100	
84	87	88	90	91	92	94	95	97	98	100	
73	75	78	81	84	86	90	92	95	98	100	
76	79	82	85	88	91	93	95	96	98	100	
67	74	79	82	85	89	92	94	96	98	100	

the infant mortality rate would have been still higher than for the urban area as a whole.[11] One reason for low infant mortality in the wealthier London parishes was that many infant children were sent to the country-side to be wet-nursed, and some of these would have died outside the parish. A high proportion of endogenous deaths is compatible with this explanation, because children probably left home a few days after they had

11. Wrigley 1977: 299, 286 table 3 and 292 table 8 demonstrate these points. The two riverside parishes, St Dunstan's and St Mary's, consistently displayed higher infant mortality rates than the other parishes. For a fuller examination of differential mortality between inland and riverside parishes as well as an analysis of socio-economic differences in mortality, see Chapter 5 below. Other series of infant mortality rates for pre-industrial England are contained in Jones 1976; West 1974: 43–4; Hollingsworth 1977; 327 table 2; and Schofield and Wrigley 1979. For Stockholm, see Hofsten and Lundström 1976: 120 table 7.2; and for Berlin, Wrigley 1961: 101 table 24.

Table 2.3. *Endogenous and exogenous components of infant mortality rates before 1653 (1,000q_0)*

Parish and dates	Legitimate baptisms	Infant deaths	Rate	Endogenous		Exogenous	
				%	Rate	%	Rate
Allhallows Bread Street, 1538–1653	1,513	125	83	45	37	55	46
St Peter Cornhill, 1580–1650	1,726	185	107	37	40	63	67
St Christopher le Stocks, 1580–1653	1,076	59	55	44	24	56	31
St Michael Cornhill, 1580–1650	2,199	239	109	46	50	54	59
St Dunstan in the East, 1605–53	3,018	707	234	69	162	31	72
St Mary Somerset, 1605–53	2,033	520	256	61	155	39	101
Allhallows London Wall, 1570–1636	1,710	284	166	45	75	55	91
St Botolph Bishopsgate, 1600–50	2,618	401	153	27	42	73	111

Table 2.4. *Revised endogenous and exogenous components of infant mortality rates before 1653 (1,000q_0)*

Parish and dates	Total births	Infant deaths	Rate	Endogenous		Exogenous	
				%	Rate	%	Rate
Allhallows Bread Street, 1538–1653	1,562	174	111	60	67	40	44
St Peter Cornhill, 1580–1650	1,769	228	129	50	65	50	64
St Christopher le Stocks, 1580–1653	1,115	98	88	64	56	36	32
St Michael Cornhill, 1580–1650	2,261	301	133	56	74	44	59
St Dunstan in the East, 1605–53	3,103	792	255	72	184	28	71
St Mary Somerset, 1605–53	2,079	566	272	64	175	36	97
Allhallows London Wall, 1570–1636	1,839	413	225	63	142	37	83
St Botolph Bishopsgate, 1600–50	2,809	592	211	50	106	50	105

Table 2.5. *Underbaptism rates before 1653 (per 1,000 live births)*

Parish and dates	Dummy births	Total births	Underbaptism rate
Allhallows Bread Street, 1538–1653	49	1,562	31
St Peter Cornhill, 1580–1650	43	1,769	24
St Christopher le Stocks, 1580–1653	39	1,115	35
St Michael Cornhill, 1580–1650	62	2,261	27
St Dunstan in the East, 1605–53	85	3,103	27
St Mary Somerset, 1605–53	46	2,079	22
Allhallows London Wall, 1570–1636	129	1,839	70
St Botolph Bishopsgate, 1600–50	191	2,809	68

been born, and once the period of greatest risk had passed.[12] The only parishes where there is evidence that there may have been some under-registration are the very large parish of St Botolph Bishopsgate (where only a sample with surnames beginning A to C, was studied) and Allhallows London Wall. But even in these parishes it is difficult to argue that the standard of recording was very poor.

The rates presented so far relate only to the deaths of those children to whom a corresponding baptism could be matched. There are burials of infants in the registers for whom there was no corresponding baptism, because the child had died before it could be baptized. Since all children were christened relatively close to birth in the seventeenth century, it might be safely assumed that all these deaths occurred in the first month of life. The entries of these children in the burial register normally took the form 'Chrisom' (although a chrisom child is not technically one which died unbaptized). There was a variety of forms of entry used where the child was not named, but often it was specified that the child had died before christening.[13] In these cases, we manufactured a date of birth that was the same as the date of burial. The addition of these dummy births produces rates as in Table 2.4 and Figure 2.3. These are obviously more plausible than the unrevised figures because they show a higher proportion of endogenous infant deaths. It is therefore possible to calculate underbaptism rates in Table 2.5 as the number of dummy births divided by the total number of births (including dummy births). Except in St Botolph's and

12. This point is discussed in detail in Chapter 7 below. At Lyons in the eighteenth century, infant mortality rates were apparently low because children were commonly sent to the hospital and also away for nursing. Garden 1970: 108–10.
13. Steel 1968/73: I, 72. It could be argued that the burial of unbaptized children would not necessarily be recorded in the parish registers. However, the Canons of 1603 (1 Jac. I, lxviii) order that: 'No minister shall refuse to delay to bury and corps that is brought to the church or church-yard (convenient warning being given him thereof before), in such manner and form as is prescribed in the said book of Common Prayer.' Quoted in Wrigley 1977: 290, n. 16.

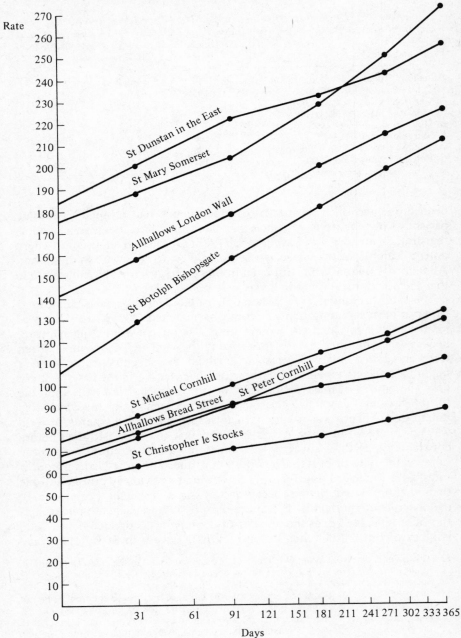

Figure 2.3 Revised cumulative infant mortality rates before 1653.

Allhallows London Wall, these rates are very similar to the omission rate of $3\frac{1}{2}$ per cent of births in the baptism registers estimated from a national sample in this period by Wrigley. There are obviously many ways in which these data may be manipulated, and many assumptions that can be made in the attempt to improve the accuracy of the estimates of the extent to which baptisms under-counted births, for example by making allowance for the interval between birth and baptism, as Wrigley illustrates. The main point for the discussion is that the biometric method effectively suggests that the underbaptism rate here did not differ markedly from that in other English parishes.

We can thus reach the important conclusion that registration was of a generally high standard before 1653 and that there was little difference in the quality of the registers between parishes typical of different social areas. The biometric method of analysing the under-registration of baptisms may be shown to be reliable by considering a period when it is possible to estimate the quality of the registers by alternative means. We can compare the results of a biometric analysis of infant mortality in the 1690s with B. M. Berry and R. S. Schofield's material on the interval between birth and baptism, and D. V. Glass's data from the tax returns made on births, marriages and deaths under the Act of 1694.[14] Glass compared the parish registers with these returns and showed how births were seriously under-registered in the 1690s. He estimated the true number of births from the totals of baptisms contained in the two lists by making the assumption that since each list had been compiled independently, there was an equal chance of the exclusion of an event from each list. This assumption may not be completely justified because the two data sets may not have been equally defective records. Although the administration of the provisions of the act were completely outside the hands of the church, it is possible that the collectors would have checked their information against the parish registers. Nevertheless, there is little doubt that Glass was correct in thinking that baptisms were under-registered. In Table 2.6, his data have been used to calculate underbaptism rates which are certainly high. Berry and Schofield's analysis of the interval between birth and baptism shows that this had indeed lengthened by the 1690s, as Table 2.7 demonstrates when compared with Table 2.1, confirming that registration had deteriorated, although not as rapidly as it did during the eighteenth century.

In Table 2.8, endogenous and exogenous infant mortality rates have been calculated, including dummy births, for four of the sample parishes in the 1690s, so that the results are directly comparable with those set out in Table 2.4. The period for which this was done varies in order to include a reasonably large number of events in the calculations. The physical appearance of the registers gave no suggestion that the standard of

14. 6 & 7 Wm & M. c. 6. Glass 1966: xxxvi table 10; and Glass 1972: 283 table 5.

Table 2.6. *Glass's estimates of underbaptism rates in the 1690s (per 1,000 live births)*

Parish and dates	Baptisms in parish register	Calculated total births	Underbaptism rate
St Matthew Friday Street, 1696–9[a]	26	36	278
St Mildred Poultry, 1696–9[a]	37	47	213
38 parishes within the walls, 1696–9[b]	3,094	4,131	251
2 parishes outside the walls, 1696–9[b]	283	325	129
St Botolph Bishopsgate, 1696–7[c]	372	461	193

Sources: a. Glass 1966: xxxvi–xxxvii tables 10 and 11.
   b. Glass 1972: 283, table 5.
   c. Hollingsworth 1971: 139.

registration had declined, but we can see that in all these parishes except St Peter Cornhill the proportion of endogenous deaths had fallen by the 1690s, and we have seen that this is evidence for deteriorating registration, though not perhaps to as great an extent as Glass suggested. There are, however, other factors which confirm the impression that parochial registration had become less reliable. First, in the graph of the cumulative distributions of infant deaths at this time in Figure 2.4, the data fit a straight line far less easily than for the period before 1653 (Figure 2.3). Although this may be partly due to smaller sample sizes, it must also be due to inconsistencies in registration. This means that the estimation of endogenous infant mortality rates will be subject to a much wider margin of error than in the earlier period. Secondly, the endogenous rates must be overestimated for the 1690s because of the increasing interval between

Table 2.7. *Interval in days (± 0.5) by which the stated percentile of 80 sample births had been baptized in the 1690s and 1700s*

Parish and dates	25%	50%	75%	Semi-inter-quartile range	% of incomplete entries
St Vedast Foster Lane, 1697–8 (½ sample)	0	1	13	6	0
St Thomas the Apostle, 1704–6 (½ sample)	1	9	16	8	5
St Benet Paul's Wharf, 1703–4	1	8	16	8	0
St Martin Orgar, 1696–1702	1	6	13	6	9
St Mary Aldermary, 1702–6	2	12	20	9	10
St Mary Aldermanbury, 1695–9	0	3	12	6	1
Christ Church, 1702	2	6	14	6	0

Source: Berry and Schofield 1971: 456, table 1.

Table 2.8. *Endogenous and exogenous components of infant mortality rates in the 1690s ($1,000q_0$)*

Parish and dates	Total births	Infant deaths	Rate	Endogenous		Exogenous	
				%	Rate	%	Rate
St Peter Cornhill, 1691–1700	284	61	215	72	154	28	61
St Michael Cornhill, 1691–1700	195	33	169	46	78	54	91
St Mary Somerset, 1691–1700	292	53	182	47	85	53	97
St Botolph Bishopsgate, 1690	364	64	176	35	62	65	114

birth and baptism by this time. Since endogenous infant mortality rates are calculated for the period after baptism, a lengthening interval between birth and baptism would mean that a greater proportion of all infant deaths would be classed as endogenous (Wrigley 1977: 296). Thirdly, underbaptism rates as calculated in Table 2.9 show that the proportion of dummy births had fallen rapidly by the 1690s – in itself strong grounds for believing that registration was deteriorating – indicating that the number of infant deaths which occurred before baptism was not known (Wrigley 1977: 309).

Table 2.9. *Underbaptism rates in the 1690s (per 1,000 live births)*

Parish and dates	Dummy births	Total births	Underbaptism rate
St Peter Cornhill, 1691–1700	5	284	18
St Michael Cornhill, 1691–1700	1	195	5
St Mary Somerset, 1691–1700	0	292	0
St Botolph Bishopsgate, 1690	14	364	38

Other evidence for the better quality of the parochial registration system before 1653 is that all eight sample parishes recorded stillbirths. This was done consistently throughout the period in St Peter Cornhill, St Michael Cornhill, St Dunstan in the East and St Mary Somerset, and from 1617 in St Botolph Bishopsgate. In the other parishes, Allhallows Bread Street, St Christopher le Stocks, and Allhallows London Wall, they were noted from time to time. The fact that the parish clerks bothered to register stillbirths when they were not required to do so suggests that they were also careful when they recorded other vital statistics. In Table 2.10, still birth rates have been calculated as the number of still births per thousand live births. These rates were high when compared with eighteenth- and nineteenth-

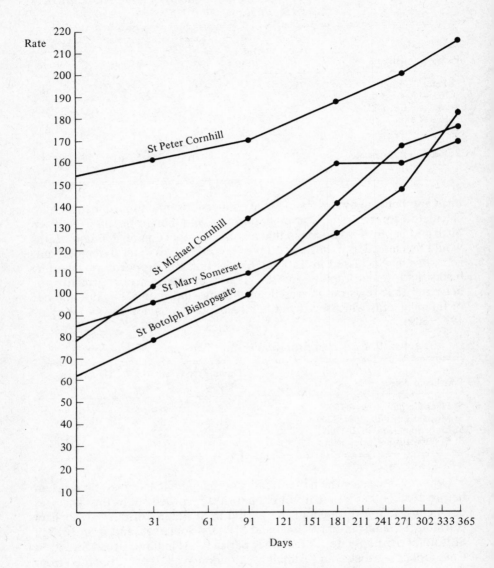

Figure 2.4 Cumulative infant mortality rates in the 1690s.

Table 2.10. *Stillbirth rates before 1653 (per 1,000 live births)*

Parish and dates	Stillbirths	Live births	Stillbirth rate
Allhallows Bread Street, 1538–1653*	17	1,562	11
St Peter Cornhill, 1580–1650	88	1,769	50
St Christopher le Stocks, 1580–1653*	14	1,115	13
St Michael Cornhill, 1580–1650	75	2,261	33
St Dunstan in the East, 1605–53	103	3,103	33
St Mary Somerset, 1605–53	62	2,079	30
Allhallows London Wall, 1570–1636*	11	1,839	6
St Botolph Bishopsgate, 1617–50	112	2,101	53

* In these parishes, the recording of stillbirths in the burial registers was obviously defective.

century Swedish experience.[15] In contrast, stillbirths were not recorded in the four parish registers selected for biometric analysis of infant mortality in the 1690s.

It should be noted that all the results presented so far refer to individuals who were also members of families. The results would not have been markedly affected by the numbers of illegitimate children and foundlings (who may or may not have been illegitimate) because the total of these for the sample parishes taken together was small, but their inclusion would raise infant mortality rates in the 1690s in the richer parishes. The mortality rate for illegitimate or abandoned children would be higher than for children who were members of families. This is an interesting topic, but not one which may be pursued in this context.[16]

We may now study individual London parish registers more closely, because the detail contained in some of them is suggestive of their careful compilation. The parish register of St Peter Cornhill gives the dates of birth and baptism for a period from 30 November 1574 until 1 April 1605, and this allows the accuracy of this particular register to be analysed more thoroughly, although it is hardly likely that it will be typical of all London registers during this period. In this register were recorded 66 infant deaths and 744 baptisms, giving an infant mortality rate of 89 and an endogenous rate of 42, or 47 per cent of the total rate. There were also 9 dummy births, giving a revised total of 75 infant deaths, 753 births and an infant mortality rate of exactly 100. The endogenous rate was 53 which in this case is the

15. Glass 1973: 182, n. 4. In nineteenth-century England, stillbirths may have amounted to between 4 and 5 per cent of all births. The use of stillbirths as a guide to the accuracy of vital registration data is also discussed by Knodel and Shorter 1976.
16. There is no question that during the eighteenth century illegitimacy and the abandoning of children attained very serious proportions, and this would obviously affect the quality of registration. Whether it had done so by the 1690s is not clear from the evidence presented for these four sample parishes, though it was undoubtedly a factor in the general deterioration of parochial registration. In the discussion of London fertility in Chapter 7 below, it will be shown that it is unlikely that non-marital fertility made a very large contribution to total fertility before the Civil War.

proportion of endogenous infant deaths. These revised endogenous infant mortality rates for 1574 to 1605 are slightly lower than those for the longer period from 1580 to 1650, but it would still be difficult to argue that, because the proportion of endogenous infant deaths was higher, the standard of registration was not as complete over the longer period.

Cumulative monthly infant mortality rates for St Peter Cornhill are shown in Figure 2.5. The interval between birth and baptism was short, as

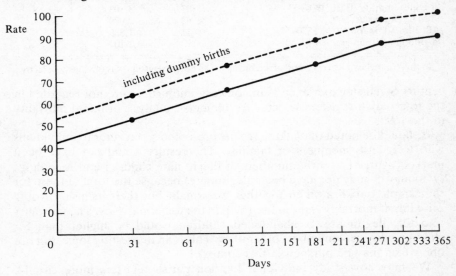

Figure 2.5 Cumulative infant mortality rates in St Peter Cornhill, 30 November 1574 to 1 April 1605.

Table 2.11 demonstrates, a quarter of the children being christened within three days, half in five days and three quarters in seven days. The detail in this register is sufficient to demonstrate that where the child died very close to birth, within seven days, the birth–baptism interval was shorter (Table 2.11). It would therefore appear that steps were taken to avoid a child dying unbaptized. Although the numbers involved are small, it would seem unlikely that the effect persisted beyond the first week, or at most the first two weeks. This procedure was obviously effective since it kept down the number of 'chrisom children', as Table 2.12 demonstrates. It is particularly interesting that no child died unbaptized before the possible disruption to registration brought about by the 1593 plague. Afterwards, it seems that the quality of registration deteriorated slightly, as there is evidence that the christening custom changed towards the end of the sixteenth century with a gradual lengthening of the birth–baptism interval. This is shown in Table 2.13, drawn from the work of Berry and Schofield, which illustrates that

The accuracy of the London parish registers

Table 2.11. *St Peter Cornhill, 30 November 1574 to 1 April 1605: distribution of birth–baptism intervals by age at death*

Birth–baptism interval (days)	All infants		Infant died 0–7 days	
	No.	Cumulative %	No.	Cumulative %
0	15	2	4	17
1	36	7	5	39
2	58	15	3	52
3	74	26	1	56
4	84	37	3	69
5	93	50	1	74
6	84	62	3	87
7	89	74	0	87
8	63	83	1	91
9	47	90	0	91
10	30	94	0	91
11	17	96	2	100
12	12	98		
13	3	98		
14	4	99		
15+	10	100		
Not known	25			
Totals	744	100	23	100

The cumulative percentages exclude those cases where the length of the birth–baptism interval cannot be calculated.

Table 2.12. *St Peter Cornhill, 1574 to 1605: annual totals of dummy births and stillbirths*

Year	Dummy births	Stillbirths	Year	Dummy births	Stillbirths
1574	0	1	1591	0	4
1575	0	1	1592	0	1
1576	0	2	1593	1	0
1577	0	2	1594	0	0
1578	0	1	1595	3	1
1579	0	4	1596	0	1
1580	0	4	1597	0	2
1581	0	2	1598	2	2
1582	0	2	1599	0	0
1583	0	0	1600	0	1
1584	0	2	1601	0	1
1585	0	2	1602	1	3
1586	0	1	1603	1	1
1587	0	4	1604	0	0
1588	0	1	1605	1	0
1589	0	1			
1590	0	1	Total	9	48

Table 2.13. *Interval in days (± 0.5) by which the stated percentile of sample births in St Peter Cornhill, London, had been baptized, and the percentage of all baptisms which took place on Sunday*

Period	25%	50%	75%	Semi-inter-quartile range	% baptisms on Sunday	% of incomplete entries
1574–8	2	3	5	2	65	2
1585–9	3	5	7	2	84	2
1596–8	5	7	9	2	82	2
1601–4	5	7	10	2	69	1
1655–6	6	8	14	4	—	2

Source: Berry and Schofield 1971: 462 table 7.

the birth–baptism interval had lengthened by the beginning of the seventeenth century, and remained more or less unchanged into the Commonwealth period.[17] Further evidence that steps were taken to try to ensure that children did not die unbaptized is given in Table 2.14, showing that in St Botolph Bishopsgate infants baptized on a weekday were more likely to die within the first month of life than those christened on a Sunday.

Table 2.14. *St Botolph Bishopsgate, 25 March 1600 to 25 March 1604: day of the week of baptism and frequency of early burial*

	Baptized on Sunday		Baptized on a weekday	
	No.	%	No.	%
Age at burial				
0–7 days	20	5	25	15
8–28 days	12	3	12	7
29–365 days	75	19	23	14
Survivors and out-migrants	297	73	105	64
Total	404	100	165	100

Source: Hollingsworth 1971: 137 table 5.

It is not known why dates of birth as well as baptism were recorded in St Peter Cornhill during the last quarter of the sixteenth century. However, the reason for the same data being available during the later 1640s for St Vedast Foster Lane (97) and St Thomas the Apostle (96) is that early in 1645 the Long Parliament, in its attempt to establish Presbyterianism in

17. It would seem that the register of St Peter Cornhill was exceptional in ensuring that children would not have died unbaptized before 1593. In several other wealthier parishes, chrisom children were recorded throughout the sixteenth century. These include Allhallows Bread Street, St Dionis Backchurch and St Clement Eastcheap.

England, ordered that services would no longer follow the Prayer Book and that a Directory should be substituted instead. At the same time it was ordered that dates of birth and death as well as of baptisms and burials should be recorded in the parish registers.[18] The instructions were not widely followed, probably because the legality of such a measure was in question until the regicides had done their work. Also, there was much confusion concerning ecclesiastical matters, for although many priests had been sequestered and replaced by puritans, the gathered churches had not fully come into being as separate identities. In fact, of the parishes mentioned in Berry and Schofield's discussion of the age at baptism throughout England in this period (1971: 456 table 1), these were the only two where the ordinance was followed at all. In St Vedast, the recording of births was not begun until 1647 and the order concerning deaths was never followed. St Vedast and St Thomas were of average social status, being located in the second and third quartiles respectively in terms of the distribution of wealth in 1638. Cumulative distributions of birth–baptism intervals are shown in Table 2.15, and they make a very interesting comparison with the data for St Peter's (Table 2.11). Although about half the children had been christened within five days of birth in all three parishes, there were more children baptized on the day of birth in St Vedast and St Thomas and there was a greater proportion of baptisms delayed beyond a week from birth. Since the number of infants involved was relatively small, it is not possible to decide whether those children dying within a week from birth were christened sooner. The small numbers also mean that it is difficult to calculate endogenous mortality rates, but the evidence suggests that under-registration of births was not serious. However, the main figures connected with infant mortality are outlined in Table 2.16 for these two parishes, and it is clear that the data are comparable with those presented for other parishes elsewhere in this chapter, particularly in terms of the extent to which the creation of dummy births inflates the infant mortality rate. The difference in levels of infant mortality between the two parishes reflects little more than the variations in social status of their inhabitants.

The registration experience in the parishes of St Vedast and St Thomas in the later 1640s marks a transition from ecclesiastical to civil registration. As soon as the principle of Independency had been accepted, the parochial

18. 'That there shall be provided at the charge of every Parish or Chappelry in this Realm of England, and Dominion of Wales, a fair Register Book of Velim, to be kept by the Minister and other Officers of the Church; and that the Names of all Children Baptized, and of their Parents and of the time of their Birth and Baptizing, shall be written and set down by the Minister therein; and also the Names of all Persons Married there, and the time of their Marriage; and also the Names of all Persons Buried in that Parish, and the time of their Death and Burial'. An Ordinance for taking away the Book of Common Prayer, and for establishing and putting in execution of the Directory for the publique worship of God (4 January 1644/5), in Firth and Rait 1911: I, 582.

Table 2.15. *St Vedast Foster Lane, 26 January 1647 to 23 August 1653, and St Thomas the Apostle, 22 March 1645 to 23 August 1653: distribution of birth–baptism intervals by length of interval*

Birth–baptism interval (days)	St Vedast Foster Lane		St Thomas the Apostle	
	No.	Cumulative %	No.	Cumulative %
0	44	24	37	19
1	14	32	18	28
2	9	36	10	33
3	10	42	7	37
4	4	44	6	40
5	10	49	9	45
6	15	58	18	54
7	11	64	17	63
8	12	70	11	68
9	8	74	15	76
10	10	80	6	79
11	15	88	10	84
12	5	91	8	88
13	4	93	7	92
14	6	96	11	97
15+	7	100	5	100
Not known	9		4	
Totals	193		199	

The cumulative percentages exclude those cases where the length of the birth–baptism interval cannot be calculated.

registration system had to be re-established along non-sectarian lines with births and deaths being recorded by civil registrars. This was instituted by the Marriage Act passed by the Nominated Parliament in 1653. Once Laudianism had been defeated in the English church, its opponents

Table 2.16. *St Vedast Foster Lane and St Thomas the Apostle: infant mortality data*

	St Vedast	St Thomas
Infant deaths	15	26
Live baptisms	193	199
Infant mortality rate (per 1,000 baptisms)	78	131
Dummy births	3	9
Revised infant deaths	18	35
Revised live births	196	208
Revised infant mortality rate (per 1,000 live births)	92	168
Underbaptism rate (per 1,000 live births)	15	43
Stillbirths	8	13
Stillbirth rate (per 1,000 live births)	41	63

These data refer to the same periods listed in Table 2.15.

immediately disagreed over the way the church should be reconstructed. This is not the place to pursue the question of the accuracy of the civil registers, although D. McLaren has recently suggested that, at least in certain parts of the country, the viewpoint that the registration system generally broke down may be in need of some revision.[19] So it does not follow that registrations in these two parishes are typical of London in general.

Even where the parochial registration system gives an accurate record of the vital events occurring in each parish, there remains an important objection to the use of these data for the calculation of demographic measures. The method by which such indices of population change may be computed from parish registers is family reconstitution, developed in France by L. Henry and successfully applied to English historical demography by E. A. Wrigley, which to be effective requires a relatively stable population. Rates of migration in London, however, were undoubtedly high, first, because the population maintained its numbers and grew only through migration from outside the capital, a point that is already well known, and secondly, because the size of individual parishes was very small within the urban area, so that moving house would far more often have entailed crossing parish boundaries than in most parishes in England, especially those which consisted of more than one settlement. Thus, although the representativeness of the results varies with the demographic parameter being calculated, it is likely that the unreconstitutable minority of events would be far larger for an urban parish than for a rural parish, which might preclude the completion of an effective family reconstitution study. The one advantage of the London social system for nominative demographic work, which involves matching one event with another, is that, although rates of migration were high, rates of persistence of population were not low. Once a family had been established in a parish it frequently remained there for many years, often until the death of one of the marriage partners. A certain amount of inter-parish migration actually facilitates reconstitution, because the introduction of new surnames helps to avoid the difficulty of ambiguity in record linkage.

A modified form of partial reconstitution may therefore be adopted to take account of the degree of mobility inherent in London society. For the

19. A study of sample parishes for the period after 1653 would be inappropriate in the sense that each parish did not have its own registrar (McLaren 1974). The text of the Act with respect to registration states: 'And that a true and just accompt may be always kept, as well of Publications, as of all such Marriages, and also of the Births of Children, and Deaths of all sorts of persons within this Commonwealth'. An act touching Marriages and the Registring thereof; and also touching Births and Burials (24 August 1653), in Firth and Rait 1911: II, 716. It would be a particularly interesting topic, although outside the scope of this chapter, to investigate the course and extent of the deterioration of registration between the outbreak of Civil War and the 1690s. The system certainly broke down, at least temporarily, as a result of the Great Plague and Fire of 1665–6.

best results, the period studied should finish with the establishment of civil registration or at the very latest in 1665. There are gaps in many registers resulting from the physical destruction caused to London parishes by the Great Fire and from the effect of the religious settlement after the Restoration, so that reconstitution is difficult during the 1660s. There were also boundary changes at this time. The period studied cannot effectively begin until after about 1580 in most parishes, or even later, because many burial registers do not contain sufficient information before this date for events to be matched with confidence. Since the family reconstitution technique is best suited to the derivation of vital rates over a relatively long period, the London registers are thus accurate for just long enough to allow meaningful rates to be obtained, and comparisons between a variety of parishes at the same time to be made.[20] The population was sufficiently stable for reconstitution during this period because people migrated to the city when they were young, often to enter apprenticeship or domestic service, and then married and settled in a parish. It would, however, be especially difficult and not practical to link the partners of a marriage back to their own births which had probably occurred outside London. This aspect of family reconstitution is of less importance when dealing with a short period and many of the complications, and also the time taken, are reduced by eliminating the attempt to make links between one generation and another. Indexes to printed parish registers have been used to facilitate the computation of specific measures, such as age at marriage for London-born girls. A short-period reconstitution also helped to avoid the problem of name changes at marriage.

The study technique was to copy the baptisms directly on to standard family reconstitution forms (FRFs) as used by the SSRC Cambridge Group for the History of Population and Social Structure. The marriage register was then worked through to enable the date of marriage, the maiden name of the wife and the rank of the marriage (whether it was the first, second or subsequent marriage) to be added to the FRFs where appropriate. By this stage it had become apparent where household heads had married more than once, either because it was stated in the register or because children were born to mothers with different names. Further FRFs were then completed to cover these additional families. The next task was to copy the burials on to slips of paper before matching the entries to the baptisms listed on the FRFs. This helped to avoid incorrect linkages, as the slips made it possible to work through the data more than once in order to resolve ambiguous links and to ensure a reasonable standard of accuracy. Apart from these modifications, the procedure followed was the same as that outlined by Wrigley (1966c).

20. These comments do not, of course, rule out the possibility of reconstitution studies of the London parish registers being undertaken for other periods.

Given that the London parish registers are accurate for the period from 1580 until 1650, it is possible to collect together a set of family reconstitution forms from which demographic measures may be computed in the normal way. The degree of mobility in London means that three important measures cannot be calculated from this material: the age at marriage, which may be studied only for the few people who were born and married in the same parish, age-specific fertility rates, and adult mortality rates.

One of the most characteristic features of the population of pre-industrial England was its mobility (Laslett 1977: 50–101), and it has to be demonstrated here that inter-parish migration within London was not so much greater than elsewhere that the results of a reconstitution study might be called into question. As has been noted, the key to successful reconstitution is a high rate of persistence of the population in one parish over time. Measuring the rate of persistence demands either the analysis of nominative listings of inhabitants compiled at successive points in time, or linking the results of reconstitution studies with such listings. The nature of the data does not help the analysis because when the registers were good before 1653 there were few listings, whereas at the end of the seventeenth century when the accuracy of the registers is questionable, there is much to be learnt from the listings. For the later period, Glass's work on enumerations for 1695 and 1696 made under that 1694 Act for the parish of St Benet Paul's Wharf (1972: 281–2) indicates that although the population in the parish was very mobile, high mobility was mainly restricted to certain groups in the population such as servants and others in migratory occupations whose families cannot in any case be reconstituted. Before 1653, the only list covering almost the whole of London was that of householders recorded in 1638 which is analysed in Chapter 4. However, a few of the London vestry minute books and collections of churchwardens' accounts also contain yearly lists of householders.[21]

The turnover of names in the lists for three parishes, St Christopher le Stocks (26), St Bartholomew by the Exchange (20), and St Margaret Lothbury (49), has been analysed to calculate persistence rates. Such lists for consecutive years are not commonly found. Although these three parishes were adjacent to each other, they represented quite a wide range of socio-economic characteristics. In St Christopher, the lists, which are contained in the churchwardens' accounts, give the names of the householders who contributed to the parish clerk's wages and paid a fee for the use of the pews in church. In the other two parishes, St Bartholomew and St Margaret, the lists were of contributors to poor rates and are contained in the vestry minute books. Persistence rates calculated from these data are contained in Tables 2.17, 2.18 and 2.19. It is clear from the content of the lists that they were revised annually, and although each year's list for each

---

21. The most useful introduction to this class of records is Cox 1913.

Table 2.17. *The persistence of householders in St Christopher le Stocks*

Date	Names on list	1 year later		5 years later		10 years later	
	No.	No.	%	No.	%	No.	%
1576	53	49	92	31	58	14	26
1577	62	56	90	32	52	—	
1578	60	50	83	29	48	16	27
1579	56	52	93	32	57	15	27
1580	58	47	81	30	52	19	33
1581	60	51	85	29	48		
1582	68	54	79	—			
1583	63	55	87	33	52		
1584	64	50	78	33	52		
1585	62	54	87	32	52		
1586	63	50	79				
1587–8	64	51	80				
1589	70	57	81				
1590	63						

Source: Freshfield 1885.

parish was compiled by a different person, there seems little cause to doubt their general accuracy, because the total number of householders in each year was nearly constant. Those who were too poor to pay were also recorded as, in St Christopher, were those in arrears. The interesting point which emerges, and which is encouraging for family reconstitution studies, is the relatively high rate of persistence, defined as the proportion of the population that stayed in the parish for ten years. That these rates were slightly lower during the Civil War may be accounted for by the social dislocation which occurred in these years. If we accept that about 50 per cent of the population remained within English villages for ten years (Laslett 1977: 50–101; Prest 1976), then the rate for London householders of 25 to 40 per cent suggests that the stability of London's population has been underestimated. There are certainly sufficient stable elements in the London social structure to permit reconstitution studies to be undertaken, and in particular the wide range of socio-economic characteristics of these three parishes encourages such studies.

The key concept in family reconstitution is that of observation. The immense advance over earlier genealogical studies in demographic research made by Henry in his formulation of the reconstitution method is that he developed a set of rules by which the population at risk may be determined with precision. Demographic rates are calculated only from those FRFs meeting specific requirements, which may vary according to the measure being investigated, so that the proportion of the population which is of use changes when different calculations are made. Family reconstitution relies on the assumption that the characteristics of the

Table 2.18. *The persistence of householders in St Bartholomew by the Exchange**

Date	Names on list	1 year later		5 years later		10 years later	
	No.	No.	%	No.	%	No.	%
1626	64	53	83	37	58	19	30
1627	61	54	89	38	62	24	39
1628	65	55	85	35	54	26	40
1629	72	63	88	42	58	28	39
1630	73	62	85	42	58	28	38
1631	73	65	89	39	53	25	34
1632	74	63	85	40	54	26	35
1633	69	59	86	37	54	26	38
1634	71	62	87	37	52	19	27
1635	76	60	79	42	55	25	33
1636	86	68	79	42	49	—	
1637	78	64	82	44	56	24	31
1638	77	66	86	40	52	25	32
1639	75	64	85	34	45	21	28
1640	76	67	88	39	51	21	28
1641	72	64	89	—			
1642	75	71	95	28	37		
1643	74	49	66	32	43		
1644	72	59	82	32	44		
1645	67	—		30	45		
1646	—						
1647	76	71	93				
1648	78	60	77				
1649	72	58	81				

Source: Freshfield 1890.
* These figures exclude the poor, because it is difficult to distinguish householders, and also shops.

Table 2.19. *The persistence of householders in St Margaret Lothbury*

Date	Names on list	1 year later		5 years later		10 years later	
	No.	No.	%	No.	%	No.	%
1642	125	112	90	62	50	37	30
1643	132 (104*)	107	81	64	48	35*	34
1644	131	102	78	72	55	—	
1645	139	102	73	76	55	38	27
1646	142	99	70	70	49	37	26
1647	136	112	82	76	56	—	
1648	132 (99*)	117	89	58*	59	41	31
1649	144	112	78	—		47	33
1650	136	120	88	75	55	—	

Source: Freshfield 1887b.
* These figures exclude the poor living in the parish.

reconstituted population are similar to those of the whole population inhabiting any parish, but it is undoubtedly the most successful method of obtaining demographic rates for smaller areas.[22] Although projection models are currently being developed to derive rates from aggregate series of births and deaths, they are of greatest value when used on the national and regional scale, since a relatively closed population is important for success. Such models also require an accurate age-structure of the population to be known for some point in time.[23] Family reconstitution remains of great value for work on any scale below that of a large region, and in particular when making comparisons between social groups. In this study, such comparisons involve a detailed examination of parishes typical of particular social areas of London.

We can now compare infant mortality rates calculated for the reconstituted population with the rates calculated so far in this chapter for the total population. Again it must be assumed that the accuracy of registration of the reconstituted population is the same as that for the total population in each parish. Much of this study will be based on the results from four parishes: St Peter Cornhill, St Michael Cornhill, St Mary Somerset and Allhallows London Wall. Endogenous and exogenous components of infant mortality rates calculated by independent observation of children within the parish are given in Table 2.20 and the distributions of infant deaths are shown in Figure 2.6. These rates have been calculated by including the deaths of unbaptized children which took place while the family was in observation and in this respect they are comparable with the data in Table 2.4. However, they exclude deaths occurring in plague

Table 2.20. *Endogenous and exogenous components of family reconstitution infant mortality rates excluding deaths in plague periods* $(1,000q_0)$

Parish and dates	Population at risk	Infant deaths	Rate	Endogenous		Exogenous	
				%	Rate	%	Rate
St Peter Cornhill, 1580–1650	1,100	115	105	47	49	53	56
St Michael Cornhill, 1580–1650	1,402	195	139	59	82	41	57
St Mary Somerset, 1605–53	1,045	277	265	64	170	36	95
Allhallows London Wall, 1570–1636	868	160	184	55	102	45	82

22. A very useful critique of the family reconstitution method is contained in Åkerman 1977.
23. Projection models are discussed in Lee 1974.

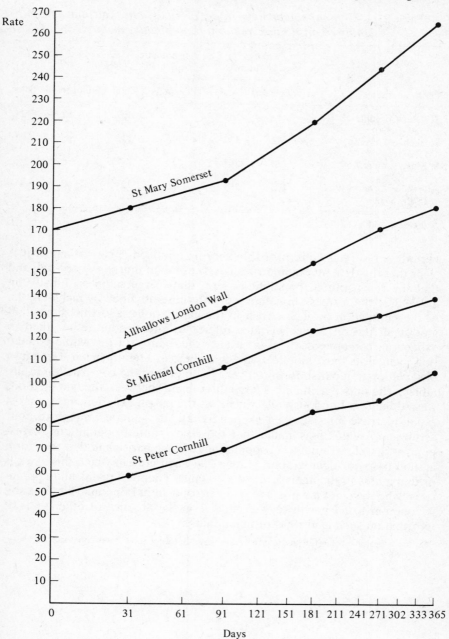

Figure 2.6 Cumulative family reconstitution infant mortality rates.

Table 2.21. *Comparison between infant mortality rates calculated from family reconstitution and simple nominative methods*

Parish and dates	Family reconstitution[a]		Nominative methods[b]		Difference	
	Endogenous	Total	Endogenous	Total	Endogenous	Total
St Peter Cornhill, 1580–1650	49	105	65	129	−16	−24
St Michael Cornhill, 1580–1650	82	139	74	133	+8	+6
St Mary Somerset, 1605–53	170	265	175	272	−5	−7
Allhallows London Wall, 1570–1636	102	184	142	225	−40	−41

Sources: a. Table 2.20
　　　　　 b. Table 2.4.

periods when rates were probably very high indeed.[24] Nevertheless, it is clear that the data fit a biometric analysis of infant mortality very well and that the reconstituted populations form quite large samples. Finally, in Table 2.21 these rates are compared with those obtained by including the whole population of each parish in the calculations, and this shows that almost all the difference in rates relates to endogenous rather than to exogenous components. This is because the figures for the whole population include its most mobile elements, whereas a family has to remain in observation in a parish for a full year to enter into the construction of life tables. The only parish with a large discrepancy between the two methods was Allhallows London Wall, which was the parish experiencing the most rapid increase in size (see Appendix 2). In general, therefore, our assumption seems reasonable that the reconstituted populations correspond very well with the total populations of each parish and that they form a good basis for demographic study. The main area in which this work is incomplete is in the analysis of single adults, mainly servants and apprentices, who were not members of families resident in London. This omission is common to all parish register studies in the absence of other sorts of information such as listings of inhabitants.

24. See Chapter 5 for a full discussion of the way life tables have been constructed.

CHAPTER 3

THE GENERAL GROWTH OF POPULATION IN LONDON

The population of London was growing continually throughout the two and a half centuries before the first national census of 1801. Since no census-type listings of inhabitants existed for large areas of the city before 1695, numbers have to be estimated from other sources, principally the bills of mortality. The current opinion about the population of London is indicated by the estimates given in Table 3.1 which are based upon a careful examination of most previous authorities.[1] Nothing is claimed for them other than that they provide a good general guide to the course of population change in London over three centuries, and they show that it was a very large city indeed and that it was growing especially rapidly after 1550. London more than doubled in size during the second half of the sixteenth century, from about 70,000 in 1550 to around 200,000 by 1600. It doubled in size again in the first half of the seventeenth century, from 200,000 in 1600 to 400,000 in 1650. The city's population grew nearly threefold during the seventeenth century, and almost tenfold between the middle of the sixteenth century and the middle of the eighteenth. However, the most rapid changes occurred during the period considered in this book, from 1580 when London numbered just 100,000 inhabitants to 1650 when it contained 400,000 people. This fourfold growth in seventy years was faster than in any other period before modern times.

Table 3.1. *Estimates of the population of London, 1500–1800*

Year	Estimated total
1500	50,000
1550	70,000
1600	200,000
1650	400,000
1700	575,000
1750	675,000
1800	900,000

Sources: Creighton 1891a: 482–90; Russell 1948: 275, 298; Wrigley 1967: 44.

1. The figures from 1600 onwards are taken from Wrigley 1967: 44–51. The most useful of the older sources is Creighton 1891a.

Estimates of the population of London are usually made from the totals of christenings included in the bills of mortality. If it is assumed that the birth rate was constant, this series of totals gives an indication of the course of demographic growth. The size of London at different periods may then be established from estimates of the actual birth rate. The chief difficulty with using the bills of mortality is that most of the originals are missing, probably destroyed in the Great Fire of 1666. An important series of annual totals was printed by Graunt but it is very difficult to check because the parish registers do not all survive in complete form, and bills exist only for some years with the totals of burials, but not christenings, subdivided by parish. These data are summarized in Appendix 1.[2]

There are three further problems involved in estimating the population of London from the bills of mortality. The first is concerned with the definition of the area of the city considered, because the number of parishes incorporated into the jurisdiction of the bills increased as the built-up area expanded during the period. The estimates given here will incorporate the whole of the area within the bills, which assumes that the periodic increases accurately reflected the growth of the townscape.[3] Secondly, the accuracy of the bills of mortality must be considered. We have shown that the bills, compiled in association with the registers, which were found to be reliable, were a better source than has frequently been thought. Nevertheless, a small degree of under-recording in the bills must be incorporated into the estimates. Thirdly, any calculations of the population of London depend on accurate estimates of the birth rate, which are very difficult to obtain, as Chapter 7 will make clear. For all these reasons, accurate estimates of the population of London are not easy to make, but it is possible to outline the general course of the changes that occurred.

The study of the bills of mortality may be supplemented by the analysis of a sample of ten parish registers.[4] These were not drawn on any basis that might be considered statistically correct since all the registers do not survive, and since it is necessary to exclude not only parishes where there were gaps in the registers, but also small parishes which might be especially susceptible to random fluctuations. Nevertheless, it was intended to cover a wide variety of parishes and the sample includes parishes from both wealthy and poor areas as well as those in the middle of the socio-economic spectrum, and inland parishes and those nearer the riverside. The sample was restricted to parishes located within the city walls because their size

2. The most thorough study of the bills of mortality is contained in Sutherland 1972. A valuable guide is Wilson 1927: 189–215.
3. The names of the administrative divisions of London, together with a map of their locations, are given in Appendix 3.
4. The parishes included were Allhallows Bread Street, St Peter Cornhill, St Christopher le Stocks, St Michael Cornhill, St Vedast Foster Lane, St Helen Bishopsgate, St Thomas the Apostle, St Lawrence Jewry, St Mary Somerset, and Allhallows London Wall.

makes matching easier, although there was little variation in the quality of registration in a large parish such as St Botolph Bishopsgate, compared with a much smaller neighbouring parish such as Allhallows London Wall. Table 2.5 suggests that baptism registers for the city parishes undercounted births by about 3 per cent, although this figure may have risen to about 7 per cent in the larger suburban parishes. The social status of the sample parishes is discussed in detail in the next chapter. Although they varied considerably in their social and demographic characteristics, there was not a great deal of difference in the accuracy of the registers for the City of London.

Figures 3.1 and 3.2 show how closely the parish register sample mirrors the demographic trends in the bills of mortality and gives an idea of the

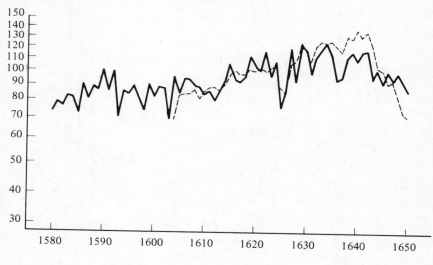

Figure 3.1 London christenings from the parish register sample (solid line) and the bills of mortality (broken line).

general trend in baptisms and burials since 1580. Index numbers have been constructed of the totals of baptisms and burials with the average of the years from 1616 and 1620 chosen as base 100. This period has been selected because it is midway between 1610 and 1625, years when the plague was practically dormant and so would have had least influence on the totals of christenings and burials. The main discrepancy between the bills and the registers came after the 1636 plague outbreak, probably because people were beginning to leave the wealthier central parishes in order to escape from plague, even though the 1636 outbreak was less serious than the earlier crises. The rapid decline in the numbers of christenings after 1642

Table 3.2 *Comparison of burials in the bills of mortality and the parish registers*

Parish	1603			1625			1665		
	Bills of mortality	Parish registers	Difference in bills %	Bills of mortality	Parish registers	Difference in bills %	Bills of mortality	Parish registers	Difference in bills %
Allhallows Bread Street (2)	33	34	-2.9	38	41	-7.3	35	36	-2.8
St Peter Cornhill (90)	141	132	+6.8	138	140	-1.4	136	134	+1.5
St Christopher le Stocks (26)	41	42	-2.4	48	42	+14.3	60	—	—
St Michael Cornhill (74)	130	129	+0.8	159	159	nil	104	105	-1.0
St Vedast Foster Lane (97)	91	95	-4.2	149	147	+1.4	144	143	+0.7
St Helen Bishopsgate (36)	98	101	-3.0	146	135	+8.1	108	—	—
St Thomas the Apostle (96)	86	83	+3.6	141	138	+2.2	163	163	nil
St Lawrence Jewry (44)	88	89	-1.1	91	85	+7.1	94	95	-1.1
St Mary Somerset (68)	197	—	—	270	263	+2.7	342	349	-2.0
Allhallows London Wall (7)	216	220	-1.8	301	302	-0.3	500	333	+50.2

The exact dates to which these figures relate are determined by the periods covered by the bills of mortality. These were 14 July 1603 to 22 December 1603; 16 December 1624 to 15 December 1625; and 20 December 1664 to 19 December 1665. The totals in the bills of mortality were taken from copies in Wilson 1927: plate 18, plate 25; and Sutherland 1963: 544 figure 3.

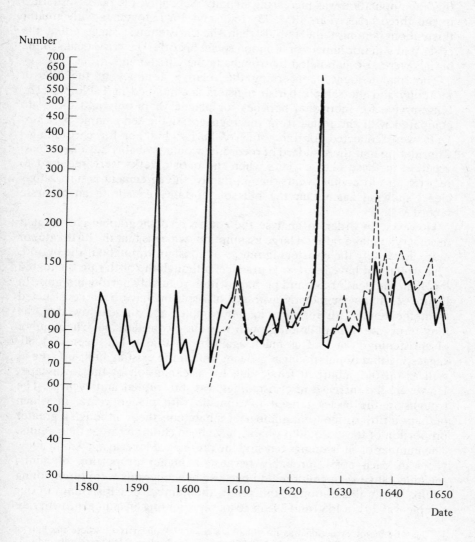

Figure 3.2 London burials from the parish register sample (solid line) and the bills of mortality (broken line).

suggests that the quality of registration in the bills deteriorated more rapidly than in the registers. Nevertheless the general trends revealed in these graphs certainly illustrate some of the salient characteristics of London's population. There are two especially striking features. First, a secular growth in the numbers of both christenings and burials indicates that the population was increasing steadily. Secondly, the peaks of burials in the three crisis years of 1593, 1603 and 1625, together with greater fluctuations amongst the burials than the christenings, suggest that the crises had a major impact on London social history. The crisis peaks in the burials were also paralleled by troughs in the christenings.

The final evidence concerning the relative accuracy of the bills of mortality and the sample parish registers is contained in Table 3.2. The bills survive for individual parishes for plague years only and these are compared with the totals from the registers of the ten sample parishes. Data were collected for the totals of burials but not for christenings. Considering that the standard of recording would probably have been least accurate in these plague years when the parish clerks were required to register far more vital events than normally, the agreement is surprisingly close, showing again that the bills of mortality constitute an accurate record.[5]

However, in order to analyse the course of demographic growth it is necessary to make rather a large assumption, which is that the birth rate, or more accurately the christening rate, was constant throughout the period. This would not have been so in practice, although the birth rate fluctuated less than the death rate, and perhaps within relatively narrow margins. In Figure 3.3 five-year moving averages of baptisms have been constructed from the ten parish registers in our sample, and these show that the long-term rate of population growth was quite considerable. The number of christenings was half as much again by 1640 as it had been in 1580, suggesting that population was growing within the existing built-up area as well as on the suburban fringe due to an expansion of the townscape. However, the increase in christenings was interrupted and cyclical. The troughs in the cycles tended to coincide with plague years, in which perhaps a fifth of the total number of inhabitants died, although a greater proportion of these would probably have been children rather than adults. The number of christenings reached the pre-plague level again within a few years of each crisis, probably because a higher proportion of adults remained alive than children and because new migrants were often young adults. As an illustration of this point, the number of christenings in our sample was 201 in 1580 and 295 in 1640, representing an annual growth rate

5. The only major exception was in Allhallows London Wall in 1665, where the bills of mortality recorded 500 burials of which 356 were from the plague, but there were only 333 entries contained in the parish register. In this parish the registers may have been unreliable after the Civil War when the church became a centre for irregular marriage.

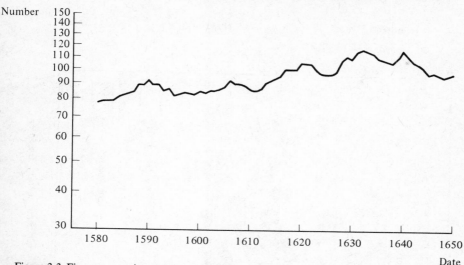

Figure 3.3 Five-year moving averages of London christenings from the parish register sample (1616–20 average = 100).

of 0.64 per cent, whilst in the ten years from 1610 to 1620 the number of christenings increased from 227 to 282, a rate of 2.19 per cent. Without the checks to demographic growth imposed by plague the increase in population might have been much greater, although higher death rates could well have come instead from other diseases, which even if endemic and less dramatic in their occurrence could still have affected population growth. There is no question, however, that the population would have been much smaller in the absence of migration to London.[6]

Although it is relatively straightforward to chart the general course of population changes in London, the problem of what figures of total population size to substitute for the index numbers, even with the assumption of a constant birth rate, is almost intractable. Creighton (1891a: 491,495) argued that in the sixteenth century, at least, London was healthier than it subsequently became, and he suggested that the birth rate would have been 29 per thousand and the death rate 25 per thousand. That is why his figures of total population size are quite high, increasing from 123,000 in 1580 to 224,000 in 1605 and 340,000 by 1634. Table 3.3 gives summary totals of baptisms, burials and marriages for our sample parishes, which indicate that in the central part of the city the numbers of baptisms were about the same as burials, so the birth rate and death rate were

6. It is interesting to note that in a recent study of the population of Venice during this period, it was found that short-term fluctuations, such as the effect of plague, did not seriously interrupt the secular course of population trends. Rapid recovery from plague was mainly attributed to migration from the countryside. Rapp 1976: 22–42.

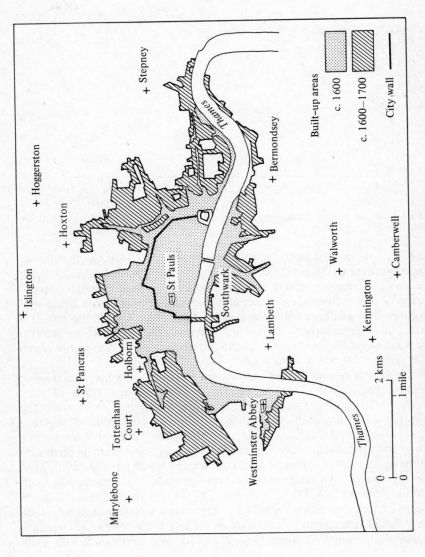

Figure 3.4 The topographical growth of London during the seventeenth century. Based on Brett-James 1935 and Darby 1973: 386 figure 82.

Table 3.3 *Summary demographic measures for London parishes,*
1580–1650

Parish	Baptisms	Burials	Marriages	Baptisms per burial	Baptisms per marriage
Allhallows Bread Street	1,044	1,006	327	1.04	3.19
St Peter Cornhill	1,805	2,145	641	0.84	2.82
St Christopher le Stocks	1,063	930	366	1.14	2.90
St Michael Cornhill	2,234	2,323	587	0'96	3.81
St Vedast Foster Lane	1,991	1,997	503	1.00	3.96
St Helen Bishopsgate	1,362	1,839	751	0.74	1.81
St Thomas the Apostle	1,552	1,740	558	0.89	2.78
St Lawrence Jewry	2,041	1,891	535	1.08	3.81
St Mary Somerset	2,834	3,864	1,133	0.73	2.50
Allhallows London Wall	2,204	3,091	1,782	0.71	1.24
Total sample	18,130	20,826	7,183	0.87	2.52

similar also. In the peripheral parishes, however, which are the last two in the table, the birth rate was much lower than the death rate, although this differential may have been underestimated for London as a whole because more people lived in the suburbs than in the city by the end of the period. Estimates of the population of London must also take the expansion of the built-up area into consideration. Places like Westminster and Hackney were incorporated into the bills of mortality as Distant Parishes in 1636, but they were much less urbanized and less clearly a visible part of the townscape even fifty years later.[7] The absence of accurate mapping in this period makes a study of the extent of the built-up area from this angle inconclusive. Therefore, all that is claimed for Figure 3.4 is that it gives an idea of the extent of growth in London during the seventeenth century. The nature of the data makes it imperative that our study is based on administrative areas, which is why areas covered by the bills of mortality are used.

Estimates of the course of population growth in London are given in Table 3.4. These have been based on totals of christenings in the bills of mortality as listed in Appendix 1 plus an additional 5 per cent to allow for under-registration of christenings. This correction factor has been chosen to incorporate a low rate of omission in the small central parishes and a higher rate in the larger suburban parishes (Table 2.5). Population totals are given in thousands and are based on a range of values between birth rates of 30 and 35 per thousand. These rates are consistent with the

7. The best guide to the topographical growth of London during the seventeenth century remains Brett-James 1935. For an interesting case-study see Power 1978b.

Table 3.4. *Estimates of the population of London, 1580–1650 (thousands)*

Year	City and Liberties	City, Liberties and Out-Parishes	City, Liberties, Out-Parishes and Distant Parishes
1580	107–125		
1593	128–150		
1600	143–167		
1605		195–228	
1610		204–237	
1615		230–269	
1620		235–275	
1625		209–244	
1630		279–326	
1635		301–351	
1640		326–380	391–456

These totals have been obtained by applying low and high estimates of the birth rate of 30 and 35 per thousand respectively to the numbers of christenings given in Appendix 1 plus a 5 per cent addition to account for under-registration of christenings.

conclusion about London fertility, outlined in Chapter 7, that although marital fertility was very high, the birth rate may have been lower because a high proportion of the population was not married. The resulting population estimates are also compatible with the figures in Table 3.1 and I. Sutherland's own analysis of population totals from the bills of mortality (1972: 296 figure 1, 310 table 6).

The combined data from the sample parish registers (Figure 3.5) confirm the general trends of a steadily rising population; approximately equal birth and death rates in normal years; the catastrophic effects of plague in crisis years; and a marriage rate sensitive to the crises. The rise in the marriage rate after 1645 is due entirely to the fact that one parish, Allhallows London Wall, had become a centre for irregular marriage during the Civil War period. All these features are also evident in the graphs for the individual parishes in Appendix 2, although the trends are visible to different degrees in each. Thus plague affected the wealthier parishes to a less marked extent than the poorer ones and the rate of population growth was slower in some parishes than others. In no parish did baptisms exceed burials to any extent, yet in the poorer parishes the death rate was considerably greater than the birth rate. Perhaps the most remarkable feature of the individual graphs is their degree of consistency with the overall pattern, which adds to our confidence in the data from the parish registers. They also demonstrate the range of variation which may have existed.

It is possible to return to the data contained in the bills of mortality to confirm that the rate of demographic growth was much greater in some

Number

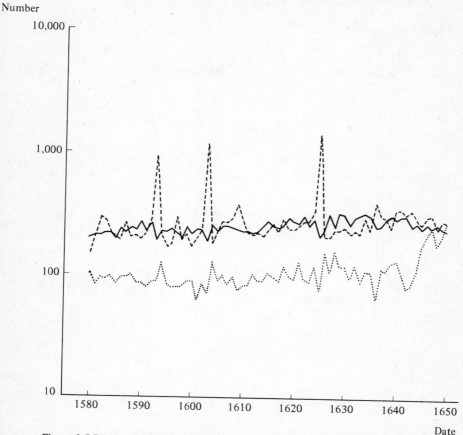

Figure 3.5 Baptisms (solid line), burials (broken line) and marriages (dotted line) in London Parish register sample.

areas of the city than others. The bills give a total of christenings only for the whole of London but the burials, excluding those attributable to plague, are subdivided into annual figures for the parishes within the walls and in the Liberties, the Out-Parishes and, from 1636, the Distant Parishes. The plotted figures (Figure 3.6) show how the rate of growth of population was greatest in the Out-Parishes and least in the city itself, which is to be expected. Thus although the trends in population growth were similar throughout London, there were important variations between individual areas of the city.

Not only did the population of London as a whole grow especially rapidly during the late sixteenth and early seventeenth centuries, but this was also the period when its long-term rate of growth was greatest, at least before modern times. It is more difficult to use the bills of mortality after

61

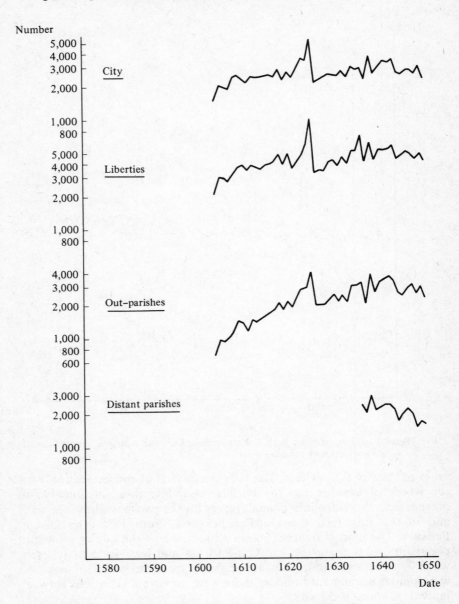

Figure 3.6 Burials in administrative areas of London from the bills of mortality.

1650 to calculate the total population of London because of the problems of under-registration of events, and because the assumption of a constant birth rate would not be reasonable over such very long periods. However, despite their general nature, the estimates in Table 3.1 show quite convincingly that whilst the population doubled between 1550 and 1600 and doubled again between 1600 and 1650, it increased by only half as much again in the succeeding half century and at an even slower rate in the first half of the eighteenth century. It cannot be argued that the rate of growth appeared especially fast in the period before the Civil War because of a markedly low initial population during the early Tudor period. The opinion that London was always very important and grew throughout the pre-industrial period is one which tends to oversimplify the issues, since the rate of population growth and the nature and extent of the links between London and the remainder of the country varied considerably.

It is only possible to give broad reasons why London may have grown so rapidly during this period, but two especially important causes stand out. In the first place, if urban growth were occurring, London was more likely to increase in size at the beginning of the period because there were so few other large towns, whilst by 1750 their number had grown sufficiently for there to be far more destinations for migrants than earlier. Secondly, and of greater importance, the growth of population in London had to be related to changes in the economy of the whole country because, as we have seen, the capital depended upon a regular supply of migrants from the countryside even to maintain its size. There is some evidence that during the early years of the seventeenth century, wages in London for skilled workers were much higher than in the countryside, an obvious attraction to migrants (Hutchins 1899).

The increase in London's population from about 7 per cent of the English national total in 1650 to about 11 per cent in 1750 (Wrigley 1967: 45) therefore reflected variations in the rates of demographic growth in both London itself and England as a whole. The exact nature of English population movements are much less clear than those for London, but the data drawn from a national sample of 404 parishes assembled by the SSRC Cambridge Group for the History of Population and Social Structure demonstrate that the population grew quite rapidly between 1550 and 1650 when there were large surpluses of baptisms over burials, whilst in the half century from 1650 to 1700 the population increased only slightly and burials kept pace with baptisms (Smith 1978: 205 figure 8.2). It should be pointed out that during the sixteenth and seventeenth centuries London was growing in population size at the same time as the population of England was increasing, and when the rate of growth of London slowed considerably, the national population was static. London always grew more rapidly than the remainder of England. By the eighteenth century, when the population of England was again rising, economic growth was

63

Table 3.5. *Regional origins of migrants to London*

Origin	Freemen 1551–3		Apprentices 15 companies 1570–1640		Inns of Court members 1590–1639		Apprentices 9 companies 1674–90		Freemen 1690	
	No.	%	No.	%	No.	%	No.	%	No.	%
Home Counties	144	17.6	1,459	19.0	1,839	18.5	1,124	31.7	227	20.3
South midlands	70	8.5	1,343	17.5	949	9.5	602	16.9	256	22.9
North midlands	114	13.9	1,082	14.1	729	7.3	374	10.6	160	14.3
Eastern counties	78	9.5	675	8.8	1,505	15.1	625	17.6	65	5.8
Western counties	52	6.4	1,244	16.2	2,028	20.3	216	6.1	201	18.0
North east	189	23.1	576	7.5	736	7.4	154	4.4	54	4.8
North west	113	13.8	675	8.8	705	7.1	142	4.0	70	6.3
South	17	2.1	330	4.3	536	5.4	218	6.2	51	4.6
Wales	21	2.6	261	3.4	526	5.3	65	1.8	25	2.2
Scotland and Ireland	16	2.0	31	0.4	409	4.1	22	0.7	7	0.6
Abroad	4	0.5	—		—		—		2	0.2
Total	818	100.0	7,676	100.0	9,962	100.0	3,542	100.0	1,118	100.0

Sources: Ramsay 1978; 528 table 1; Elliott 1978: 158 table 1, 159 table 2; Prest 1972: 33 table 6; and Glass 1976: 229 table 10.10.

Note: The counties included in each regional grouping are:

Home Counties	Essex, Hertfordshire, Kent, Middlesex, Surrey
South midlands	Bedfordshire, Berkshire, Buckinghamshire, Northamptonshire, Oxfordshire
North midlands	Derbyshire, Leicestershire, Nottinghamshire, Staffordshire, Warwickshire
Eastern counties	Cambridgeshire, Huntingdonshire, Lincolnshire, Norfolk, Rutland, Suffolk
Western counties	Cornwall, Devon, Dorset, Gloucestershire, Herefordshire, Somerset, Wiltshire, Worcestershire
North east	Durham, Northumberland, Yorkshire
North west	Cheshire, Cumberland, Lancashire, Shropshire, Westmorland
South	Hampshire, Sussex

Table 3.6. *Regional origins of London apprentices per 10,000 population in 1630 and 1660*

Origin	1570–1640			1674–90		
	Apprentices	Population of area of origin	Apprentices per 10,000 population	Apprentices	Population of area of origin	Apprentices per 10,000 population
Home Counties	1,459	1,062,436	13.7	1,124	1,120,054	10.0
South midlands	1,343	381,326	35.2	602	357,919	16.8
North midlands	1,082	419,481	25.8	374	453,092	8.3
Eastern counties	675	738,928	9.1	625	756,435	8.3
Western counties	1,244	1,176,842	10.6	216	1,172,779	1.8
North east	576	624,462	9.2	154	703,082	2.2
North west	675	533,934	12.6	142	558,921	2.5
South	330	258,313	12.8	218	243,469	9.0
England	7,384	5,195,722	14.2	3,455	5,365,751	6.4

Sources: Apprentices – Table 3.5
Population – British Parliamentary Papers, 1843, xxii, 1841 Census Enumeration Abstract, pp. 36–7.

occurring in a sufficiently large number of areas to mean that urban growth would no longer be concentrated almost entirely in London.

To indicate the pattern of migration, Table 3.5 shows the regional origins of several groups of migrants to the capital. This kind of tabulation can be assembled only for certain groups in the population, and mainly only for male migrants. The information which has the widest coverage is for apprentices from fifteen city companies and for members of the Inns of Court during the period between 1570 and 1640. This may be set into comparative perspective with data for freemen admitted between 1551 and 1553, apprentices enrolled between 1674 and 1690 and freemen admitted in 1690. There are similarities in migration patterns between these groups which suggest that the figures give some indication of the influence of London in the country as a whole. Table 3.6 estimates the relative importance of the different regions in sending migrants to London by relating the number of apprentices listed in Table 3.5 to estimates of the population of the various counties in 1630 and 1670 made by John Rickman and published in the 1841 census. He estimated the population from the numbers of baptisms, marriages and burials in each county but assumed that birth, marriage and death rates were the same as in 1801.[8] Although this means that Rickman's population totals are probably too high, the same error runs throughout the calculations so the figures are likely to show the correct trends. Between 1570 and 1640, the midlands contributed a disproportionate number of migrants and large numbers also came from northern England. In contrast, a much smaller number of migrants than might be expected came from the Home Counties. The pattern after 1674 was very different. The relative importance of the peripheral northern, midland and western counties declined as provincial cities grew in these areas, and a far higher proportion of migrants came from the Home Countries, southern England and the eastern counties. This table demonstrates how strong were the links between London and the remainder of England in the period before the Civil War.

The reason that a study of the origins of apprentices gives a good indication of the importance of migration to London is because apprentices comprised such a high proportion of the population of the city, as shown in Table 3.7. Around 1600, there were 4–5,000 enrolments each year, which would imply that there were a further 28–35,000 serving out a minimum seven-year term. So there was a possible total of about 32–40,000 apprentices in the capital at any one time, reduced to between 27,000 and 34,000 if only 85 per cent survived their terms. This suggests that apprentices comprised about 15 per cent of the population in the early seventeenth century. By 1700, not more than 5 per cent of the population were apprentices. The declining significance of apprenticeship during the

8. The data are discussed in Griffith 1929.

Table 3.7. *Estimates of the proportion of apprentices in the population of London, 1600 and 1700*

	1600	1700
Total population	200,000	575,000
Annual number of apprentices bound	4,000–5,000	3,400–4,080
Apprentices serving a minimum seven-year term	28,000–35,000	23,800–28,560
Total apprentices	32,000–40,000	27,200–32,640
Depletion, 85% survivorship during term	27,200–34,000	23,120–27,744
Percentage of total population	13.6–17.0	4.0–4.8

Sources: Population – Table 3.1
　　　Apprentices – approximate calculations and tentative estimates drawn from Eliott 1978:214–17.

seventeenth century has important implications for the structure of population in London which influences the analyses of fertility, marriage and mortality which follow. In particular, in the first half of the seventeenth century, there were very large numbers of young, unmarried men in the capital, a fact which must be considered in any discussion of the composition of the population. The figures also suggest that one of the important ways London grew during the period was through the recruitment of apprentices.

In discussing the structure of London population, the alien community must be taken into account. It reached a significant size in the last third of the sixteenth century, although it never approached the proportions attained in Norwich where by 1583 there were 4,679 aliens recorded out of a total population of perhaps only 13,000 (Ketton-Cremer 1957: 118–27). This massive influx of Protestant settlers of all social groups from the Low Countries and France is one of the least well known episodes in English social history. The reason for the mass movement was the renewed persecution of Protestants on the continent; for example, after the Duke of Alva had been appointed Captain-General in the Spanish Low Countries in 1567, it has been estimated that 18,000 people were executed in five years. The wave of immigration was intensified with the aftermath of the Massacre of St Bartholomew's Day in Paris in 1572, but came to an end when Henry IV published the Edict of Nantes in 1598 guaranteeing freedom of religious belief in France. Enormous social and administrative problems were caused by the rapid influx of migrants, both in several of the towns of eastern England and in London, and as a result the government took much care in collecting data on their numbers.[9]

There are several problems involved in attempting to analyse the size of

9. The best general accounts of immigration to England are: Wagner 1960: 219–29; Steel 1968/73: II, 741–80; and Burn 1846.

the alien community and to calculate the proportion of Londoners who were aliens. The definition of an alien is not clear. An alien was usually considered to be somebody from another nation so that people who came to London from other parts of the British Isles, for example from Scotland, would be classed as aliens. However, most London aliens originated from the Low Countries and France. Aliens should not be confused with foreigners or sojourners, terms which refer to individuals of English birth but coming from outside London. A further point of some importance is that although families may be identified as containing aliens, it is not apparent whether all other family members were also aliens. This problem of identification occurs when an alien married a London girl or hired his servants on arrival in England.

Table 3.8. *The size of the London alien community*

Date	Alien population	Total population	Per cent alien
1567	4,700	100,000	4.7
1571	4,850	100,000	4.9
1573	5,315	100,000	5.3
1593	5,450	150,000	3.6
1635	3,600	350,000	1.0

Sources: Alliens – Scouloudi 1938: 29–30, 43.
London – Total population including the distant parishes estimated from Tables 3.1 and 3.4.

There are two main sources of information from which the size of the alien community might be estimated. These are the lay subsidies of the period which only list taxpayers, and the surveys contained in the State Papers which consist of house-by-house listings of the alien community (Kirk 1900–7). The latter are of obvious importance because they enumerate the whole alien population including children. In the estimates of the size of the alien community given in Table 3.8, based on the work of I. Scouloudi (1938), the alien community is taken to consist of heads of families, their wives, children and other relatives, but excluding servants, listed in the surveys for the whole of London, including Westminster. These estimates show that in the 1570s and 1580s the alien community consisted of up to 5 per cent of the total population living in all areas of the city. By the 1630s, the community was very small and included only about 1 per cent of the population. Although it is difficult to estimate the rate of immigration of aliens from the continent, the history of the alien community is a good illustration of the point that urban populations could not maintain their size without a constant influx of new migrants. The alien community would obviously tend to lose its identity as its members were gradually assimilated into the native English population, particularly as there was no new migration to help maintain the distinctiveness of the community. The aliens, who deserve much fuller study, certainly represented a significant part of the population of London in the sixteenth century, but were far fewer because of the decline in the number of immigrants by the first half of the seventeenth century.[10]

10. The demographic history of aliens may be studied from the registers of the Dutch and French churches (Moens 1884 and 1896–9). These contain records of baptisms and marriages only. Burials of aliens were recorded in the registers of the Anglican parishes in which the deceased had been resident. It is often difficult to distinguish aliens in the Anglican registers.

CHAPTER 4

LONDON SOCIAL STRUCTURE IN 1638

So far, I have concentrated on the examination of population trends in London as a whole. However, it is well known that in early modern times there were wide variations in demographic experience between places which were situated near each other. In the very long term, one of the more important themes in population history has been the gradual elimination of these local differences, so that by modern times the range of variation in population trends within a country, city or area and between city and countryside has become very much smaller than at the beginning of the parish register period. The magnitude of local demographic variations depends of course on the size of the area under consideration. The smaller the area and population being observed, the sharper the contrasts. The demographic performance of any area must therefore be a weighted average of the many different local variations within its boundaries. These comments apply equally well to the study of a city and of the countryside, especially in a city like London which was as large, or even larger, than important country regions. Just as there were marked contrasts between the demographic experience of urban and rural areas in the early modern world, so there were equally wide variations within each sector.

We have seen that the most accurate way of obtaining reliable demographic rates from parish registers is by the technique of family reconstitution, and that the success of this method depends on the study of relatively small areas in depth. Therefore, in order to use parish studies to draw conclusions about the population trends of a whole society or area, and to examine the contrasting demographic processes which made up these trends, it is necessary to select with some care the parishes for which special analyses have been made. If different social areas can be identified within the city, individual parishes can be chosen for detailed reconstitution studies. In this way, the evidence from the family reconstitutions can be used both to build up a picture of the historical demography of London as a whole, and to illustrate the range of demographic experience which existed between different areas of the city.

D. V. Glass (1966, 1972) has demonstrated that by 1695 residential differentiation within London was no longer characterized by the localization of occupations, but that the capital was clearly divided on the basis of the wealth of its inhabitants: individuals of similar means lived close to

70

each other. This suggests that social areas may be readily distinguished. In general, the wealthiest Londoners lived in the central parishes of the city, whilst the poor were normally to be found in the peripheral parishes located around the walls and along the riverside. The wealthier members of London society, as might be expected, lived in larger households and employed more servants and apprentices. J. Langton (1975) has shown that this zoning was also a feature of other British cities during the Restoration period, for example Dublin, Newcastle and Exeter. What is especially significant about London is that the social differentiation which existed in the city in 1695 was equally apparent in the period before the outbreak of the Civil War. Urban social areas may be identified from as early as 1638.

The evidence for the distribution of wealth in London in 1638 comes from a bound manuscript in Lambeth Palace Library entitled *Settlement of Tithes 1638*.[1] This is a nominal listing of every householder, drawn up on a parish basis for eighty-seven of the ninety-seven parishes within the walls and seven parishes just outside the walls. For each parish, the names of the householders together with the moderate rent of each house (i.e. the value of each property, not any money transaction) and the actual amount of tithe paid are given.[2] The list was compiled by each parish as the result of an Order by the King-in-Council dated 22 April 1638 in response to a grievance by the London clergy that they were not receiving in full tithes due to them.[3] At this time, the Laudian high church movement was reaching its zenith, and Laud himself was sympathetic to the claims of the London clergy as Bishop of London until 1633. He was succeeded in this position on his appointment to Canterbury by one of his closest disciples, William Juxon. The fact that Juxon was also Lord Treasurer of England is of some significance, for questions of church government and the extent to which episcopal authority might be asserted over the laity were issues of some substance. In reality, the clergy sought only a modest increase in the actual tithe collected. They were more concerned with principles than with revenue (Hill 1956: 283).

For these reasons, it could be argued that the 1638 list may not have been accurate. However, almost all counts made in the seventeenth

---

1. Cod. Lambeth Ms 272. This was printed in Dale 1931. Some of the spelling in the manuscript has been modernized, and for some parishes the figures have been converted from Roman to Arabic numerals. Jones 1980 has also completed an interesting analysis of this listing.
2. The amount of tithe paid in 1638 was omitted from the printed version and it bore no relationship to the amount assessed.
3. The original discussion in the Privy Council is recorded in the *Privy Council Registers*, III, 127–8. The records of the City of London show that the debate over this issue went back at least till 1620 and it was raised again in 1633–4 as well as in 1638. See Overall 1878: 135–8. The background to the controversy over the London tithes is contained in Hill 1956: 175–88.

century from which population sizes have been estimated, whether the hearth taxes, the poll taxes, or the 1695 assessments, were compiled for fiscal purposes, and so there seems little reason to doubt that the 1638 list is as good a source as any for the social structure of London on the eve of the political breakdown that was to lead to open, armed conflict. The list was clearly written, on paper of about foolscap size, in three columns. Each local assessment was sent in by the individual parishes and these were bound together, with a much more recent index at the front of the book. Some of the parish lists were written by the incumbent himself, in his own handwriting. Despite the fact that, like the parish registers, the returns for each parish were not compiled in a consistent way, the 1638 listing is by far the most detailed and the most important known for the period before the Civil War. It is the only one giving nominative rather than aggregative data for almost the whole of London.

Nearly all the entries made in 1638 are quite straightforward, with only a few where there might be some ambiguity. The greatest problem in interpreting the entries on the list is concerned with those properties referred to as 'tenements', since there is no evidence as to what a tenement was like. Graunt (1662: 59) mentions this kind of property only in the context that as the population of London was increasing, tenements were built in areas which were formerly gardens. There is also some confusion in the various parish lists on this point for whilst some incumbents included a mass of low-rental accommodation and no tenements in their return, others noted down tenements but very few low-rental houses. Whether the conclusion to be drawn is that the housing stock of the various parishes differed in these respects is uncertain. Whilst it may be assumed that a tenement was a very large house divided into a mass of relatively low-standard accommodation for many families, this point is not clear from the information given on the list. Where the number of tenements is not indicated, they are estimated at one for every £2 rental value of the property concerned. This must be a conservative estimate as many houses were listed at less than £2 moderate rent. The number of houses and tenements calculated on this basis for each parish is given in Appendix 3.

Because the 1638 count is not well known, it is important to establish it as generally reliable. The easiest way to do this is to compare it with lists made in 1631 and 1695. It may be shown that plausible estimates of the population of London on the eve of the Civil War may be compiled from the data. The assessments of 1631 and 1638 are the only ones made between 1580 and 1650 which cover a substantial part of the city. For the later seventeenth century, the list made in 1695 is normally considered to be the most useful.

The original version of the 1631 count no longer survives, and aggregate figures as printed by Graunt were used in this analysis. The count was taken to assess food requirements of the city in a year of shortage, economic crisis, trade depression, unemployment and high food prices generally in England.[4] Whilst many authorities consider that this list is inaccurate because its method of compilation is not known, the totals seem to agree well with other estimates of the population of London within the walls, and it is important to remember that the figures do not cover the whole of the area contained within the bills of mortality. For the present, attention will be concentrated only on the analysis of the ninety-seven parishes within the walls.

When the so-called Marriage Duty Act of 1695[5] was passed to raise money to pursue the war with France, it provided for a nominal listing of inhabitants to be made as well as for the registration by civil authorities of all births, marriages and deaths. Although the Act was obviously meant to cover the whole country, records survive for only a few areas, which fortunately include most London parishes where there are data for eighty-six of the ninety-seven parishes within the walls. This material formed the basis for Gregory King's work and has subsequently been used in an important study of the size of the London population in the period by P. E. Jones and A. V. Judges and, more recently, in a detailed analysis of London social structure at the end of the seventeenth century by D. V. Glass.[6] It is generally thought to be a remarkably accurate list of the population of London at this time. When Glass compared King's data with that presented by Jones and Judges for those parishes for which King had access to the original returns, he showed that there was a very close agreement for most of them (1965: 175 table 2, 195 table 1, 197 table 2). Although some authorities have questioned the reliability of King's analysis of national population and social structure in 1695, their comments should not apply to those places where he collected accurate local information, which include London itself.[7] In my analysis, the material used for 1695 was that printed by Jones and Judges (1935: 58–63), supplemented for a further three parishes from what is known as King's 'L.C.C. Burns Journal' (1973b: 124–7).

Probably the best and the most obvious way of testing the plausibility of the 1638 listing is to compare it with the 1631 population count. However,

4. The list was originally printed in Graunt; II, 405–6. The Privy Council was obviously concerned with food shortage in London at this time and wrote to the Lord Mayor and Aldermen on 28 April 1631 with instructions to find out how much corn was needed to provision London for a year. *Acts of the Privy Council*, 1630 June–1631 June, no. 909, p. 311. By 6 December 1631, an estimate of the total population of the City and Liberties and the quantity of wheat required to feed it had been made. Overall 1878: 389. For the general background, see Leonard 1900: 188; and for a masterly survey of the problems of economic fluctuations, Supple 1959. The latest authority to comment on the 1631 list is Sutherland 1972: 307–8.
5. 6 & 7 Wm & M. c. 6.
6. King 1973a: 34–6; Jones and Judges 1935; Glass 1966; 1972; and 1976. Some of the results of the analysis of this material have also been used in Chapter 2.
7. See for example, Holmes 1977.

a technical problem is involved here in that the 1638 survey was conducted on a parochial basis whilst the figures for 1631 were listed by wards. It is therefore necessary to estimate the number of houses in the ten missing parishes in 1638, and then to aggregate the figures upwards from a parish to a ward basis. The simplest method by which this could be done is to show that there was some correlation between the number of houses in 1638 and the total in 1695. A reasonable objection to this argument is that the figures for 1638 and 1695 would not be comparable because of the destruction of much of the townscape caused by the Great Fire of 1666. Those areas which were destroyed may not have been repopulated by similar social groups, but, in practice, this problem does not appear to have affected the results markedly, and the social geography of the city was not greatly altered by the rebuilding. There were seventy-five parishes for which the number of houses is known for both periods. A Pearson's product moment correlation coefficient was calculated between the two data sets as +0.80, which is significant at the 1 per cent level. This is an encouraging result, so that the number of houses in the missing parishes could be estimated as being in the same ratio to the number of houses in 1695 as were the total number of houses in the seventy-five parishes in 1638 to 1695. These parishes contained 9,763 houses in 1638 and 8,400 in 1695, so the totals for the missing parishes in 1638 were estimated from the 1695 totals by using a multiplier of 1.15. In two parishes, the information was missing for both years, so here the procedure was simply to allocate 1/97th of the total number of houses to each parish. On this basis, it was calculated that there were 12,180 houses in the London parishes within the walls in 1638.

A second technical problem to be overcome in aggregating from parish to ward totals is that it is not clear that their boundaries were coterminous. Although there is some resemblance between their boundaries, legally they defined different rights and the parishes cannot entirely be fitted within the ward boundaries.[8] In John Stow's *Survey of London*, the names of the parish churches in each ward are given, so to overcome the problem, the assumption was made that the parishes contained in each ward were those whose churches were located within their boundaries. Figures were then aggregated upwards on this basis. The totals of population in 1631 and houses in 1638 by ward are given in Appendix 4. The correlation between the number of houses in 1638 and of people in 1631 was +0.88, which is again significant at the 1 per cent level. The figures appear to be sufficiently well correlated to overcome the boundary problems indicated. It therefore seems possible to undertake further work. If there were on average 6.1 persons per house in 1638, the same as in 1695, it may be

8. This fascinating subject is discussed in greater detail in Brooke and Keir 1975: 130–3, 165–9.

calculated that there were 74,298 people within the walls of the City of London in 1638, compared with 71,029 in 1631 and 69,581 estimated by Jones and Judges for 1695 (1935: 58–63 table 3). Obviously the way in which these figures were assembled makes it quite clear that they can be used only as a guide, but the results are not implausible.

An alternative way of assessing the accuracy of the 1638 survey is to compare totals for individual parishes with listings assembled for other purposes. These were sometimes contained in the more carefully kept vestry minute books and churchwardens' accounts. The results of this exercise for three parishes for which the lists survive for a period close to 1638 are given in Table 4.1. It is not practical to compare individual names

Table 4.1. *Comparison between numbers of householders recorded in the 1638 survey and in other parochial lists*

Parish	1638	Other list	Date	Reason for compilation
St Bartholomew by the Exchange	99	99	1638	Poor rate[a]
St Christopher le Stocks	63	72	1641	Payments to lecturer[b]
St Margaret Lothbury	117	125	1642	Poor rate[c]

Sources: Freshfield 1887b; 1885; 1890.
Notes: a. There were seventy-five names common to the two lists. The discrepancies relate to the poor and the numbers of shops in this parish.
b. In the four quarters of 1642–3, the numbers of parishioners paying to maintain the lecturer were 64, 65, 64 and 63 respectively.
c. There were 102 houses and 15 tenements in 1638. The figure for 1642 includes the poor living in the parish and the disagreement between the two totals is probably because the number of tenements has been estimated at one household for every £2 rental value.

except where both lists relate to 1638, because rates of persistence were such that only about nine households out of ten could be expected to remain within the same parish after a year, and between five and six after five years.[9] The close comparison between the number of householders enumerated in 1638 and recorded in other similar lists shown in Table 4.1 is misleading for some groups in society. For example, in St Bartholomew's, where two assessments were compiled in 1638, only seventy-five names of heads of households were common to both lists out of a total of ninety-nine recorded on each. This may reflect increased residential mobility among the poor.

The reliability of the 1638 listing may be tested in a third way by cross-matching heads of households counted in 1638 with heads of families reconstituted from the parish registers, as shown in Table 4.2 for five

9. See above, Chapter 2.

Table 4.2. *Cross-matching names in the 1638 assessment and heads of families on family reconstitution forms*

	St Peter Cornhill, 1580–1650		St Christopher le Stocks, 1580–1653		St Michael Cornhill, 1580–1650		St Mary Somerset, 1605–53		St Botolph Bishopsgate,[b] 1600–50	
	No.	%	No.	%	No.	%	No.	%	No.	%
Householders on list[a]	123	100	63	100	153	100	144	100	68	100
Matched links with family reconstitution forms	83	67	44	70	104	68	97	67	45	66
On list, not in registers	40	33	19	30	43	28	47	33	23	34
Not identified on list	—		—		6[c]	4	—		—	

Notes: a. Including the incumbent.
b. Surname sets A to C only were reconstituted, excluding the tenements, the householders of which were not named.
c. These refer to an entry where no surname is given on the list.

parishes. The problem with this exercise is that two very different kinds of data are being compared, an enumeration of householders taken at one particular time and heads of families built up from vital registration records compiled over a long period. This in modern terms is the distinction between the census and vital registration of births, marriages and deaths. Once it is realized that a certain proportion of couples were childless and would therefore not have appeared on family reconstitution forms as compiled for this study, and considering the problem of comparing two very different kinds of data, the results are not too discouraging. It is, however, difficult to say why the leakage amounted to as much as 30 per cent of all cases. Perhaps it is a reflection of the fluidity of London society. A similar percentage of matched links in each of the parishes suggests a constant omission factor and again tends to give confidence in the accuracy of the data.

But, however reasonable the 1638 list may have been, given the method of its compilation, there must have been at least some omissions from it. The question of the reliability of the 1695 'census' also has implications for other seventeenth-century assessments from which population sizes may be calculated, even though Jones and Judges rightly considered the 1695 list to be the most accurate of contemporary enumerations (1935: 48; Glass 1966: xviii). Doubtless the majority of omissions were accounted for by those people who were very poor. Gregory King carried out a post-enumeration survey of the two parishes of St Benet Paul's Wharf and St Peter Paul's Wharf. An omission rate for the two parishes combined may be calculated at about 15 per cent from the data he collected (Glass 1966: xxviii–xxix). In his last essay on the subject, Glass (1976: 219–21) suggested that at least a quarter of the total population of the city was omitted from the 1695 assessments, and a greater proportion still from the 1692 poll tax. This may be a little pessimistic.

In his reply to Robert Harley's criticisms of his work in political arithmetic, in what is often referred to as the 'Kashnor Manuscript', King (1972: 791) suggested why these omissions had occurred:

For the parishes in England, there is scarce an assessor but knows every man, woman, and child in the parish, but it is much otherwise in London, where the parishes have one with another 800 houses and 4,000 souls and where an assessor shall scarce know 5 families on each side of him. So that I am of opinion my allowance for these regular assessments (for it was such only I could make any use of) is very near the matter.

This assessment of the quality of his population estimates is unrealistic because Gregory King was well aware that most London parishes were very much smaller than the type-example he gave. Indeed, it is difficult to argue that, at least within the walls, people were less likely to know each other than in rural parishes, except of course in the case of some individuals in the population who were very mobile, for example the apprentices and servants. In those large parishes around the walls, however, it must have been very difficult to make accurate population counts in the seventeenth century. Gregory King appears to have been less than fair to his own work in London, although the question of parish size also has a bearing on the accuracy of the 1638 listing. There is little reason to think that the 1638 assessment does not provide as good a source as the 1695 material from which the degree of social stratification in London might be outlined. The count taken in 1638 is especially important because it was compiled at an early date before the outbreak of the Civil War.

Having discussed the reliability of the 1638 listing, what it can indicate about the social structure of the city may now be assessed. In Figure 4.1, the proportion of 'substantial householders' living in property valued at £20 rent or above in each parish has been mapped and a very clear ecological structuring of the population is revealed. The poorer parishes were those located around the city walls and along the riverside, whilst the central parishes were far more likely to have been wealthy. This pattern is of course what Glass found for 1695 (1966: xxiii map 2). Figure 4.1 for 1638 was therefore constructed in a similar way to his, except that the proportions of substantial householders in each parish were divided into quartiles rather than six classes for greater simplicity. The aim was to isolate relatively rich and relatively poor parishes, so the basis for

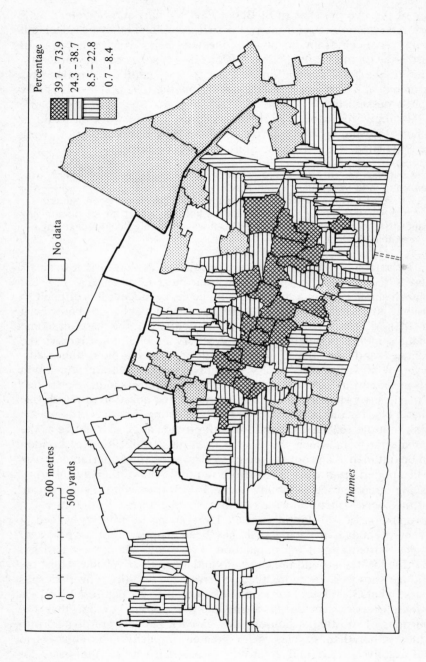

Percentage

▨	39.7 – 73.9
▥	24.3 – 38.7
▥	8.5 – 22.8
▥	0.7 – 8.4

☐ No data

500 metres

500 yards

0

0

Thames

Figure 4.1 Proportion of substantial households in 1638.

distinguishing the wealthier groups is not crucial to the argument.[10] It is an important point that the social areas evident in 1695 had been present from as early as 1638. A comparison of the two maps suggests that the distributions of wealthy and poorer households were more constricted and clearly defined in 1638 than in 1695, by which time the parishes with high proportions of wealthier households were more widespread geographically. Figure 4.1 demonstrates that spatial differentiation was an important feature of the social structure of London.[11]

The data presented so far could also suggest that such an argument may be more apparent than real. For example, a map constructed on the basis of quartiles would overemphasize differences between parishes if the proportions of substantial householders in each parish were quite similar. Perhaps the most important feature of the distribution of wealth was the growth of a middling group of householders. The ordinary Londoner had average means by the standards of the time, being neither especially wealthy nor poor. The proportion of householders valued at £20 and above is an arbitrary measure of the social distribution of wealth so it might be valuable to examine the range of wealth in some parishes in greater detail. In Table 4.3, the percentages of the population inhabiting houses with different rents by £10 groups are shown for two parishes typical of each quartile. It is clear that although there were poor inhabitants living in wealthy parishes, and a few rich people in poor parishes, there were also definite tendencies for people of similar means to live in quite close proximity to each other. There was only a wide spread of different kinds of properties in the wealthiest parishes, where a relatively high proportion of householders lived in accommodation valued at above £20 rent. Almost everybody was poor in the poorest parishes, and there were very few houses valued at above £20. In the middle two quartiles, there was relatively little difference between individual parishes. Although there were wide variations between the wealthiest and poorest London inhabitants, there were many householders of middling wealth, neither rich nor

10. In the eighty-six parishes in 1638 for which it was possible to distinguish substantial households, there were 2,238 out of a total of 10,698 households, or 21 per cent. For eighty parishes in 1695, 27 per cent of the households were substantial (Glass 1966: xx–xxi). It could be argued that the larger parishes contained a smaller proportion of substantial householders but a similar number to the smaller parishes and hence the method outlined here would possibly obscure the distribution of wealth. A glance at the figures in Appendix 3 shows that the large, very poor parishes were inhabited by very few substantial householders as well as having a very small proportion of their populations included in this category.
11. More comments on the 1638 assessment are contained in Pearl 1979. In the period 1658–60, a further collection for the poor was made in London which was organized centrally by the corporation and was in addition to the normal poor rate. The proceeds were then redistributed throughout the city. The poorest parishes which received back more than they contributed were all located around the walls and along the riverside, on the periphery of the city (Herlan 1979).

Table 4.3. *Distribution of householders by value, 1638*

	Quartile															
	I St Peter Cornhill		I St Christopher le Stocks		II St Michael Cornhill		II St Bartholomew by the Exchange		III St Dunstan in the East		III St Margaret Lothbury		IV St Mary Somerset		IV Allhallows London Wall	
Value £	No.	%	No.	%	No.	%	No.	%	No.	%	No.	%	No.	%	No.	%
0–9	18	14	13	21	58	40	34	35	99	37	41	43	102	72	128	66
10–19	34	27	24	38	31	21	40	41	98	37	33	34	29	20	58	30
20–9	35	27	16	25	45	31	6	6	27	10	7	8	4	3	1	1
30–9	27	21	5	8	4	3	11	12	18	7	7	8	2	1	1	1
40–9	7	5	1	2	4	3	3	3	12	5	4	4	3	2	3	1
50–9	4	3	—		1	1	2	2	4	2	1	1	1	1		
60–9	2	2	1	2	1	1			1	0	1	1				
70–9	1	1	1	2			1	1							1	1
80–9			1	2									2	1		
90–9									5	2	1	1				
Total	128	100	62	100	144	100	97	100	264	100	95	100	143	100	192	100

Householders who are not named on the list are excluded from this analysis.

poor, who lived in parishes between the centre and the periphery. The main point demonstrated by Table 4.3 is that the quartiles drawn on the map represent divisions between the parishes which can be sustained by closer examination of the data, and they suggest a general guide to the social distribution of wealth in London.

In Table 4.4, which attempts to summarize the distribution of wealth outlined in Table 4.3, the data for individual parishes in each quartile have been amalgamated and the proportions of householders valued at different rents have been given. The data show that although the middle half of the parishes may have been very similar, the proportion of poor householders increased rapidly with declining socio-economic status and the wealthier parishes also contained far more householders living in reasonable or good properties valued at above £20 rent than in the poorest quartile. These data show that by 1638 traditional social structure had already largely broken

Table 4.4. *Proportions of householders by value in each quartile, 1638*

Value	Quartile			
£	I	II	III	IV
0–9	17%	38%	40%	69%
10–19	33%	31%	36%	25%
20+	50%	31%	24%	6%

See text for method of construction.

down, for residential differentiation did not occur on the basis of guilds, trades, or occupations, but in terms of the social distribution of wealth.

Superficially, London resembled G. Sjoberg's type-example of the pre-industrial city: 'The preindustrial city's central area is notable also as the chief residence of the elite. Here are the luxurious dwellings . . . The disadvantaged members of the city fan out toward the periphery, with the very poorest and outcastes living in the suburbs, the farthest removed from the center' (1960: 97–8). Given the fact that the early modern English city was organized on the basis of foot transport, and since the elite could afford the highest rents, it is hardly surprising that they would have lived in the central part of the city. But there the similarity ends, for the social processes which underpinned their common spatial form were both different from, and more complex than, those imagined by Sjoberg. For example, in the English pre-industrial city, of which London is an example, the elite did engage in business activities and the economy of the city was not occupationally zoned. In fact, the unit of production was small in London, home and workplace were not physically separated, and the distinction between the family and the firm had not yet emerged. Whilst Sjoberg imagined that extended- and stem-family units would be the norm,

English social structure was firmly based around the nuclear family. In general, this was true of both town and countryside. The formation of nuclear families had an important influence on the population dynamics of the city. Since urban mortality rates were reckoned to be high, and because the majority of adults were migrants to London, even if the intention had been to form stem families, most in fact would have been nuclear. The way that modernizing London differed from the traditional pre-industrial city underlines the important point that the same spatial characteristics may conceal very different social processes at work. A further point to note is that although the locational pattern of social groups within London was similar in 1638 and 1695, important changes occurred in the social structure of London during the course of the seventeenth century (cf. Wrigley 1967; Langton 1975).

CHAPTER 5

THE MEASUREMENT OF MORTALITY RATES

It is well known that mortality rates were invariably high in the pre-industrial city, but little attention has been concentrated on assessing how high these rates actually were. In this chapter it will be shown how life tables may be calculated for children of London parishes in the period before the establishment of civil registration in 1653, by the method of partial family reconstitution outlined in Chapter 2. This technique has the advantage over the reconstructions pioneered by M. F. and T. H. Hollingsworth[1] because it may be applied to all those parishes with registers that are sufficiently complete for the normal process of family reconstitution, and not simply to those three parishes for which ages at death are given in the burial registers (St Peter Cornhill from 1579 to 1604, Allhallows London Wall between 1578 and 1598, and throughout the period from 1600 in St Botolph Bishopsgate). The subject of this chapter will be the normal background level of mortality which prevailed. In the next chapter, attention will be turned to the impact of the plague crises. Because of the unusual age-incidence of plague mortality, where the victims were more likely to be children than adults, the tables presented here eliminate plague deaths in order to obtain estimates of the normal levels of mortality in London.

It is difficult to measure short-term fluctuations in mortality rates within a period of less than about fifty years by family reconstitution methods – a further reason why epidemic plague mortality requires separate treatment. The expectation of life at birth has to be estimated from infant and child mortality rates using model life tables, because it is almost impossible to construct adult life tables from the results of family reconstitution studies. Ages at death of few adults are known, such a small proportion being born in London. Such estimates must be subject to wide margins of error, because very little work has been done on the relationships between adult and child mortality rates. In particular, it is not known whether adult rates will fit model mortality schedules as well as those for children discussed here, a point which has important implications for calculations of the expectation of life simply from knowledge of child mortality rates.

1. Hollingsworth 1971. Despite its limitations, this is an important study because it shows that the calculation of mortality rates from London parish registers is a practical proposition.

Nevertheless, the expectation of life at birth is a good measure of mortality experience because it is not affected by the age-structure of the population.

The results presented here will be based on an analysis of the registers of four London parishes: St Peter Cornhill (90) and St Michael Cornhill (74), two wealthy parishes located adjacent to each other in the centre of the city; and two very poor parishes, St Mary Somerset (68), situated in the western sector of the city along the riverside, and Allhallows London Wall (7), just inside the city wall in the north-eastern part of the city (see Appendix 3). Although the rates apply only to these four parishes, they ought to be typical of the range of values that prevailed in London, because these parishes have been selected from widely contrasting socio-economic areas of the city. All the parishes studied in detail had populations of around 1,000 in 1638. They were thus not too large to make ambiguities in record linkage a problem when completing the reconstitutions, but were of sufficient size to ensure that the sample would be representative. The two poorer parishes were increasing in population during the period but this does not affect the calculation of mortality rates, because the method used requires the population at risk in each age group to be independently determined.

It is convenient to begin by presenting uncorrected life tables as in Table 5.1. In parish register demography, the chief problem in calculating death rates is that the population at risk is not known, for the parish registers contain only the record of individuals buried. Family reconstitution allows both the age of individuals at death to be calculated, and also the population at risk to be determined independently from the mortality record, by calculations of the length of time individuals were in observation on FRFs. A family enters observation at the date the couple married, or at the date of baptism of the first child, and remains in observation until the date of burial of the last surviving parent, if this is known, or otherwise until the date of burial of the first parent. If these dates are not known, or it is not known which parent died first, the family passes out of observation when the youngest child in the family was baptized. These rules may seem complicated, but once all the vital events occurring in each parish have been gathered on to family reconstitution forms the calculation of life tables is a relatively straightforward exercise for child deaths. The method followed was exactly the same as that described in detail by L. Henry and E. A. Wrigley and it is therefore unnecessary to discuss it here.[2] The success of the method depends on the independent determination of the period of observation of a family within the parish. Hence the life tables will be more accurate up to age 9 than in the 10–14 age-group, during which time some children may already have left the parental home for

---

2. Henry 1967: 125–9; and Wrigley 1972a: 247–9. The rates presented in this chapter will refer only to legitimate children; it is unlikely that more than 5 per cent of all births would have been illegitimate at this time as is suggested in Chapter 7.

Table 5.1. *Child life tables for the sexes combined*

Age	Deaths	Population at risk	Rate 1,000q_x		Survivors 1,000l_x
St Peter Cornhill, 1580–1650					
0	115	1,100	105	(107)	1,000
1–4	106	716	148	(152)	895
5–9	15	326	46	(64)	763
10–14	6	194	31	(61)	728
15					705
1–14	127	599	212	(255)	705
					705
St Michael Cornhill, 1580–1650					
0	195	1,402	139	(142)	1,000
1–4	139	891	156	(168)	861
5–9	30	361	83	(113)	727
10–14	5	147	34	(60)	667
15					644
1–14	174	690	252	(306)	644
					644
St Mary Somerset, 1605–53					
0	277	1,045	265	(265)	1,000
1–4	143	581	246	(249)	735
5–9	18	194	93	(110)	554
10–14	6	87	69	(119)	502
15					467
1–14	167	460	363	(411)	467
					467
Allhallows London Wall, 1570–1636					
0	160	868	184	(185)	1,000
1–4	87	489	178	(199)	816
5–9	16	154	104	(137)	671
10–14	4	71	56	(132)	601
15					567
1–14	107	351	305	(400)	567
					567

The rates in brackets include deaths occurring in plague periods. See text for the duration of these.

service and apprenticeship.[3] To ensure that the tables are constructed from reasonable samples, it is imperative that the rates derived by family reconstitution methods are based on the analysis of long time periods, and it would help comparability if these could be the same for all parishes. However, since the registers of St Mary Somerset and Allhallows London Wall, the two poorer parishes, contain sufficient detail for the matching exercise to be performed with confidence only between the dates indicated

3. Recent research has suggested that children left home in pre-industrial England much later than is commonly thought. Wall 1978.

in Table 5.1, it is impossible to make all the time periods the same. Although it is unlikely that the characteristics of London mortality experience changed markedly during this time, the fact that rates are based on periods which included a different number of plague crises might affect the comparability of the life tables. All those deaths occurring during the main epidemics, from the beginning of June until the end of November in each of the crisis years 1593, 1603 and 1625, have been excluded from the calculations. All deaths from plague cannot be eliminated because causes of death were not consistently stated in the registers, but the remaining plague deaths would be too few to influence the rates significantly. The rates given in brackets in Table 5.1 show the result of including plague deaths, and the effect was most marked for the older children aged 10–14, partly because relatively few deaths occurred in this age-group. These life tables also include those unnamed children, often termed 'chrisoms' in the registers, which died close to birth before they could be baptized, while the family was in observation. There were 10 of these in St Peter's, 36 in St Michael's, none in St Mary's and 25 in Allhallows.

In most family reconstitution studies, it is possible to calculate adult as well as child life tables. The former are derived from the married population only, with some margin of error arising from the assumption of burial dates for a small proportion of the population. Therefore, the mortality experience of individuals aged between fifteen and marriage cannot be measured. The expectation of life is calculated by fitting model life tables to the rates so as to estimate the mortality experience of those people in that mobile age-group between childhood and marriage. In this study, where an insufficiently large number of ages at marriage are known due to the many young migrants to London who subsequently married there, it is almost impossible to calculate adult life tables by the method of family reconstitution. In turn, this means that the expectation of life may be estimated only to within very broad margins by fitting model life tables to infant and child mortality rates. It is, however, difficult to argue from child life tables to mortality experience at all ages, and there is no point of entry to see which model tables might be appropriate in the adult age range. At Colyton, in Devon, for example, mortality rates did not move in step with model life tables and were higher for adults than for children. The overall expectation of life at birth would therefore be lower than that estimated by fitting model life tables to child mortality experience.[4]

Demographers often used model schedules to estimate vital rates when the data are incomplete. The reliability of the child life tables for London parishes given in Table 5.1 may be assessed by comparison with model life tables. An obvious problem with this exercise is that model life tables are constructed from real-world life tables which can be drawn only from

4. Wrigley 1972a: 270. Similar arguments are made in Smith 1978: 212.

Table. 5.2. *Expectations of life at birth and mortality levels in Princeton model life tables*

Age	Rate $1,000q_x$	Expectation of life (e_o)					
		Model West		Model North		Model South	
St Peter Cornhill, 1580–1650							
0	105	53	(15)	51	(14)	56	(16)
1–4	148	34	(7)	36	(8)	42	(10)
5–9	46	31	(6)	43	(11)	34	(7)
10–14	31	34	(7)	38	(9)	30	(5)
1–14	212	34	(7)	38	(9)	39	(9)
St Michael Cornhill, 1580–1650							
0	139	46	(12)	43	(11)	49	(13)
1–4	156	31	(6)	36	(8)	39	(9)
5–9	83	—		31	(6)	20	(1)
10–14	34	31	(6)	36	(8)	25	(3)
1–14	252	29	(5)	34	(7)	34	(7)
St Mary Somerset, 1605–53							
0	265	29	(5)	26	(4)	27	(4)
1–4	246	21	(2)	24	(3)	30	(5)
5–9	93	—		26	(4)	20	(1)
10–14	69	—		19	(1)	—	
1–14	363	—		24	(3)	25	(3)
Allhallows London Wall, 1570–1636							
0	184	39	(9)	36	(8)	39	(9)
1–4	178	29	(5)	34	(7)	37	(8)
5–9	104	—		24	(3)	—	
10–14	56	—		24	(3)	—	
1–14	305	24	(3)	29	(5)	30	(5)

Mortality levels are given in brackets.

nineteenth- and twentieth-century mortality experience, yet age patterns of disease mortality could have been very different in earlier periods. Changes in the incidence of disease, of which the most celebrated example was the disappearance of plague after 1665, would be of obvious importance in this respect. The most convenient set of model life tables is that derived by Coale and Demeny (1966), who realized that age patterns of mortality varied between different populations with the same overall expectation of life. They constructed four families of tables, which they termed North, South, East and West. These labels have no special significance; the data from which the tables were constructed were drawn mainly from these geographical divisions of Europe. Within each family, Coale and Demeny published life tables for males and females for twenty-four mortality levels, beginning at level 1 where the female expectation of life at birth is twenty years. The difference in the expectation of life between each level is two and a half years in the female tables. Model life tables for the sexes combined were calculated by taking a simple average of the male and female rates as given by Coale and Demeny and have been used throughout this analysis.

If the rates in Table 5.1 are consistent with model mortality experience they should fit an appropriate model life table. Therefore, the rates calculated for each age-group should correspond with the model life tables in one of the four families at the same mortality level. The expectations of life and mortality levels in the West, North and South families corresponding to each individual London mortality rate have been indicated in Table 5.2. For example, in St Peter Cornhill, the life table death rate for children aged 1–4 was 148 per thousand, which corresponds to level 7 in the West tables where the overall expectation of life was thirty-four years. The rate for age-group 5–9 was 46 per thousand which is level 6, and for the 10–14 age-group it was 31 per thousand or level 7. For children aged 1–14, the rate was 212 per thousand for which level 7 is again appropriate. Because the mortality levels are almost the same for each death rate, there is good reason to argue that these rates are plausible. However, at age 0, the death rate was only 105 per thousand or level 15, which suggests that mortality has been underestimated in this age-group. The rates in model North and model South tables do not fit the data for St Peter's quite as well as model West. The mortality rates for each age-group in the four parishes have been analysed in this way in Table 5.2. This shows that the mortality pattern in the North family fits the actual overall mortality experience of these parishes much more closely than the other families. However, model West fits the lowest mortality parish, St Peter Cornhill, best except for infants, and there is some suggestion that model South tables are most appropriate in the two highest mortality parishes up till age 4.[5] At present, it is convenient to rely on the model North tables which have been found to correspond closely to English mortality experience from the beginning of the seventeenth century until the middle of the nineteenth century (Schofield and Wrigley 1979). These estimates apply only to normal years; the plague years would ensure that the expectation of life would have been slightly lower than suggested here.

Two especially interesting features of London mortality experience are brought out in Tables 5.1 and 5.2. These are, first, the contrast in death rates between the two wealthier and the two poorer parishes, and secondly, low infant mortality compared with the rates for children aged 1–14. The second feature was least marked in St Mary Somerset, where the

5. It is interesting to note that child mortality in the Paris region in the first half of the nineteenth century corresponded to the model South pattern. Van de Walle and Preston 1974: 102. Child mortality at Geneva in the first half of the eighteenth century could also have fitted the South pattern. Perrenoud 1978: 219.

pattern of mortality appears to be different from the other parishes and the high rates mean that the contrast with them is especially sharp. Low infant mortality rates relative to child mortality experience is characteristic of the North family of model life tables, but it is even more pronounced here because if the rates were entirely consistent with the North pattern of mortality, the expectations of life to which the rates correspond would be identical at each age-group. This important point will be returned to later.

Table 5.3. *Representativeness of the child life tables*

Parish and dates	In observation at age 0	No. of births	Percent of births in observation
St Peter Cornhill, 1580–1650	1,100	1,769	62
St Michael Cornhill, 1580–1650	1,402	2,261	62
St Mary Somerset, 1605–53	1,045	2,079	50
Allhallows London Wall, 1570–1636	868	1,839	47

It could of course be argued that the rates presented in Table 5.1 do not indicate the range of values which could be found in early Stuart London because only those families which could be reconstituted enter into the calculations and are therefore not representative of all the whole population of each parish. This problem could be more marked in London than in country parishes because migration was such an important component of demographic change. However, the repr esentativeness of the results depends on the demographic parameter being calculated, and a family has to be in observation in a parish for only a year to be of some use in the construction of life tables. The experience of both migrants and London-born inhabitants is therefore included. In Table 5.3, the number of individuals in observation in the first year of life is given as a percentage of the total number of legitimate births and the results are not too discouraging.[6] It would seem that the lower percentages of individuals in observation in the two poorer parishes of St Mary Somerset and Allhallows London Wall may be related to the greater level of migration of families, which itself must have been partly a result of higher death rates. Even if adult and child mortality rates had moved in step with each other, it does not necessarily follow that the experience of the unreconstitutable popula-

6. In Colyton, 68 per cent of all births were in observation in the first year of life for the whole period from 1538 to 1837. Wrigley 1972a: 255. At Geneva, 87 per cent of births were in observation in the first year of life during the seventeenth century. Perrenoud 1978: 218.

Table 5.4. *Child life tables by sex*

Age	Sexes combined			Males			Females		
	Survivors $1,000l_x$	Rate $1,000q_x$	North e_0	Survivors $1,000l_x$	Rate $1,000q_x$	North e_0	Survivors $1,000l_x$	Rate $1,000q_x$	North e_0
St Peter Cornhill, 1580–1650 and St Michael Cornhill, 1580–1650									
0	1,000	107	51 (14)	1,000	107	49 (14)	1,000	107	50 (13)
1–4	893	155	36 (8)	893	167	32 (7)	893	144	38 (8)
5–9	757	65	36 (8)	749	59	37 (9)	765	71	35 (7)
10–14	708	31	38 (9)	705	33	34 (8)	710	31	40 (9)
15	686			682			688		
1–14	686	234	36 (8)	682	242	34 (8)	688	229	38 (8)
St Mary Somerset, 1605–53 and Allhallows London Wall, 1570–1636									
0	1,000	218	31 (6)	1,000	235	30 (6)	1,000	200	33 (6)
1–4	782	215	29 (5)	765	235	25 (4)	800	195	30 (5)
5–9	614	103	24 (3)	585	111	20 (2)	644	85	30 (5)
10–14	551	62	21 (2)	520	84	—	589	45	30 (5)
15	517			476			562		
1–14	517	340	26 (4)	476	377	22 (3)	562	297	30 (5)

tion, particularly single people, would be similar to what can be measured for those families that can be reconstituted. Nevertheless, the results reported here should indicate the range of values of London death rates that prevailed.

The contrast in mortality rates between the wealthier and poorer parishes may now be pursued in a little more detail by a brief examination of sex differences in mortality rates. Because an analysis of death rates for males and females separately for each parish means that sample sizes would be rather small, it was decided to treat the two wealthier and two poorer parishes together as in Table 5.4. This table does not include 'chrisom' children because their sex was frequently not identified in the registers. It is interesting that there was little difference in mortality rates between males and females in the wealthier parishes, yet the difference was quite considerable in the poorer parishes where only 476 boys survived to age 15 compared with 562 girls. Little comparative work has been completed on sex differences in child mortality. However, in his revised analysis of the demography of the British peerage, T. H. Hollingsworth (1977: 328 table 3) presented life tables for males and females separately which showed that fewer boys than girls survived childhood, but not to as marked an extent as in the poorer London parishes.

It is clear from these life tables that mortality was considerably higher in London than elsewhere in England. In Table 5.5, life tables in summary form are presented for four English villages and also for the British peerage.[7] It is surprising that there were such similarities in the infant and child mortality experience of the four contrasting English parishes. They demonstrate that the expectation of life at birth was lower in London, even in the wealthier parishes, although this tendency was perhaps most marked at child rather than infant rates. A second feature of this table is that the children of peers had a lower expectation of life than did the population as a whole, but there were no greater contrasts between the experience of the peerage and of Londoners. It is also apparent that model North tables again provide a good fit. Although there was thus a distinct mortality differential between metropolitan and rural areas of England, London death rates were not as high as elsewhere. Table 5.6 demonstrates that the expectation of life was lower in many French villages in the late seventeenth and eighteenth centuries than in some London parishes a century earlier, apart from during plague years. The expectations of life at birth have been estimated here using the model West life tables which provide the best fit in most French parishes. In some places such as Tourouvre in Normandy, with a mixed economy of farming, forestry, and crafts and trades – a village under severe population pressures and which became a

---

7. Infant and child mortality rates until age 10 are given for a further selection of parishes in Smith 1978: 210–11 table 8.3.

Table 5.5. *Comparative English life tables*

Parish or group	Dates	Age	Survivors 1,000l_x	Rate 1,000q_x	North e_0	
British peerage	1550–1699	0	1,000	166	38	(9)
		1–14	834	188	31	(6)
		15	677			
Bottesford, Leics.	1600–49	0	1,000	160	41	(10)
		1–14	840	154	46	(12)
		15	711			
Colyton, Devon	1538–99	0	1,000	120–40	46	(12)
		1–14	870	124	51	(14)
		15	762			
	1600–49	0	1,000	126–58	43	(11)
		1–14	858	176	43	(11)
		15	707			
Shepshed, Leics.	1600–99	0	1,000	126	46	(12)
		1–14	874	119	51	(14)
		15	770			
Terling, Essex	1550–1624	0	1,000	128	46	(12)
		1–14	872	142	48	(13)
		15	748			
	1625–99	0	1,000	124	46	(12)
		1–14	876	143	48	(13)
		15	751			

Sources: Calculated from Hollingsworth 1977: 340 table 10; Levine 1977: 68 table 5.7, 99 table 6.8, 125 table 8.4; and Wrigley 1972a: 267 table 16.

centre for migration to Canada – and also at Coulommiers and Chailly-en-Brie in the Paris region, the expectation of life for children was just as low as it was in the poorer parishes of seventeenth-century London. The expectation of life was also low in the only urban parish included in this sample, Ingouville, a suburb of Le Havre.

Further comparative material for a large city in the seventeenth century, Geneva, is presented in Table 5.7. This suggests that although the expectation of life was gradually improving, mortality was generally more severe than in London, especially in the first half of the century. Overall death rates in Geneva were about the same as those for the poorer London parishes. However, in comparing the figures, it must be remembered that the experience of the plagues would depress the expectation of life in London by a few points.

Attention must now be turned to what is one of the most difficult problems concerned with mortality in London, the causes of low mortality rates, which are particularly noticeable in the two wealthier London parishes. The most obvious possibility is that infant deaths were being under-registered to a marked extent. However, this argument is unlikely to

Table 5.6 *Comparative French life tables*

Parish	Dates	Age	Survivors $1,000l_x$	Rate $1,000q_x$	West e_0
Crulai	1688–1719	0	1,000	236	34 (7)
		1–14	764	192	36 (8)
		15	617		
Tourouvre-au-Perche	1670–1719	0	1,000	285	29 (5)
		1–14	715	315	21 (2)
		15	490		
Saignhin-en-Mélantois	1740–9	0	1,000	259	31 (6)
		1–14	741	247	29 (5)
		15	558		
Ingouville	1730–70	0	1,000	286	29 (5)
		1–14	714	352	19 (1)
		15	463		
Sotteville-lès-Rouen	1760–90	0	1,000	244	31 (6)
		1–14	756	264	26 (4)
		15	556		
Coulommiers and Chailly-en-Brie	1670–95	0	1,000	269	29 (5)
		1–14	731	364	19 (1)
		15	465		
Boulay	1750–99	0	1,000	196	39 (9)
		1–14	804	226	31 (6)
		15	622		
Thézels-Saint-Sernin	1747–92	0	1,000	191	39 (9)
		1–14	809	183	36 (8)
		15	661		

Sources: Gautier and Henry 1958: 163; Charbonneau 1970: 173, Deniel and Henry 1965: 587; Terrisse 1961: 291; Girard 1959: 498; Polton 1969: 25; Houdaille 1967: 1076; Valmary 1965: 153.

be correct, both because the parish registration system effectively recorded births at this time and also because it has been shown in Chapter 2 that high proportions of infant deaths were endogenous. It will be recalled that the data on the distribution of infant deaths for the four sample parishes presented in Table 2.20 and Figure 2.6 fit a biometric analysis of infant mortality very well and, if under-registration of deaths had been widespread, this would have been very unlikely. The fact that large numbers of infant deaths were occurring close to birth in the wealthier parishes gives confidence in the infant mortality rates, as does the effective recording of stillbirths in three of the parishes (Table 2.20). It was also interesting that the difference in infant mortality rates between the wealthier and poorer parishes was mainly in the endogenous rates. Short birth intervals shown in Table 5.8 are another feature of London demography which is particularly suggestive of good registration because the effect of missing births is to

Table 5.7. *Comparative life tables for seventeenth-century Geneva*

Dates	Age	Survivors $1,000l_x$	Rate $1,000q_x$	North e_0	
1625–49	0	1,000	271	24	(3)
	1–14	729	386	21	(2)
	15	447			
1650–74	0	1,000	265	26	(4)
	1–14	735	339	26	(4)
	15	486			
1675–99	0	1,000	246	29	(5)
	1–14	754	346	26	(4)
	15	493			

Source: Perrenoud 1978: 219–23.

lengthen the apparent mean intervals between them. It thus seems unlikely that low infant mortality rates were caused by defective registration.[8]

A more probable explanation of low infant mortality rates is that even though the rates given in Table 5.1 reflect very well the actual levels of infant mortality within the boundaries of the parishes shown, they do not explain the fate of all children born there during the relevant period, because wealthier parents were sending their newly born infant children out of the parish to be wet-nursed. It therefore follows that infant mortality rates would be particularly low in the wealthier parishes because children were dying away at nurse.[9] A very high proportion of endogenous infant

Table 5.8. *Mean birth intervals of birth parities 1–6 (in months)*

Parish and dates	Interval	No. of observations
St Peter Cornhill, 1580–1650	23.0	128
St Michael Cornhill, 1580–1650	22.7	143
St Mary Somerset, 1605–53	26.7	135
Allhallows London Wall, 1570–1636	24.1	123

8. The calculation of birth intervals and their use in measuring marital fertility is fully discussed in Chapter 7.
9. See Chapter 7 for detailed evidence about the existence of this practice and the way it helped to contribute to high fertility in London.

deaths is also consistent with older infants dying away at nurse. These would, of course, have been from exogenous causes and were not included in the registers of the London parishes where nurse-children had been born. It therefore becomes necessary to assess the mortality rates of all children born in the parishes under consideration whose parents continued to live there, rather than just those born and dying there. Essentially the problem is to estimate the number of deaths of children at nurse while they were outside the parish. The work which follows will have to be approximate and it is included to give an idea of the level of mortality which may have prevailed. The method by which this can be done is in principle quite simple and it is based on a technique first outlined by L. Henry. It makes the assumption that if two children in one family are given the same forename, the first child would already have died when the second was christened. If the first child had not apparently died, it may be assumed that its burial had not been recorded in the parish register and it may be counted as an underburial. The number of underburials allows inflation ratios from burials to deaths to be calculated.[10] The assumption is that parents would not have called two children by the same name even if one of them were not living at home. It is very difficult to find evidence to substantiate this point, particularly with respect to English registration experience.[11]

The method proceeds by a consideration of the fate of the older child at the baptism of its younger brother or sister. This means that the sexes have to be considered separately, although for reasons of space the results will be combined in the tables which follow. At the birth of its younger brother or sister, each child is first classed as either living, dead, or of unknown fate,

10. The main references to this method of correcting for the under-recording of burials are: Henry 1967: 25–6; 1976: 15–17; Charbonneau 1975: 96–100; Perrenoud 1975: 229; and Bideau 1976: 116–19. Other methods which have been developed to measure the under-registration of deaths in parish registers are unsuitable for this study. Census or confirmation lists do not exist and the method based on the intervals between successive births is inapplicable because short birth intervals could have occurred when a child was sent to be nursed as well as after an infant death. See Henry 1968: 72–8.

11. The parish register of St Peter Cornhill contains the following mention of a christening on 16 April 1692: 'Abraham (being the second son of that name) son of Abraham and Jane Hemingway.' Another example of such a baptism occurred at Lancaster parish church on 12 September 1696: 'Geo: ye 2nd of yt name s. of Tho: Medcalfe of Lancaster.' Presumably such entries were unusual to warrant a special comment by the parish clerk. Neither was recorded until the 1690s, after the period considered here. At Saignhin-en-Mélantois, two children were hardly ever given the same forename in the eighteenth century if the older had not died when the younger was baptized, but this was not uncommon at the end of the seventeenth century and the beginning of the eighteenth. It is also interesting that no child was recorded as having died on the same day as it was born until 1732, and in the period 1700–19 there were only 8 recorded deaths of children aged less than a month compared with 53 in the period 1720–39. This would suggest that once the standard of registration of events improved, a younger child would not be recorded as having the same forename as his older brother or sister were he or she still living. Deniel and Henry 1965: 564.

Table 5.9. *Fate of the older child at the baptism of his younger brother or sister for the sexes combined*

| | Fate of older child at birth of younger child | | | | | | | |
| | Living (v) | | Dead (m) | | Unknown (i) | | Total | |
Forename of younger child	No.	%	No.	%	No.	%	No.	%
St Peter Cornhill, 1580–1650								
Same	2	1.60	33	22.92	32	6.37	67	8.69
Different	123	9 8.40	111	77.08	470	93.63	704	91.31
Total	125	100.00	144	100.00	502	100.00	771	100.00
St Michael Cornhill, 1580–1650								
Same	1	0.72	41	18.81	37	5.60	79	7.76
Different	138	99.28	177	81.19	624	94.40	939	92.24
Total	139	100.00	218	100.00	661	100.00	1,018	100.00
St Mary Somerset, 1605–53								
Same	0	0.00	57	17.65	19	5.48	76	9.92
Different	96	100.00	266	82.35	328	94.52	690	90.08
Total	96	100.00	323	100.00	347	100.00	766	100.00
Allhallows London Wall, 1570–1636								
Same	1	0.88	18	11.46	17	5.23	36	6.04
Different	113	99.12	139	88.54	308	94.77	560	93.96
Total	114	100.00	157	100.00	325	100.00	596	100.00

and secondly it is ascertained whether or not the younger child had been given the same forename as his older brother or sister. A child is classed as alive unless it is known to have died or to have left the sample by being married. The remaining children who did not appear in the burial register were placed in the category whose fate was unknown. These could either have migrated, or their deaths not been recorded by the parish registrars. A difficulty was presented by the incidence of twins, but these were always treated as if they were two separate individuals. The data are set out in Table. 5.9. It is now possible to work through an example to show how a multiplier from burials to deaths may be calculated using the data from St Peter Cornhill. The problem is essentially to estimate what proportion of those children whose fate was unknown at the birth of their younger brother or sister had in fact already died (a). From Henry's work, $i = am + (1 - a)v$ where $a = (i - v)/(m - v)$. The values of i, v and m may be calculated as the percentages of the total number of children in each category either living, dead or of fate unknown. Thus, $i = 6.37$ per cent (32/502), $v = 1.60$ per cent (2/125), and $m = 22.92$ per cent (33/144). The factor a may then be calculated as $(6.37 - 1.60)/$

Table 5.10. *Calculation of deaths from burials*

Parish and dates	Burials at ages 0–3	Multiplier	Deaths	No. to be distributed
St Peter Cornhill, 1580–1650	212	1.778	377	165
St Michael Cornhill, 1580–1650	317	1.821	577	260
St Mary Somerset, 1605–53	411	1.334	548	137
Allhallows London Wall, 1570–1636	240	1.866	448	208

$(22.92 - 1.60) = 4.77/21.32 = 0.224$. The total number of deaths which have not been recorded as burials is therefore $0.224 \times 502 = 112$. The number of burials was 144 so the total number of deaths was 256 (144 + 112). The multiplier from burials to deaths will be 1.778 (256/144).

The multiplier should now be applied to the total number of deaths to be calculated. This has been done in Table 5.10, multipliers for the other parishes being obtained in exactly the same way as for St Peter Cornhill. The number of underburials has then to be distributed according to an assumption about the age incidence of deaths of nurse-children. The key to this problem is that the risk of children dying declines with increasing age and is thus highest closest to birth. It follows from this point that the age at which children were put out to nurse will affect the proportions of nurse-children dying at particular ages. Some examples of the distribution of deaths by age are given in Table 5.11, drawn from seventeenth- and eighteenth-century French experience. An important point is demonstrated by the data for Cormeilles, where a higher proportion of nurse-children died during the first year of life after 1668 than earlier, because infants were put out to nurse rather closer to birth (Berthieu 1975: 263). It is not in dispute that the great majority of nurse-children died as infants and the number still at nurse after the first four years of life was minimal; they had either died or been returned to their parents.

There are two important pieces of evidence which suggest that children were put out to nurse very soon after birth. First, fertility was very high indeed where women did not have to care for their own infant children. For example, it is unlikely that birth intervals would have been so short in the wealthier St Peter Cornhill and St Michael Cornhill parishes shown in Table 5.8 if children were not being put out to nurse. Subsequent birth intervals were generally shorter after an early infant death than if an infant died after the first month of life (Table 7.11). Secondly, both endogenous

Table 5.11. *Proportion of nurse-children dying at particular ages in France*

Age	Lyons 1761–70	Meulan 1670–1729[a]	Meulan 1670–1869[a]	Meulan 1740–89[b]	Beauvaisis 1770–99	Paris Region 1774–94	Thiossey-en-Dombes 1740–1814	Cormeilles-en-Parisis 1640–67	Cormeilles-en-Parisis 1668–1729	Cormeilles-en-Parisis 1730–89
0	67%	57%	62%	77%	79%	59%	88%	59%	68%	53%
1	⎰18%	⎱43%	⎱38%	⎱23%	15%	24%	⎱12%	27%	24%	21%
2	⎱				4%	10%	⎰	8%	6%	8%
3	⎰12%				1%	4%	⎰	2%	2%	6%
4	⎱				1%	3%		2%	1%	1%
5–9	2%				⎰0.4%	—		1%	—	1%
10+	1%				⎱	—		—	—	—
Number	2,000	138	495	236	2,339	815	249	85	300	427

Sources: Garden 1970: 138 table 25; Lachiver 1969a: 126 table 26, 131 table 29; Ganiage 1973: 274 table 2; Galliano 1966: 159 table 7; Bideau 1973: 53 table 3; and Berthieu 1975: 264.

Notes: a. Nurse-children dying at Meulan
b. Nurse-children from Meulan dying elsewhere

and exogenous infant mortality rates were low (Table 2.20); if infants were not being sent to nurse until they were, for example, six months old, the effect on the total infant mortality rate would not be very great, owing to infants being at highest risk closest to birth. There are obviously a number of ways in which these deaths of nurse-children may be distributed but the following is probably not too far wide of the mark:

0	80%
1	15%
2	4%
3	1%
4+	nil

Altering these percentages slightly would have little effect on the total number of deaths and on consequent rates. It is now possible to recalculate the life tables, remembering that the population at risk will remain the same, only the number of children dying will be increased.

At this point it becomes difficult to proceed, because the multipliers are so high that their reliability must be considered. In fact, it is unlikely that the values of the multipliers are precise because their calculation depends on the fate of children in that relatively small proportion of families which gave two children the same forename. Also, there were a very large number of children in all parishes whose fate was unknown (see Table 5.9), and this would cause a further degree of uncertainty about the multipliers. If the proportion of children having the same forename as a younger brother and whose fate was unknown (i) was equal to the proportion living (v), all those whose fate was unknown would in fact have been living at the birth of their younger brother or sister, since the underburial rate (a) would be zero. There would need to be only a very small increase in the number of cases with two living children with the same name in the same family to produce a major fall in the inflation ratio.

Most of these problems affect all the studies where this method of estimating the number of deaths occurring from the total number of burials recorded is used. However, it is very unlikely that parents in St Mary Somerset and Allhallows London Wall were sending their children away to be nursed because they were very poor, and so it would seem that other reasons for deaths apparently exceeding recorded burial must be found. One explanation is that the assumption that two children in the same family would not have been given the same forename unless the older child had died is not always valid. In other words, in some families two living children were given the same forename, and high marital fertility in London might make this more probable because some parents had upwards of ten children. An alternative explanation is that temporary absences of people from their own homes would mean that burials would have been recorded in the registers of other parishes. Such a hypothesis would obviously also have an equal effect on christenings, and it is therefore implausible, because birth intervals were so short that it is unlikely that many baptisms were missing on family reconstitution forms (Table 5.8).

In view of these uncertainties about London mortality experience, it is best to make high and low estimates of death rates by age. Any plausible estimates should incorporate all the features of London child mortality experience that have already been discussed. These are: lower infant mortality in the wealthier parishes compared with the poor areas; low infant mortality relative to child mortality rates; higher infant mortality along the riverside irrespective of the socio-economic status of the parish; and the possibility that some children were dying whilst they were temporarily away from their parents' home. Some of the rates would be lower than those calculated by using the multipliers, because there seems to be little case to inflate the infant and child mortality rates in, for instance, St Mary Somerset. The lowest possible estimates are the uncorrected life tables (Table 5.1). So, it is reasonable to establish broad margins within which the true rates should lie. The criteria by which these estimates have been made for different ages are:

High estimates
0–4 The rates for all the parishes were inflated by the use of the calculated multipliers.
5–14 The uncorrected data plus 10 per cent for temporary absences.
Low estimates
0–14 The uncorrected data.

Revised mortality rates calculated according to these assumptions are presented in Table 5.12 and the mid-points between the high and low estimates are also given. In Figure 5.1, survivorship curves have been plotted which are based on these estimates. The main conclusion to be drawn from the mortality rates for children aged 1–14 is that the expectation of life at birth was between 30 and 35 years in the wealthier central parishes and about 20 to 25 years in the poorer areas. The inclusion of plague deaths would reduce these expectations by a few years. Both differential mortality and the extent of the contrasts between the parishes may be considered surprising and important conclusions. Some of the poorer districts were obviously exceedingly unhealthy for children. Mortality for London overall must have been between these extremes; most parishes were not quite as poor as St Mary Somerset and Allhallows London Wall, nor as wealthy as St Peter Cornhill. Even though they were poor, the suburban parishes were not as densely built-up as the areas just within the walls, so mortality was probably a little lower than in the poorer parishes discussed here. But to say that, on the whole, the expectation of life at birth for Londoners in the period before the Civil War was between 25 and 30 years is reasonably correct. This of course also assumes that adult mortality rates were not inconsistent with those for children.

100

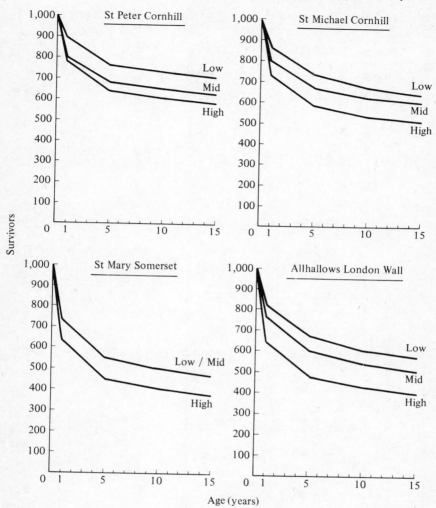

Figure 5.1 Survivorship curves. The high and low estimates were taken from Table 5.12 and the middle curve from Table 5.15.

It is relatively straightforward to explain variations in mortality experience between wealthier and poorer parishes in terms of differences between socio-economic areas within the pre-industrial city. This point is very well illustrated by the experiences of the two Cornhill parishes, St Peter's being the wealthier of the two and having lower mortality, but is weakest in the case of St Mary Somerset, where the expectation of life was lower than in Allhallows London Wall by about five years, although both

101

Table 5.12. *Revised child life tables*

Age	High estimate			Low estimate			Mid-point		
	Survivors $1{,}000l_x$	Rate $1{,}000q_x$	North e_0	Survivors $1{,}000l_x$	Rate $1{,}000q_x$	North e_0	Survivors $1{,}000_x$	Rate $1{,}000l_x$	North e_0
St Peter Cornhill, 1580–1650									
0	1,000	217	31 (6)	1,000	105	51 (14)	1,000	161	38 (9)
1–4	783	185	31 (6)	895	148	36 (8)	839	167	34 (7)
5–9	638	51	41 (10)	763	46	43 (11)	699	49	43 (11)
10–14	605	34	36 (8)	728	31	38 (9)	665	33	36 (8)
15	584			705			643		
1–14	584	253	34 (7)	705	212	38 (9)	643	234	36 (8)
St Michael Cornhill, 1580–1650									
0	1,000	269	26 (4)	1,000	139	43 (11)	1,000	204	34 (7)
1–4	731	205	29 (5)	861	156	36 (8)	796	181	31 (6)
5–9	581	91	29 (5)	727	83	31 (6)	652	87	29 (5)
10–14	528	37	34 (7)	667	34	36 (8)	595	36	34 (7)
15	508			644			574		
1–14	508	304	29 (5)	644	252	34 (7)	574	279	31 (6)
St Mary Somerset, 1605–53									
0	1,000	370	—	1,000	265	26 (4)	1,000	318	21 (2)
1–4	630	284	21 (2)	735	246	24 (3)	682	265	21 (2)
5–9	451	102	24 (3)	554	93	26 (4)	501	98	26 (4)
10–14	405	76	—	502	69	19 (1)	452	73	—
15	374			467			419		
1–14	374	406	21 (2)	467	363	24 (3)	419	385	21 (2)
Allhallows London Wall, 1570–1636									
0	1,000	358	19 (1)	1,000	184	36 (8)	1,000	271	26 (4)
1–4	642	246	24 (3)	816	178	34 (7)	729	212	29 (5)
5–9	484	114	21 (2)	671	104	24 (3)	574	109	24 (3)
10–14	429	62	21 (2)	601	56	24 (3)	511	59	21 (2)
15	402			567			481		
1–14	402	373	24 (3)	567	305	29 (5)	481	339	26 (4)

parishes were very poor. This general conclusion is important not only because mortality rates differed in London, but also because it is not really adequate just to show that there were variations in wealth between parishes in order to argue that residential differentiation occurred in London. The argument that residential areas, defined on the basis of wealth, did exist is considerably strengthened by demonstrating that parishes typical of these areas also had especially distinctive patterns of child mortality (Table 5.12) and birth intervals (Table 5.8), which are indicative of marital fertility levels. It is also important that these striking variations occurred from as early as the period before the outbreak of the Civil War.

The contrast in mortality rates between the two poorer parishes is worth pursuing in a little more detail. The essential question is whether the difference in multipliers and in mortality rates between these two parishes, St Mary Somerset and Allhallows London Wall, reflects differences in the quality of the registers or reflects genuine variations in mortality rates between riverside and inland parishes. As the difference is apparently greatest for infants (Table 5.1), data on infant mortality are presented for these and two additional parishes in Table 5.13. The infant mortality rate has been calculated in all four parishes as the number of infant deaths per thousand live baptisms, not simply for those children which entered into observation for the purpose of constructing life tables. This rate is thus less accurate than the rates derived by family reconstitution methods in Table 5.1, because it includes the fate of those children born in the parish but dying elsewhere. The two additional parishes are St Botolph Bishopsgate adjacent to Allhallows London Wall and of similar social status, but just outside the walls; and St Dunstan in the East, along the riverside in the eastern part of the city. St Dunstan's was wealthier than the other riverside parish, St Mary Somerset. The data suggest that there was a genuine difference in infant mortality rates between riverside and inland parishes irrespective of the social status of the parish concerned. There remains the possibility that the gap between the two kinds of parishes could be narrowed by including those children who died before they could be baptized. Revising the rates by taking dummy births into account increases the level of infant mortality in Allhallows and St Botolph's to a greater extent, but the distinctiveness of the riverside parishes is still apparent. To show that the revised infant mortality rates are acceptable, the endogenous component of these rates has been given in the final column of Table 5.13. From the table we see that infant mortality was particularly high in St Mary Somerset and that the registers were better kept there than in Allhallows London Wall.

There is some evidence, although not enough to be conclusive, that part of the difference in the expectation of life between riverside and inland parishes could be accounted for by the nature of the water supply. This

Table 5.13. *Infant mortality data for the poorer parishes*

Parish and dates	Infant burials	Legitimate baptisms	Infant mortality rate	Dummy births	Infant deaths	Total births	Revised infant mortality rate	Under-baptism rate	Endogenous rate
St Dunstan in the East, 1605–53	707	3,018	234	85	792	3,103	255	27	184
St Mary Somerset, 1605–53	520	2,033	256	46	566	2,079	272	22	175
Allhallows London Wall, 1570–1636	284	1,710	166	129	413	1,839	225	70	142
St Botolph Bishopsgate, 1600–50	401	2,618	153	191	592	2,809	211	68	106

Sources: Tables 2.3, 2.4 and 2.5

subject was discussed by John Stow in his well known *Survey of London.* He drew attention to the fact that the riverside parishes drew their water directly from the Thames.[12] The remainder of the city was supplied from wells, by water conveyed by pipes and conduits from wells, from other rivers in the London area, or from the Thames, in other words by a variety of means.[13]

An alternative explanation of the contrasts in mortality rates between St Mary Somerset and Allhallows London Wall relates to differences in weaning practices. It has been demonstrated that where death rates are high mortality rises at weaning.[14] At such high rates, model life tables do not fit actual adult life patterns very well, and model tables are also least accurate because there are few real-world life tables to base them on. In such situations, the fitting of model life tables to the data for infant mortality is a less reliable method, and a difference in infant mortality rates would be explained by earlier weaning in the parish with higher infant mortality rates, and weaning after the first birthday in the parish with lower rates. In the latter example, a jump in rates would occur early in the second year of life and could be concealed in the overall rates presented by age-group 1–4. The basic data on this point are given in Table 5.14, but

Table 5.14. *Child mortality rates*

Parish and dates	Age					
	0 Exogenous	1	2	3	4	1–4
St Peter Cornhill, 1580–1650	56	46	49	42	20	148
St Michael Cornhill, 1580–1650	57	75	39	21	30	156
St Mary Somerset, 1605–53	95	127	81	30	31	246
Allhallows London Wall, 1570–1636	82	78	65	21	26	178

12. 'Thames water conveyed into men's houses by pipes of lead, from a most artificial forcier standing near unto London bridge and made by Peter Moris Dutchman in the year 1582, for services of the city, on the east part thereof.
    'Conduits of Thames water by the parish churches of St Mary Magdalen and St Nicholas Cole Abbey near unto Old Fish Street, in the year 1583.'
    'One other new forcier was made near unto Broken Wharf to convey Thames water into men's houses of West Cheap, about Paul's. Fleet Street, &c, by an English gentleman, named Bevis Bulmer, in the year 1594.' Stow 1908: I, 18. The spelling has been modernized.
13. Stow 1908: I, 175–92. Other useful accounts of London's water supply at this time are given in Foord 1910: 252–69; and Sunderland 1915: 11–37.
14. Cantrelle 1975: 105–9. For the argument that infant mortality was often higher in the absence of breast feeding, see Knodel and Kintner 1977.

they are unconvincing because a marked increase in mortality at age one which might be attributed to weaning is difficult to detect. The advantages of breast feeding for infant survival diminish with age and its effects are felt to a lesser extent towards the end of the first year. Another problem with this table is that underburial rates were higher in Allhallows London Wall than St Mary's (Table 5.10), but the point that weaning was later in Allhallows can really only be demonstrated if the deaths which were not recorded in the registers as burials were distributed in quite different ways in the two parishes. This could of course be correct if childrearing practices varied greatly between them, but such assumptions about the extent to which the rates should be corrected introduce more than an element of circularity into the argument. The most convincing evidence that weaning was early in St Mary Somerset is that the infant mortality rate did not follow the straight line distribution but began to kink upwards after three months, the opposite of the situation in the other parishes (Figure 2.6). However, there was no increase in mortality during the second year of life in Allhallows London Wall. Another difficulty with the weaning hypothesis is that high infant mortality should lead to short birth intervals, which was the case in St Mary's, yet the intervals were even shorter in Allhallows (Table 5.8), which is itself an argument that the level of infant mortality recorded in Allhallows may have been too low. But this assumes that births were well registered and deaths were not, which is improbable. So although the case that differences in mortality rates between the two poorer parishes which experienced high mortality may be related to weaning practices is interesting, it will remain unsubstantiated until death rates in early childhood can be measured with greater precision.

Although there is little doubt from the survivorship curves in Figure 5.1 that there was an important contrast in mortality experience between the wealthier and poorer London parishes, it is also clear that there was a wide margin of error between the low and high estimates. The low estimates are certainly not implausible, though the infant mortality rate in the two Cornhill parishes and possibly the 0–4 rate in Allhallows London Wall are less likely to be accurate. The problem with the high estimates is whether the method by which the rates were inflated is correct. To what extent can the experience of less than 10 per cent of families which gave two children the same forename also be applied to all reconstituted families (Table 5.9)? Unfortunately, it is the only method that may be used in this study to inflate the burials. The best reason for supposing that the resulting multipliers are too high is that it is far more likely for births to be under-registered than deaths, if only because the interval between birth and baptism was likely to be longer than between death and burial. There is little evidence in Figure 2.9 to suggest that birth registration was not generally good. It is therefore difficult to accept that deaths were not also effectively recorded except where children were dying away at nurse. The high estimates would thus appear to be too pessimistic.

The range of possible child mortality rates illustrated in Figure 5.1 may be narrowed down by using model life tables fitted to the uncorrected data in Table 5.1 in the 1–14 age-group to estimate the infant mortality rate. This works especially well in the two Cornhill parishes. In St Peter Cornhill, the best fit is model West at level 7 which gives an infant mortality rate of 231. Model North, level 9 would also be adequate and the rate would be 170. Splitting the difference gives a rate of exactly 200. Model North, level 7 would also be required in St Michael Cornhill, giving a rate of 203. The rates for St Mary Somerset could well be realistic and do not require inflation, and if they did it would only be by a small amount. Level 3 would probably be the best fit, in either the North family or the South family. The most difficult parish is Allhallows London Wall. If the rates are not inflated, infant mortality would be lower than in the wealthier Cornhill parishes, which is unlikely. It is most probable that the age patterns of mortality would be closer to the experience of the Cornhill parishes than to St Mary's in which case model North would apply, probably at level 5. In this example, the rates for ages 1–4 should be inflated as well as the rates for infants. It is still uncertain why deaths were not completely recorded in Allhallows London Wall. Working in this way provides best estimates of child mortality rates which lie between the optimistic and pessimistic assumptions, but which are different from the mid-points. The corresponding rates and number of survivors are shown in Table 5.15.

Table 5.15. *Summary life tables*

Age	St Peter Cornhill, 1580–1650		St Michael Cornhill, 1580–1650		St Mary Somerset, 1605–53		Allhallows London Wall, 1570–1636	
	Survivors $1,000l_x$	Rate $1,000q_x$	Survivors $1,000l_x$	Rate $1,000q_x$	Survivors $1,000l_x$	Rate $1,000q_x$	Survivors $1,000l_x$	Rate $1,000q_x$
0	1,000	200	1,000	203	1,000	265	1,000	242
1	800	148	797	156	735	246	758	208
5	682	46	673	83	554	93	600	104
10	651	31	617	34	502	69	538	56
15	631		596		467		508	

Given the present state of research, these are best estimates of child mortality rates in London. It should be possible to estimate the overall expectation of life at birth from these rates by the model life table method. But as indicated at the beginning of this chapter, there are grounds for

Table 5.16. *Expectation of life at birth in seventeenth-century London and Geneva*

Place and group	Expectation of life, e_0
London	
St Peter Cornhill, 1580–1650	34–6
St Michael Cornhill, 1580–1650	29–31
St Mary Somerset, 1605–53	21
Allhallows London Wall, 1570–1636	24–6
Geneva, 1625–84	
Social Group I	35.9
Social Group II	24.7
Social Group III	18.3

Sources: London, see text: Geneva, Perrenoud 1975: 236 table 11

believing that in pre-industrial England, levels of adult mortality were higher than those for children.[15] An overall expectation of life calculated in this way may be too optimistic. The most plausible overall mortality estimates therefore result from establishing the expectation of life from child mortality rates between the pessimistic and mid-point figures in Table 5.12. Figures of 34 to 36 years in St Peter's, 29 to 31 years in St Michael's, 21 years in St Mary's and 24 to 26 years in Allhallows seem possible, and these are given in Table 5.16. Technically, such a method of working is less than satisfactory, and the validity of the results is much greater for infant and child rates than for adults. It should also be emphasized that these rates refer to the normal background level of mortality, and do not include the effect of plague epidemics, which would further depress the expectation of life. Mortality differentials would also be accentuated because plague was more severe in the poorer than the wealthier parishes. Before more satisfactory estimates of the expectation of life at birth can be made, much more work is required on mortality in early modern England generally, and especially on the relationships between the mortality experience of children and adults.

There remains the question of the extent to which these estimates of mortality experience in contrasting London parishes are plausible. The most convincing argument in support of the rates presented here comes from comparison with A. Perrenoud's recent family reconstitution study of civil registers in seventeenth-century Geneva, then a city of about 15,000 inhabitants. He showed that there were significant variations in the

15. See for example, Schofield and Wrigley 1979; and Smith 1978: 212.

expectation of life between different social groups and that mortality for the lowest status inhabitants was very high indeed. Some comparative data are presented in Tables 5.7 and 5.16 which demonstrate that London appears to have been slighlty healthier than Geneva before 1650, despite its much larger size. There were wide variations in mortality rates between social areas of groups in both cities. This conclusion contrasts with other evidence which suggests that fertility may have been far more sensitive to socio-economic conditions in the past than mortality.[16] It is often argued that mortality was strongly influenced by the environment and that different groups living in the same city were subject to the same risk of dying. Urban conditions caused mortality to be severe. The conclusion that there could be wide variations in mortality between different socio-economic groups within the same city is therefore of some importance. It also shows that such distinctions were not merely a product of those urban conditions brought about by industrialization but had existed for a much longer period.

London mortality rates in the first half of the seventeenth century did not represent a maximum from which they continually declined into the nineteenth century. The subsequent history of the London death rate is not easy to establish because of increasingly defective parochial registration, which creates difficulty in constructing accurate life tables from family reconstitutions after 1660. The main problem complicating the evidence is the rise of religious nonconformity, and the associated likelihood that many families were using more than one registration system, or none at all. Nevertheless, some features of London mortality changed relatively little between 1550 and 1850, especially when compared with mortality rates at the present time – in particular, deaths were predominantly of infants and children rather than of adults (Forbes 1976). There is little doubt about the main outlines of mortality. During the mid nineteenth century, Farr (1885: 131) suggested that 'The mortality of the city of London was at the rate of 80 per 1,000 in the latter half of the seventeenth century, 50 in the eighteenth, against 24 in the present day.' Clearly the expectation of life had deteriorated in London during the course of the seventeenth century, as it had done in England as a whole. George (1965: 35–42) implied that the London death rate reached its peak in the early eighteenth century at the time of the gin-drinking period. Brownlee's (1925) work on the London bills of mortality supports this case, although he was wrong to assume that the population of London was constant in the eighteenth century and that migration was not an important component of demographic change. The disappearance of plague after 1665 did not necessarily lead to a reduction in mortality rates because occasional epidemic crises were replaced by an

16. See for example, Charbonneau 1970: 167–70; Terrisse 1961: 291; and Bideau 1976: 123 table 7.

increase in mortality from a number of other endemic diseases. For example, P. E. Razzell (1977: 128) has argued that smallpox became more virulent around this time. In the non-plague years between 1629 and 1636, it accounted for only 2.8 per cent of burials recorded in the bills of mortality, but had risen to 8.2 per cent from 1720 to 1730. Smallpox was a disease that was easily identified by contemporaries.

To set this analysis of London mortality rates firmly into perspective, it must be remembered that many industrial towns in the middle of the nineteenth century experienced conditions which were equally poor and probably even worse. When the expectation of life at birth was 40.2 years in England and 51.0 years in the most favourable county, Surrey, it was only 24.2 in Manchester, lower than in London two hundred years earlier; and doubtless in some areas of both cities, and others like Liverpool and Glasgow, it must have been below 20 years (Wrigley 1969: 173). Much the same was true of Paris, Berlin and Stockholm in the later nineteenth century, where mortality rates were very high indeed. Mortality in London in the first half of the seventeenth century was not so high as to have a marked effect on the course of population growth that could not be overcome by migration from outside the capital.

The calculation of demographic rates in this chapter depends on a number of assumptions, especially concerning the characteristics of appropriate model life tables and the extent to which the number of deaths has to be inflated to take account of the mortality of nurse-children. Yet however the figures are manipulated, it is difficult to escape the general conclusion that there were important differences in mortality rates between the wealthier and poorer parishes, and that the expectation of life at birth among the poorer parishes was low. Overall, mortality was much higher than for what is known about the experience of the rural parishes in England, but it was not as high as in some places in continental pre-industrial and early industrializing Europe (Weber 1899: 349; Van de Walle and Preston 1974; Hofsten and Lundström 1976: 119 table 7.1). Whether the mortality of adults was also consistent with the pattern in model North life tables is another open question, yet it is clear that half the London-born children did nor survive to adulthood. Having examined the background level of mortality in London, it is time now to turn to the impact of short-term fluctuations in the death rate caused by the plague crises.

CHAPTER 6

THE EFFECT OF PLAGUE ON MORTALITY EXPERIENCE

The mortality rates for London parishes which have been presented so far refer to the background level of mortality and do not include the effect of the plague epidemics. There were very serious plague crises in 1563, 1593, 1603, 1625 and 1665, and a lesser outbreak in 1636. There were relatively few plague deaths outside these years, but in the worst crises the annual death rate was well over 200 per thousand. In this chapter it will be argued that it is easy to misunderstand the effect of plague. The continuous supply of migrants from the countryside meant that even when the crisis mortality rate was so high, the population was replenished very rapidly after the end of the outbreaks. Outside these plague years, the great majority of deaths in London may be attributed to other diseases, and the disappearance of plague did not necessarily lead to a significant narrowing of the gap between deaths and births. The crises themselves, however, were very serious for their duration, and, as with mortality in general, their impact was unequally distributed between the different areas of the city.

Despite the social dislocation caused by its occurrence, plague was a relatively infrequent epidemic disease, although it was also endemic for much of the period in some of the poorer parts of the city. As T. McKeown has recently written:

By simple arithmetic it can be shown that a high death rate from an infrequent epidemic infection has much less effect on the general level of mortality and rate of population growth than the constant high death rate from endemic infections which killed the majority of all newborn children within ten years of birth.[1]

This point may be easily illustrated by comparing the experience of three model populations over a hundred-year period as in Table 6.1. In all three models, it is assumed that the initial population was 1,000 and that the number of newcomers being born or migrating in each year equalled the extent to which the original total was depleted by deaths. This would hardly be unrealistic of many central London parishes, which were not increasing in size; growth in the capital was occurring mainly on the periphery, in the Liberties and suburbs. In Population A, the crude death rate in normal years was 20 per thousand but there were five plague crises

1. McKeown 1976: 69. These assumptions about endemic mortality are appropriate for the poorer London parishes as Chapter 5 argues. This point is also a main focus of Shrewsbury 1970.

during the century when the death rate shot up to 200 per thousand. There were thus 2,900 deaths during the hundred years, and a crude death rate of 29 per thousand. In contrast, if the normal death rate doubled to 40 per thousand, as in Population B, but there were no crises, the total number of deaths would be 4,000, giving a death rate of 40 per thousand. The case of London is probably best reflected in Population C. Here the normal death rate was 35 per thousand, but in the five crisis years, it shot up to 200 per thousand. The overall death rate would be 43 per thousand. An average rate of 200 per thousand in plague years would not be an unrealistic assumption (Table 6.4). Obviously the background level of mortality was more important over a long period of time than the effect of mortality crises in determining the extent to which the death rate exceeded the birth rate, and consequently the number of migrants that would be required to prevent the early modern metropolitan population from declining. These models simplify the situation – the age-incidence of plague is distinctive in that younger people were normally affected to a greater degree than adults, which would have repercussions throughout the demographic system – but even so the background level of mortality was of greater significance over a long period than the short-term plague crises.

The effect of the plague crises was that death rates varied widely over short periods. The plague was an important part of London demographic experience because of the severity of its impact. All Londoners were conscious of the onset and effects of plague. Many of the very wealthiest inhabitants left the city for the duration of the crises. The epidemics were especially serious in 1593, 1603 and 1625, the last two outbreaks being particularly bad when about a fifth of the population died in each. There was a lesser epidemic in 1636, and, just outside the period covered here, equally catastrophic outbreaks in 1563 and 1665. Five major epidemics occurred during the course of a century. Their effects would have been even more far-reaching had the combined effect of fertility and especially migration not meant that the city recovered its former population very quickly after each crisis.

It would be convenient to begin a study of the demographic impact of the plague by trying to establish its importance in relation to other causes of death. It is often argued that the official figures contained in the bills of mortality underestimate the actual number of deaths because of the difficulty of notifying burials to the authorities in time of crisis,[2] but it may partly have been due to the almost complete collapse of registration in some parishes. The data used here will be drawn from those registers where a continuous record was kept throughout the plague periods, and in fact the analyses of plague mortality from the parish registers in Tables 6.3, 6.5, 6.6 and 6.7 do not imply that the number of burials reported in plague

2. See, for example, Bell 1924: 151, 330; and Wilson 1927: 206–7.

Table 6.1. *Death rates in model populations under various mortality assumptions*

	Population A		Population B		Population C	
Initial population	1,000		1,000		1,000	
At risk over 100 years	100,000		100,000		100,000	
No. of deaths, death rates:						
95 years	1,900	(20 per thousand)	3,800	(40 per thousand)	3,325	(35 per thousand)
5 years	1,000	(200 per thousand)	200	(40 per thousand)	1,000	(200 per thousand)
Total deaths	2 900		4,000		4,325	
Death rate over 100 years	29		40		43	

Table 6.2. Deaths from specific causes per 1,000 deaths from all causes

Cause	Allhallows London Wall, 1578–98	St. Botolph Aldgate, 1583–99	London bills of mortality, 1629–36	London bills of mortality, 1706–10	Southern Sweden, 5 regions, 1749–73	Sweden, 1799–82
Plague	239	236	125	0	0	0
Tuberculosis	152	224	171	153	138	113
Other infectious diseases	90	118	182	272	305	294
Total infectious diseases	481	578	478	425	443	407
Number of deaths	724	4,953	96,275	—	39,957	217,673

Sources: Forbes 1971: 100–2 table 6; Glass 1973: 190 table 3; Imhof and Lindskog 1974: 932–3; and Widen 1975: 97–9.

years was necessarily defective. Contemporary identifications of causes of death must always have been suspect – not only was medicine not well advanced, but many people died without any medical care at all. The parish clerks who entered the cause of death in the registers presumably often just wrote down what they had been told by the family of the deceased. The classification of diseases in this period is in any case very difficult because they were identified by their symptoms, rather than by causes as they are today. This creates a problem when attempting to draw conclusions from the data, and also means that any approach should be as simple as possible.[3]

Some insight into mortality from specific diseases may be obtained from an analysis of certain London parish registers where the burial register recorded causes of death. In two very poor London parishes around the walls, original paper registers survive for short periods towards the end of the sixteenth century. These were Allhallows London Wall (7) and St Botolph Aldgate (102), located just outside the city walls in the north-eastern part of the city. Similar information was given in the bills of mortality for the period between 1629 and 1636. This is not directly comparable with the parish register data because it relates to a different time period in which no major plague epidemic occurred. For comparison, material from the bills of mortality for the period from 1706 to 1710 when London mortality rates may have been very high has been added, as well as for five regions of southern Sweden between 1749 and 1773, and for the whole of Sweden between 1779 and 1782. The purpose of Table 6.2 is to demonstrate what proportions of deaths might be attributable to infectious diseases and to show how important the two most serious diseases, plague and tuberculosis, may have been.[4] There are two main points which emerge from this table. First, mortality rates were high because of infectious diseases. Of these, plague was the most important but its impact was not overwhelming. Its effect on contemporaries was because of the

3. Some of the points in this paragraph are also contained in Creighton 1891b: 509, 654, 661–2; and Forbes 1971: 99, 124.
4. The diseases included in the categories of 'tuberculosis' and 'other infectious diseases' have been taken from those suggested in Glass 1973: 203. Useful accounts of classifying diseases and the identification of contemporary causes of death are given in Forbes 1971: 102–18; and Peter 1975. The data for tuberculosis given for St Boltolph Aldgate mainly consist of deaths identified as being from 'con'. T. R. Forbes suggests that this could be an abbreviation for consumption, convulsions or perhaps for both. Convulsions were mainly a cause of infant deaths associated with summer infections (Glass 1973: 189). In Allhallows London Wall, these would probably have been included amongst the deaths where the cause was not identified, as they could have been in St Botolph's. In the bills of mortality for the years 1629–31, the number of children dying from convulsions was very small but this increased rapidly thereafter. It is therefore possible, but not proven, that deaths from tuberculosis in St Botolph Aldgate could have been overestimated. There were some plague deaths in Sweden for the earlier period which were classed with a variety of other diseases which together made up 5.9 per cent of all deaths (Imhof and Lindskog 1974: 932–3 table 4).

dramatic nature of its occurrence in epidemic crises, but other diseases were not insignificant. Many of these were endemic, like tuberculosis. In most parish registers, causes of death were not included with each entry which makes the study of endemic diseases exceptionally difficult. Of the main epidemic diseases, only plague may be readily identified in the registers because the mortality crises were so serious. Secondly, the proportion of deaths from other infectious diseases increased rapidly after plague was eliminated. People who were no longer at risk from plague found themselves at greater risk from other diseases.

At this stage of the argument, it should be pointed out that despite the amount that has been written about the plagues which affected western Europe between the mid fourteenth and early eighteenth centuries, the subject is still poorly understood.[5] Much of the problem rests with the complex nature of the disease. It is difficult to know how much of what has been learnt from case studies in early-twentieth-century China and elsewhere may be usefully applied to seventeenth-century England, because the character and virulence of diseases vary over time. Nevertheless, a medical perspective is certainly important in working towards a proper historical understanding. The plague bacillus, *Yersinia pestis*, is a disease which affects rats and which is only transmitted to men through fleas, particularly the rat flea, *Xenopsylla cheopis*, although the human flea, *Pulex irritans*, may also be a vector. There is some division of opinion about how the disease is spread. For example, it has been argued that plague can be diffused in the absence of rats if the human flea can transmit the disease. But it is generally thought that the rat flea is the more important vector and plague was most prevalent where rats and men lived in close proximity to each other. This may have been the reason why the disease was confined mainly to towns and especially to their poorer areas. Because plague was such a complex phenomenon, there are no simple explanations of its historical incidence. It is not known what determined the periodicity of the crises and why the disease completely disappeared from the capital after 1665, for London social conditions did not improve so dramatically in the succeeding century to provide a credible cause of the elimination of plague. Detailed historical research is needed for new light to be shed on the incidence of plague, and hence on its causes and importance.

The point that it is easy to overemphasize the long-term significance of plague may be pursued further by examining the contribution of the disease to mortality experience in ten sample parishes (Table 6.3). The main problem involved in constructing this table is to estimate the

5. The most important general references on plague are: Creighton 1891b; Shrewsbury 1970; Morris 1971; Chambers 1972; Clarkson 1975; Biraben 1975–6; McNeill 1977; Bradley 1977a; 11–23; Appleby 1980. The main works on the plague in London are: Bell 1924; Wilson 1927; Sutherland 1972; Forbes 1971; Hollingsworth 1971; and Appleby 1975.

Table 6.3. *Estimation of percentage mortality due to plague, 1580–1650*

Parish	Excess deaths	Total deaths	% due to plague
Allhallows Bread Street	66	1,006	6.6
St Peter Cornhill	293	2,145	13.7
St Christopher le Stocks	110	970	11.3
St Michael Cornhill	333	2,323	14.3
St Vedast Foster Lane	289	1,965	14.7
St Helen Bishopsgate	280	1,610	17.4
St Thomas the Apostle	243	1,740	14.0
St Lawrence Jewry	198	1,891	10.5
St Mary Somerset[a]	533	3,864	13.8
Allhallows London Wall	593	3,091	19.2

Note: a. The number of deaths in the 1603 plague was partly taken from the bills of mortality and the record is incomplete.

proportion of deaths that could be attributed to plague, since causes of death were not identified in most parish registers. The method followed was to subtract the normal number of deaths from the total which occurred in the three plague years 1593, 1603 and 1625, so enabling the excess number of deaths, presumably from the plague, to be calculated. Such a procedure underestimates the actual number of plague deaths, because the population at risk by the end of the plague year has declined, and thus too many deaths are subtracted. The normal number of deaths was calculated as a simple average of the burials for five years before the crisis year. The year immediately before the plague year was not included because it has been observed in several parishes that the upturn in mortality began in the autumn before the main epidemic, but the number of deaths then subsided during the winter months.[6] For example, in order to calculate the normal number of deaths which might be expected to have occurred in 1603, the mean annual number of burials was taken to be a simple average of the totals for the years between 1597 and 1601. The calculated number of excess deaths may then be expressed as a percentage of the total number of burials, so enabling the proportion of burials attributed to plague to be calculated in Table 6.3. The period covered is restricted to that considered in the remainder of this study, 1580 to 1650, so the plague years included were 1593, 1603 and 1625. The contribution of plague to total mortality experience was similar in most of the parishes analysed except the wealthiest and the poorest, and about one death in seven might be attributed to plague. This table underestimates the proportion of plague deaths in the poorer parishes because it does not take account of deaths

6. This characteristic of plague epidemics has been observed for Colyton in 1645–6; Eyam in 1665–6; in some Swedish parishes in 1710–11; as well as for some London outbreaks. See Schofield 1977: 101.

from plague outside the main crisis years which were commoner in these areas. However, it is unlikely that this point would affect the conclusions markedly.

Another way of judging the magnitude of the plague crises in individual years is to estimate crude death rates in plague years from the data contained in the bills of mortality. If the assumption of a constant birth rate is made, the population of London may be estimated for each year from the number of christenings reported in the bills of mortality. In Table 6.4,

Table 6.4. *Estimated London death rates in plague years*

Year	No. of burials	Population at given birth rate		Death rate at given birth rate	
		30	35	30	35
1593	17,844	149,700	128,029	119	139
1603	38,244	167,433	143,514	228	266
1625	54,265	244,400	209,486	222	259
1636	23,369	333,267	285,657	70	82

In estimating the population, the number of christenings was inflated by 5 per cent to allow for under-recording. See text for details of methods of estimation.

low and high estimates of the crude death rate have been made assuming birth rates of 30 and 35 per thousand. However the data are manipulated, it is clear that death rates were especially high during the crises and it also appears probable that the 1603 and 1625 epidemics were the most serious.[7] During these two crises, between a fifth and a quarter of the population of London died. These rates were much higher than in Holland where the crude death rates in Dutch towns have been estimated as 112 in 1624, 140 in 1636, 125 in 1655 and 120 in 1664 at Amsterdam, and between 120 and 135 in 1624 and 1635 in Rotterdam (De Vries 1974: 111 table 3.10; Van der Woude and Mentink 1966: 1181).

The plague death rates calculated in this way can only be estimates, because the population at risk is not exactly known. The best way of overcoming this problem is to compare death rates in plague years with those in normal years. Once again the bills of mortality may be used to analyse the situation in the city as a whole, whilst the parish registers facilitate an examination of the impact of plague on its constituent parts. The bills have already been subjected to a thorough examination by I. Sutherland. He concluded that:

7. It is also possible to estimate the death rate for the area within the walls from the number of burials in the bills of mortality and population totals estimated from counts taken in 1631 and 1638. These gave death rates of 35 and 47 respectively, whilst the method outlined above for the whole of the bills of mortality indicated rates of 35 in 1631 and 46 in 1638 where the birth rate was 35 per thousand.

In 1593 the mortality was more than four times the normal level, in 1665 more than five times, in 1603 and 1625 more than six times, and in 1563 more than seven times the normal level. Taking these figures at their face value, the mortality appears to have become slightly less severe in each successive major plague.[8]

The main problem involved in reaching this conclusion is that the bills of mortality run in a continuous series only from 1604. Hence Sutherland's method was to fit trend lines to the annual totals of christenings recorded in the bills. He then made the assumption that the birth rate was constant and took these trends to represent an index of population. This enables mortality indices to be calculated as the ratio of recorded burials to expected christenings. Sutherland's earliest figure, for 1563, is particularly suspect because the expected number of christenings was estimated only from these trends. It is therefore difficult to maintain the argument that, from the evidence in the bills of mortality, the first outbreak was the most catastrophic. The method also assumes that the rate of demographic growth was constant from as early as 1563 and that there would be no variation in the birth rate, although in fact some variation could be expected over a period as long as a century.

Nevertheless, the parish register evidence suggests that the conclusions reached by Sutherland command respect. The registers were analysed using the different method of calculating the number of times burials in plague years exceeded those in normal years. The total of burials for the normal years was calculated in exactly the same way as above except that, since many registers did not commence until the accession of Queen Elizabeth in 1558, there was little alternative but to take the average of the four years from 1559 till 1562 as the level of normal mortality. This measure of the relative severity of a plague outbreak was termed a crisis mortality ratio.[9] Attention here will be focused on the whole year in which the crisis occurred, rather than converting the number of deaths in the actual period of the crisis to an annual total of burials and comparing this with the normal number of deaths occurring in a year. Such an approach would give much higher crisis mortality ratios. The main disadvantages of our method are the problem of establishing the exact dates of each epidemic in the absence of the identification of plague deaths in many parish registers, and the fact that the onset and duration of the crises varied between different parishes. A further problem remaining is that in those outer parishes which were gaining in population size, the crisis mortality ratio might be inflated because the population would be lower at the beginning of the normal years than at the end. Where the burial registers

8. Sutherland 1972: 299. Other authorities are agreed that the greatest proportion of the population died in 1563, although the greatest number died in 1665. Creighton 1891b: 304; and Shrewsbury 1970: 192, 487.
9. This method is similar in concept, but varied in detail, from that adopted in Flinn 1974: 287.

Table 6.5. *Crisis mortality ratios in each plague year by parish*

Parish	1563	1593	1603	1625	1636	1665	Houses/acre
Allhallows Bread Street	4.26	1.96	3.82	2.73	0.85	2.13	30.0
St Peter Cornhill	8.00	3.29	6.59	4.40	1.08	4.22	21.5
St Christopher le Stocks[a]	—	4.12	4.75	4.23	1.59	2.50	22.5
St Michael Cornhill	6.10	4.15	5.51	5.65	1.09	4.41	45.8
St Vedast Foster Lane	7.52	5.33	6.25	5.67	1.87	3.30	52.2
St Helen Bishopsgate[b]	—	3.90	6.05	6.80	1.44	4.35	13.2
St Thomas the Apostle[c]	11.61	3.98	7.06	6.17	1.13	5.86	47.1
St Lawrence Jewry	7.10	3.50	4.72	3.10	0.89	2.24	25.7
St Mary Somerset[d]	8.00	4.60	4.35	5.22	1.92	6.65	40.0
Allhallows London Wall	9.14	5.08	10.25	10.14	2.83	10.12	23.1

Notes: a. According to the register, the peak in burials in this period was in 1561 when 57 deaths were recorded.
b. The registers do not commence until 1575 and were defective in 1665. The total of burials in 1665 was taken from the bills of mortality.
c. The burial register does not begin in a complete form until 1561 and the normal level of mortality is based on the average of deaths occurring between 1565 and 1569.
d. The number of burials in 1603 was partly taken from the bills of mortality. There is no surviving record between 28 March 1603 and 19 September 1603 in the parish registers, meaning that the crisis mortality ratio is underestimated.

were not complete in the plague years, the number of deaths given in the bills of mortality were used to calculate crisis mortality ratios as the totals contained in the parish registers and the bills of mortality were in general agreement in most parishes (Table 3.2).

Crisis mortality ratios for the ten sample parishes are presented in Table 6.5. In general, these confirm Sutherland's conclusion that the relative severity of plague was declining from 1563 to 1665, particularly if only the most important epidemics of 1563, 1603, 1625 and 1665 are considered. There were also significant contrasts between the various parishes. As a general tendency, the two poorest parishes were more severely affected by plague, and this is especially noticeable in the case of Allhallows London Wall where the 1665 outbreak was as serious as that of 1563. In St Mary Somerset, a parish in which mortality rates in general were exceedingly high, the contribution of plague was less marked, possibly because of the fact that its location by the riverside meant that it would also have been affected by other kinds of water-borne infections. In the two poorer parishes, plague declined less rapidly, if at all, whilst the opposite was true of the wealthiest parish, Allhallows Broad Street.[10] In a study of the incidence of plague in Bristol during the same period by P. Slack (1977), it was also found that the poorer parishes were more severely affected by plague.

Table 6.6. *Crisis mortality ratios in plague years for peripheral and suburban parishes*

Parish	1593	1603	1625
Allhallows London Wall	5.08	10.25	10.14
St Botolph Bishopsgate	7.23	8.88	9.69
St Botolph Aldgate	6.19	7.69	6.59
St James Clerkenwell	4.08	6.48	5.68
St Margaret Westminster	2.97	4.61	4.08

The data for St Botolph Aldgate were taken from Forbes 1971: 59–61 table 1.

Plague caused greatest distress and the highest death rates in the whole of the bills of mortality in those parishes located around the city walls. In the suburban parishes some distance from the walls, the disease was much less severe and of about equal intensity to the parishes in the central area of the city. Table 6.6 illustrates how parishes further away from the city walls were less affected by plague: St James Clerkenwell and St Margaret

10. Most of the authorities on the London plagues agree that the disease occurred very unevenly between the various parts of the city. Shrewsbury 1970: 193–4, 223, 229, 268, 316, 466; and Bell 1924: 273, and map facing p. 273. They also agree that plague was mainly a disease of the poor. Creighton 1891b: 519, 663; Bell 1924: 152, 254, 327; Wilson 1927: 172; and Shrewsbury 1970: 228.

Westminster are much further from the centre of the city than Allhallows London Wall, St Botolph Bishopsgate and St Botolph Aldgate, all of which were situated around the walls. Clerkenwell and Westminster were large parishes inhabited by people of varied social status which probably means that they were on average wealthier than the poorest parishes around the walls analysed here. But it is important to bear in mind, as L. Bradley (1977b) shows in an interesting discussion of the diffusion of plague through the Lea Valley in 1603, that the transmission of the disease was complex, and it was not simply contagious between neighbouring parishes. The path of an epidemic was not easily determined by the relationship of one place to another that was already affected.

Although evidence from both London and Bristol suggests that the plague was most severe in the poorest parishes, which were probably overcrowded and presented conditions where rats and men lived close together, little correlation has been found between the density of housing per acre in 1638 and the intensity of the crises (Table 6.5). However, when Slack (1977: 55–9) analysed the distribution by street of plague victims in Christ Church parish, Bristol, in 1575 and 1603, he found that in this parish, which was of average wealth for the city, plague deaths were few in the main street but were clustered in the back alleys of the parish. Wealthier people tended to leave their homes during the crises, and thus plague was socially selective even within individual parishes.

The social structure of a metropolitan city is important in explaining the incidence of plague, but it is not sufficient to account for the disappearance of the disease, because inadequate social conditions in towns persisted after 1665. This problem of the causes of the disappearance of plague is still unresolved and it will probably remain unresolved whilst this complex disease is inadequately understood. By the seventeenth century, plague usually, but not always, flourished only in an urban environment. It is, therefore, hardly surprising that A. B. Appleby (1975) concluded that there was little relationship between standards of nutrition and the extent of disease mortality in London. His argument was based on an attempt to correlate numbers of deaths from individual diseases recorded in the bills of mortality after 1629 with the level of bread prices in the capital.

Not only was plague much more important in particular social areas of the pre-industrial metropolitan city, but it also affected certain age-groups in the population to a much greater extent than others. This has important implications for replacement rates of London population. Any serious attempt to analyse the demographic effects of the London plague crises must take account of the pioneering and important article by M. F. and T. H. Hollingsworth (1971) who attempted to calculate plague mortality rates from the parish register of St Botolph Bishopsgate for the 1603 crisis. They reached two main conclusions: first, that death rates decreased with increasing age, and secondly, that men were more susceptible to plague

Table 6.7. *Crisis mortality ratios by age-group*

Parish	1593	1603	1625
St Peter Cornhill	3.29	6.59	4.40
Infants	2.22	2.35	0.58
Children	11.67	9.83	6.54
Adults	2.67	6.21	5.06
St Michael Cornhill	4.15	5.51	5.65
Infants	0.83	3.44	2.14
Children	8.33	8.79	6.00
Adults	2.73	4.69	6.21
St Thomas the Apostle	3.98	7.06	6.17
Infants	1.79	3.33	—
Children	5.83	7.00	—
Adults	4.18	8.16	—
Allhallows London Wall	5.08	10.25	10.14
Infants	1.17	2.78	—
Children	6.39	21.80	—
Adults	5.61	9.03	—

than women. These questions may be pursued further by investigating the situation in a larger number of London parishes. One of the simplest methods of analysing the age-incidence of plague mortality is outlined in Table 6.7, where crisis mortality ratios have been calculated for four parishes, one drawn from each quartile in terms of the distribution of wealth in London in 1638. These have been tabulated by those entries described in the registers as children and adults. Children are recorded as either 'son of' or 'daughter of' and would normally have been still living at home, although not always. The numbers of infants dying have also been calculated from the parish registers. These have been subtracted from the numbers of children recorded, so enabling crisis mortality ratios for infants to be calculated. All the other burials would have been of adults. The point that emerges is that children appear to have been especially susceptible to plague compared with adults. This generalization applies to all the parishes studied except for St Thomas the Apostle in 1603. Infant mortality in plague periods probably exceeded normal levels by a lesser degree if only because infant mortality rates were quite high in any case. This must mean that a very high proportion of infants alive at the beginning of a plague year did not survive the year. It is not clear in these cases whether infants died from plague or whether the risk of dying increased because they were less well cared for during plague periods, for example if one or both parents had also died.[11] The deaths of fewer adults than children implies that

11. Schofield 1977: 118 table 12 found that infant mortality during the 1645–6 plague at Colyton was three times as great if both parents died rather than surviving the crisis.

survival from a previous epidemic granted at least some immunity from plague.

This is obviously a crude method of working. However, the calculation of mortality rates requires ages at death to be known accurately, for both children and adults, and family reconstitution allows it to be done with success (Schofield 1977: 116 table 10, 117 table 11). But, it is difficult to do for Londoners because the amount of migration to the capital meant that few people had been born in the parish in which they subsequently settled. An insufficient number of ages at burial are known from reconstitution to calculate adult life tables. Nevertheless, the problem can be overcome by analysing data for those three London parishes in which ages at death were given in the burial registers, which enables both adult and child mortality to be examined. The three parishes are St Peter Cornhill in 1593 and 1603, Allhallows London Wall in 1593 and St Botolph Bishopsgate in 1603 (where ages at death were also recorded in 1625 but not consistently for the few years preceding the crisis). Unfortunately this sample only includes one wealthy parish, St Peter Cornhill, and no parish of intermediate social status.

As the analysis depends on the use of ages at death reported in the register, it is important to show that these ages were stated with reasonable accuracy. The registers were carefully compiled and it is likely that, where they were recorded, ages at death would have been given conscientiously. However, one of the chief causes of error was that many people did not know their exact age or their date of birth. In a pre-statistical age, when the only written record of the lives of many ordinary people was contained in the parish registers, there would have been far less reason to remember these facts, especially as there were so many children christened in each family. In Table 6.8, the difference in age at death calculated by matching each register entry to a date of baptism from that given in the burial register is shown for children up until age nine. Most ages at death for children were stated correctly to within a year. This is encouraging and gives confidence in the use of the ages as stated for demographic purposes. The last row shows the results for a forty-five-parish national sample where ages recorded by the 1851 census enumerators were compared with those calculated from the Anglican baptism registers. Since this refers to a non-migrant population living in the same parish as they had been born, the majority of these cases would have been children. There is no evidence that the standard of accuracy of age-reporting in the mid nineteenth century was much better than two hundred years earlier, which suggests that the ages given in the burial registers, for children, at least, may be regarded as reasonably accurate.

For adults, the same method of checking the accuracy of the ages recorded could not be adopted, with so many Londoners being migrants. There was some evidence of 'age-heaping' in the registers, because ages

Table 6.8. *Distribution of discrepancies between recorded ages at burial in registers and calculated ages by date of baptism up to nine years*

Parish and dates	Discrepancy in years						Total
	0	1	2	3	4	5+	
St Peter Cornhill, 1579–1605	123 (69)	49 (27)	5 (3)	0 (0)	0 (0)	1 (1)	178 (100)
Allhallows London Wall, 1578–98	87 (81)	20 (19)	0 (0)	0 (0)	0 (0)	0 (0)	107 (100)
St Botolph Bishopsgate, 1603	167 (67)	68 (27)	6 (3)	4 (2)	0 (0)	3 (1)	248 (100)
45-parish national sample, 1851	1,792 (46)	1,226 (32)	406 (11)	195 (5)	93 (2)	141 (4)	3,853 (100)

Figures in brackets are percentages.

The figures for St Botolph's were taken from Hollingsworth 1971: 136 table 3.

In the forty-five-parish national sample, the discrepancy refers to all ages and is calculated between the age given in the 1851 census and that found by linking individuals to baptism entries in parish registers. The data were taken from Razzell 1972: 126 table 5.

were frequently given in round figures. Although they may have been correct to the nearest five years, too much reliance should not be placed on the actual ages as given. If all the ages were correctly stated, 40 per cent of the total ages ought to end in the possibly unpopular digits 1, 3, 7 and 9. Index numbers may be calculated such that 100 represents the theoretical maximum proportion ending in these digits. Thus, in a population where ages were always correctly given, scores would be very close to 100, which is the case for advanced countries today, whilst a score close to zero indicates that all the ages were rounded.[12] Scores are shown in Table 6.9 for the first hundred cases after the beginning of each base year. Any

Table 6.9. *Age-reporting index scores*

Parish	Date	Index score	Excluding infants
St Peter Cornhill	1580	80	85
	1590	52.5	57.5
	1600	67.5	72.5
Allhallows London Wall	1580	50	57.5
	1590	55	72.5
St Botolph Bishopsgate	1600	62.5	87.5
	1610	67.5	85
	1620	25	40
	1630	45	62.5
	1640	57.5	75

See text for method of calculation.

12. This method is explained in detail in Smith and Zopf 1970: 152–7.

missing ages were excluded. The results were disappointing, suggesting that many of the ages stated were rounded. Since a very high proportion of all deaths were of infants, those burials occurring at age 0 were excluded in the second column, which showed that age-heaping which was visible in the data may not have been as severe as first thought. The effect of the deterioration in age-reporting between 1620 and 1625 in St Botolph's is clearly evident in the table. The inference to be drawn from this evidence is that ages at burial for children (Table 6.8) were more accurate than for adults (Table 6.9), so in examining the age-incidence of the plague, the experience of all adults will be tabulated only by very broad age-groups. This will minimize the effect of possible age mis-statements whilst retaining sufficient detail for the analysis to be undertaken.

The method used by the Hollingsworths to calculate age-specific plague mortality rates was as follows. Since plague deaths were not identified in many parish registers, and such identifications of plague reported by the parish clerks and incorporated in the bills of mortality may not have been accurate, the death rates from plague were calculated by subtracting rates appropriate to the period immediately prior to the crisis year from the rates computed for the period of the crisis itself. Their conclusion that suscepti-bility to plague declined with age is of great importance. The main problem in constructing life tables for plague periods encountered by the Hollings-worths was that they did not know the age-structure of the population.[13] The amount of migration creates difficulty in estimating the exact shape of the age pyramid because the age of the migrants is not known. R. S. Schofield (1977) constructed life tables from reconstitution data for the

Table 6.10. *Excess mortality by age: St Peter Cornhill, 1593*

Age	Pre-crisis burials 1587–91 (1)	Crisis burials (2)	Recorded excess (2)–(1) (3)	Model age-structure (4)	Expected excess burials (5)	Excess ratio (3)/(5) (6)
0	1.4	4.0	2.6	3	3.0	0.87
1–4	2.0	12.0	10.0	9	9.0	1.11
5–9	0.2	16.0	15.8	10	10.0	1.58
10–19	1.8	42.0	40.2	18	18.1	2.22
20–49	9.0	36.0	27.0	41	41.2	0.66
50+	7.2	12.0	4.8	19	19.1	0.25
All	21.6	122.0	100.4	100	100.4	1.00

Model population: Model North, level 7. Expectation of life at birth 35; gross reproduction rate 2.00; birth rate 30; death rate 28; growth rate 1.83.

13. The proportion of the population surviving to age 15 in St Botolph Aldgate was not calculated by proper life table methods, so that estimates of the numbers of survivors are too pessimistic. Forbes 1971: 71 table 3.

well-known plague crisis in Colyton, Devon. In this rural parish, children were particularly susceptible to plague compared with adults, which confirms the conclusion reached by the Hollingsworths in their analysis of a suburban London parish. Schofield also developed a simpler method of analysing age-specific mortality from plague, which gave similar but less detailed and less precise results than the more formal and more elaborate calculation of life tables. It may be used in situations where the construction of life tables is impractical. His technique may also be applied to the study of the London plagues. It will be illustrated by a consideration of the 1593 crisis in St Peter Cornhill (Table 6.10). In the discussion that follows, all the results have been standardized to an annual basis. The first column of Table 6.10 shows the average number of deaths for a five-year period before the crisis in each age-group. The number of age-groups is smaller than for the Hollingsworths' larger parish of St Botolph's because of the need to avoid too few numbers in each age-group. This also helps to overcome problems of age mis-statement by adults. In the second column, the number of burials in the six months of the crisis from June to November are given on an annual basis, allowing the number of excess burials to be calculated in column 3. This will only be a rough estimate, and too small, because the pre-plague population would have declined once the epidemic had started so too few burials were subtracted. It is also likely that the age-structure of the population would change during the epidemic because of differential mortality, the very topic under consideration, and this might also affect the results. If, however, each age-group were equally at risk from plague in crisis years as from other diseases in normal years, the expected age distribution of excess burials may be calculated in column 5 from a model age-structure of the population in column 4. The age-structures have been taken from a stable population in the North family. Thus for St Peter Cornhill, where the expectation of life at birth was found to be 34 to 36 years (Table 5.15), a model age-structure was selected with an expectation of life of 35 years in the female tables, and a gross reproduction rate of 2.00. This of course assumes that mortality at all ages moved in step with what has been found for children. Given the generality of this method, the exact choice of an age-structure is not crucial. Finally, the ratio of the recorded to the expected number of excess burials may be calculated in column 6 which demonstrates the extent to which the age pattern of mortality in crisis periods differed from that in normal years.

This simple method has been discussed at some length both to explain the way it works and to show that it is capable of producing meaningful results. It has been applied to the study of the London parishes in Tables 6.10, 6.11, 6.12 and 6.13. It is apparent that the incidence of plague varied between different age-groups and its impact tended to decline with age. Similar results were found by Schofield (1977: 110 table 6, 113 table 7, 114

Table 6.11. *Excess mortality by age: St Peter Cornhill, 1603*

Age	Pre-crisis burials 1597–1601 (1)	Crisis burials (2)	Recorded excess (2)–(1) (3)	Model age-structure (4)	Expected excess burials (5)	Excess ratio (3)/(5) (6)
0	3.6	12.0	8.4	3	7.3	1.15
1–4	2.6	32.0	29.4	9	22.0	1.34
5–9	1.6	36.0	34.4	10	24.4	1.41
10–19	2.8	84.0	81.2	18	44.0	1.85
20–49	6.4	84.0	77.6	41	100.1	0.78
50+	4.8	18.0	13.2	19	46.4	0.28
All	21.8	266.0	244.2	100	244.2	1.00

Model population: Model North, level 7. Expectation of life at birth 35; gross reproduction rate 2.00; birth rate 30; death rate 28; growth rate 1.83.

Table 6.12 *Excess mortality by age: Allhallows London Wall, 1593*

Age	Pre-crisis burials 1587–91 (1)	Crisis burials (2)	Recorded excess (2)–(1) (3)	Model age-structure (4)	Expected excess burials (5)	Excess ratio (3)/(5) (6)
0	6.0	14.0	8.0	3	5.1	1.57
1–4	2.6	24.0	21.4	8	13.5	1.59
5–9	1.0	26.0	25.0	9	15.1	1.66
10–19	0.8	48.0	47.2	16	26.9	1.75
20–49	5.2	62.0	56.8	43	72.3	0.79
50+	6.2	16.0	9.8	21	35.3	0.27
All	21.8	190.0	168.2	100	168.2	1.00

Model population: Model North, level 3. Expectation of life at birth 25; gross reproduction rate 2.00; birth rate 31; death rate 40; growth rate −9.15.

Table 6.13. *Excess mortality by age: St Botolph Bishopsgate, 1603*

Age	Pre-crisis burials 1600–3 (1)	Crisis burials (2)	Recorded excess (2)–(1) (3)	Model age-structure (4)	Expected excess burials (5)	Excess ratio (3)/(5) (6)
0	46	244	198	3	78	2.54
1–4	19	436	417	8	209	2.00
5–9	7	472	465	9	235	1.98
10–19	8	556	548	16	418	1.31
20–49	35	884	849	43	1,123	0.76
50+	37	172	135	21	549	0.25
All	152	2,764	2,612	100	2,612	1.00

Model population: Model North, level 3. Expectation of life at birth 25; gross reproduction rate 2.00; birth rate 31; death rate 40; growth rate −9.15.

Table 6.14. *Comparative excess crisis mortality*

Age	St Peter Cornhill, 1593	St Peter Cornhill, 1603	Allhallows London Wall, 1593	St Botolph Bishopsgate, 1603	Colyton, Devon, 1645–6
0	0.87	1.15	1.57	2.54	2.24
1–4	1.11	1.34	1.59	2.00	1.03
5–9	1.58	1.41	1.66	1.98	1.15
10–19	2.22	1.85	1.75	1.31	1.10
20–49	0.66	0.78	0.79	0.76	0.86
50+	0.25	0.28	0.27	0.25	0.88
All	1.00	1.00	1.00	1.00	1.00

Sources: Tables 6.10, 6.11, 6.12, 6.13, and Schofield 1977: 114 table 8.

table 8) for St Botolph Bishopsgate in 1603 using the Hollingsworths' data, for Eyam, Derbyshire, in 1665–6 and for Colyton in 1645–6. These tables, and also the summary of the excess ratios in Table 6.14, illustrate some important variations between the individual parishes and crisis years and also between the experience of London and the Colyton epidemic. Older people, and especially those over fifty, were much less susceptible to plague in London, once again confirming the argument that survival of a previous crisis may have granted some immunity to plague. Since this was equally apparent in all four London epidemics studied, it would not suggest that older people were simply leaving London at the time of plague, for it is unlikely that the poorer members of the community living in Allhallows London Wall and St Botolph Bishopsgate could have afforded to do so. But the suggestion that individuals were leaving London is a far more plausible explanation for why infants and young children were not affected in crisis years to a proportionately greater degree than in normal years in St Peter's compared with the other parishes. These children would have been too young to have been exposed to previous epidemics. The practice of sending children to nurses was commonplace in a wealthy parish like St Peter's, and migration away from London may have been intensified in a time of crisis.

The most curious feature about plague in St Peter Cornhill was the effect it had on the 10–19 age-group. Many of the people included would have been servants or apprentices who had recently migrated to London and newcomers may have been as susceptible as much younger children. The nature of London mortality experience normally meant that only half the London-born children could expect to survive this age-group even in normal years. The risk for older children and young adults is very marked in the figures for the wealthier parishes, suggesting that it was a characteristic part of mortality experience there that servants and apprentices were less likely to survive an epidemic than other members of the community. It is possible that this tendency has been overestimated, because of the difficulty of estimating the number of servants and apprentices living in London. Any model age-structure underestimates the proportion of the population in the 10–19 age-group because the number of new migrants is not known, and hence the expected number of burials should be increased, which in turn reduces the excess ratio. The non-married population which had left home is the most difficult to analyse for it cannot be reconstituted.

For several reasons, the age-incidence of plague has important implications for the demographic structure of the capital. First, since adults were less likely to die in epidemics, there would still be married couples to continue the economic life of London after the epidemic had run its course. This would aid a speedy recovery from the crisis. Secondly, the argument that many marriages lasted for a long time may be sustained, because in comparison with the experience of young people, adult mortality from plague was relatively low. Thirdly, just as young adults would be most likely to die, so they were also the most mobile part of the population and this may have helped the reconstruction of London society. In short, although the analysis of the effect of plague on the age-structure of the population shows that there were important variations between parishes in different socio-economic areas of London, disruption to city life may have been temporary and not as great as has been thought. Creighton (1891b: 663–4) suggested that there was never a complete breakdown of local government or the economic life of London because so many people required employment during the crises when only the wealthier inhabitants were able to leave London. The conclusions about the age-incidence of plague therefore modify the conventional viewpoint that the effects of the plague crises were catastrophic.

The most controversial aspect of the Hollingsworths' analysis of plague mortality was their suggestion that for St Botolph's in 1603, men were affected to a greater degree than women (1971: 145). The pattern found there was not repeated in Colyton or Eyam. Table 6.15 provides some rather surprising evidence on this point. Sex ratios were calculated from the burial registers for six parishes for normal and crisis periods defined as for the other tables in this chapter, except that in St Botolph's the period of normal mortality prior to 1603 consisted of the five years from 1597 till 1601 and the crisis in 1625 lasted from May until October. The proportion by which the sex ratio in the crisis year exceeded that in normal years was then calculated in column 3 of the table for each parish. The six parishes chosen may not have been typical of the whole of London, but they do represent the wealthier and poorer areas of the city. Although, in numerical terms, more males died from plague than females because there was a surplus of men in the population, death rates from plague were not relatively higher for men than women during crisis periods, except in 1603. Also, there were quite wide variations between individual parishes in the

Table 6.15. *Sex ratios at death in plague periods (males per 100 females)*

Parish	Normal years (1)	Crisis year (2)	Ratio (2)/(1) (3)
1593			
Allhallows Bread Street	127	150	1.18
St Peter Cornhill	122	133	1.09
St Michael Cornhill	190	113	0.59
St Thomas the Apostle	93	141	1.52
Allhallows London Wall	131	102	0.78
St Botolph Bishopsgate	119	135	1.13
All	782	774	0.99
1603			
Allhallows Bread Street	150	138	0.92
St Peter Cornhill	138	159	1.15
St Michael Cornhill	105	142	1.35
St Thomas the Apostle	177	250	1.41
Allhallows London Wall	71	146	2.06
St Botolph Bishopsgate	102	148	1.45
All	743	983	1.32
1625			
Allhallows Bread Street	117	143	1.22
St Peter Cornhill	140	144	1.03
St Michael Cornhill	150	133	0.89
St Thomas the Apostle	109	120	1.10
Allhallows London Wall	128	122	0.95
St Botolph Bishopsgate	119	128	1.08
All	763	790	1.04

extent to which the relative significance of male and female mortality fluctuated. For example, in Allhallows Bread Street, the wealthiest parish, death rates for women were higher than for men in 1603 but not in 1593 and 1625, the exact opposite of the situation for the sample as a whole. By 1625, the amount of variation between the parishes had probably been reduced and the sex ratios were liable to fluctuate less in the two wealthiest parishes than in the two poorest. The study of differential plague mortality between males and females is therefore exceptionally difficult and little sense can be made of it. Why males appear to have been particularly susceptible in 1603 remains a mystery. Explanations concerned with temporary migration by the wealthier inhabitants away from London in crisis periods are in general unconvincing because similar tendencies were experienced in both rich and poor parishes. More detailed research is probably required to investigate how individual households were affected and whether the epidemiology of the disease varied between the crises.

Demographic historians sometimes argue that the main factor influencing the course of population change in early modern Europe was the death rate, because of the way epidemic infections could suddenly strike a population with very serious implications for the rate of demographic growth.[14] If this hypothesis applies anywhere, it is to the cities where the effect of epidemic crises was particularly marked. But even in London, the background level of mortality in normal years was at least as important, and probably more important, to the demographic development of the capital as was the effect of occasional crises, despite their severity. Because the natural decrease in urban populations resulted from the extent the death rate exceeded the birth rate, it would be unwise to ignore London fertility and the urban marriage pattern.

14. See for example: Helleiner 1965; Chambers 1972; and McNeill 1977.

CHAPTER 7

MARRIAGE AND FERTILITY

Graunt's ambivalent view about the level of fertility in London provides a good starting point for our analysis. First, he argued that there were more burials than christenings in London, so that the birth rate was lower than the death rate. This interpretation of low urban fertility was shared by all the seventeenth- and eighteenth-century pioneers of demography including Petty, King and Short. They suggested that fertility was lower in urban areas than in the countryside because rural areas were healthier than towns and because relationships outside marriage were so commonplace in London.[1] But, although they were correct in detecting a lower urban birth rate than death rate, their arguments about the causes of differential fertility are unconvincing. Secondly, Graunt commented that within marriage women had children about every two years (1662: 60), which suggests that fertility was very high indeed. Graunt did not draw a connection between the two conflicting passages of his book, and he therefore missed one of the main points about fertility in London: that marital fertility was high but overall fertility was lower, probably because marriage was far from universal. Thus the birth rate could be low even though married couples usually had large numbers of offspring.

Reliable estimates of the London birth rate cannot be obtained because the total population is not accurately known. The ratio of the number of baptisms to the number of burials is very close to the ratio of the birth rate to the death rate, so that if the numbers of baptisms recorded are similar to the numbers of burials, and since the death rate is known to be high, it is difficult to substantiate a viewpoint that the birth rate was low. Table 3.3 showed the numbers of baptisms and burials in ten contrasting London parishes between 1580 and 1650. In the wealthier parishes, the numbers of baptisms and burials were approximately equal, but there were fewer baptisms than burials in the poorer parishes,[2] indicating that there may have been contrasts in fertility between the two types of parish. Overall, there were 0.87 baptisms per burial, so if the death rate was 40 per thousand, the birth rate would have been about 35 per thousand. Although this is only a very rough guide to the birth rate it shows that it was at a high

---

1. These arguments are discussed in Graunt 1662: 41–6; King 1973a: 44; Kuczynski 1938 and Eversley 1959.
2. These data are presented in graphical form in Appendix 2.

level by the standards of pre-industrial England. Even if the London birth rate was higher than in the countryside, there would still have been a natural decrease, so that total population would have fallen but for migration from the countryside. It also appears that because of the continuing gap between the death rate and the birth rate there was little economic incentive to limit fertility within marriage. The factors influencing London fertility were social rather than economic. Vital rates in metropolitan cities were characterized by a high-pressure equilibrium, in comparison with a low-pressure equilibrium in many parts of rural England with much reduced fertility and mortality rates.

Urban fertility may be measured from family reconstitution by the careful calculation of birth intervals. It is better, although not essential, to know the date of marriage when calculating these intervals because they are generally found to increase for higher order births. Comparison between parishes is facilitated if the birth order of children is known. In this study, all the intervals have been calculated from the date of marriage, which allows the experience of both native-born and migrant women to be considered. Birth intervals have been chosen as the chief measure of fertility. Although age-specific marital fertility rates are in fact a more accurate measure, for these the age at marriage needs to be known, and this can be calculated only for women who were baptized and married in the same parish. Because so many Londoners were migrants, age-specific rates would not be representative and it is unlikely that a sufficiently large sample of women whose age at marriage is known could be obtained for each parish.

The data included in Table 7.1 have been based on a sufficiently large number of births to make the results representative. Birth intervals were calculated in completed months from those family reconstitution forms for which the date of marriage was known. Half a month was added to each of the intervals, because as many children would have been born in the second half of the following (incomplete) month as in the first half. The calculated intervals may overestimate the true intervals, because those children described as 'chrisoms' in the registers, and buried before they could be baptized, were excluded from the calculations. The average interval of under 27 months in all four parishes is very short, suggesting that marital fertility was high. In the two wealthier Cornhill parishes, fertility was particularly high as the mean birth intervals were only 23 months, close to the shortest recorded, and equivalent to an age-specific marital fertility rate of at least 500 live births per thousand woman-years lived.

It is difficult to understand the significance of the birth interval data presented in Table 7.1 without adding a note about the structure of intervals. According to R. G. Potter (1963: 160), 'Average birth intervals in societies practising little or no birth control vary from approximately 24

134

Table 7.1. *Mean birth intervals by birth order of children (months)*

Parish and dates	Birth order of children							
	0–1st	1st–2nd	2nd–3rd	3rd–4th	4th–5th	5th–6th	0–6th	1st–6th
St Peter Cornhill, 1580–1650	17.4 (67)	20.5 (42)	21.1 (35)	25.7 (23)	27.7 (17)	24.8 (11)	21.0 (195)	23.0 (128)
St Michael Cornhill, 1580–1650	17.3 (74)	22.0 (50)	23.3 (37)	24.3 (26)	19.7 (18)	24.6 (12)	20.9 (217)	22.7 (143)
St Mary Somerset, 1605–53	16.7 (81)	28.1 (48)	24.6 (29)	26.4 (23)	25.9 (18)	27.7 (17)	23.0 (216)	26.7 (135)
St Botolph Bishopsgate, 1600–50	16.3 (182)	26.4 (103)	26.9 (69)	25.7 (39)	29.7 (28)	26.3 (17)	22.4 (438)	26.8 (256)

The figures in brackets refer to the number of intervals from which these means have been calculated.

months to somewhat less than 36.' Birth intervals consist of various factors: a period of post-partum amenorrhoea when conception cannot take place, the interval before conception occurs, and the nine-month period from conception to childbirth. A further period must be added to account for those pregnancies which do not run to term because of foetal deaths, which were quite commonplace in a pre-industrial society. The duration of all the periods which make up birth intervals will vary, except for the time from conception to childbirth, but the most important is the period of amenorrhoea. This lengthens considerably with prolonged breast feeding, which thus becomes the main factor accounting for the length of the birth interval. It was particularly important in pre-industrial societies, compared with contemporary modern societies where women are much better nourished.[3]

Table 7.2. *Mean birth intervals in pre-industrial England (months)*

| Parish | Dates | Birth order of children | | | |
		0–1st	1st–2nd	2nd–3rd	3rd–4th
Colyton, Devon	1560–1646	11.3 (87)	25.2 (87)	27.4 (84)	30.1 (77)
	1647–1719	10.3 (23)	29.1 (23)	32.6 (26)	32.1 (18)
	1720–1769	11.9 (24)	25.1 (24)	29.8 (24)	32.9 (22)
Cardington, Beds.	1750–1781	10.8 (19)	25.7 (19)	27.4 (18)	30.9 (18)
Caversham and Mapledurham, Berkshire	1630–1706		24.2 (103)	27.5 (105)	27.5 (106)

The figures in brackets refer to the number of intervals from which these means have been calculated.
Sources: Wrigley 1966a: 93 table 8; Baker 1973: 61 table 35; McLaren 1978: 384 table 1.

Table 7.2 presents birth intervals for four parishes in pre-industrial rural England: Colyton, Cardington, Caversham and Mapledurham. Although there were wide variations in fertility experience in the four parishes, these birth intervals were much longer than those reported for London parishes. The data for four rural parishes can in no way be thought of as typical of national experience, but the difference with the London parishes is very marked. Age-specific marital fertility for four parishes, Bottesford, Colyton, Shepshed and Terling, at this time was much lower than the rate of 0.500 early in marriage which the London birth intervals suggest (Levine 1977).

3. This discussion of birth intervals and natural fertility is based on Wrigley 1969: 92–4; and Henry 1961.

Marriage was the chief regulator of fertility in a pre-industrial community. Marriage controlled the formation of new families, especially where illegitimacy was low, as in London. The marriage pattern in western Europe ensured that overall fertility would be far short of the maximum biologically possible for two main reasons: a high age at marriage and a relatively low proportion of the population ever marrying. This constituted what J. Hajnal (1965) termed the distinctive west European marriage pattern. Such a pattern was in marked contrast to eastern Europe in traditional times where universal marriage at an early age was commonplace.

Despite the difficulties discussed above of measuring the age at marriage from parish registers, London-born girls were marrying young in the capital at this time (Table 7.4). However, the London marriage pattern was curious because couples commonly married by licence as well as by banns. The widespread use of the licence system meant that marriages frequently occurred in parishes in which neither partner lived nor where the couple subsequently settled. This is the main reason why the ratios of baptisms to marriages given in Table 3.3, which should measure differen-

Table 7.3. *Age at first marriage for women*

Parish and dates	Mean	Median	No. of women
St Peter Cornhill, 1580–1650	23.7	23.0	15
St Michael Cornhill, 1580–1650	21.3	19.7	22
St Mary Somerset, 1605–53	24.7	21.5	9
St Botolph Bishopsgate, 1600–50	23.8	23.0	24

tial fertility between parishes, demonstrate no overall pattern, although the figures are also affected by the varying proportion of weddings that were remarriages. Some parish registers give places of residence of the partners at marriage, although there was no official requirement to do this. Table 7.4 shows that the proportion of endogamous marriages, that is between partners who were both resident in the same parish, was quite small, being less than a quarter of all marriages. This might be expected because London's high population gave a wide choice of marriage partners. Endogamous marriages were more common, and matches where both partners were strangers less frequent, in the poorer parishes. The relatively high proportion of cases with incomplete data must be noted because some individuals with no residence stated may have been living in the parish where they were married. The most notable feature of marriage in London revealed by this table is that almost a quarter of marriages were between partners neither of whom had any connection with the parish in which the wedding was performed. Where one partner was resident in the parish in which the marriage occurred, the other partner often came from

Table 7.4. *Residence of partners at marriage*

Residence	Allhallows Bread Street, 1594–1650		St Peter Cornhill, 1592–1615		St Michael Cornhill, 1598–1650		Allhallows London Wall, 1572–98	
	No.	%	No.	%	No.	%	No.	%
Both same parish	17	9	35	18	97	26	60	33
One partner migrant	112	56	132	67	181	49	88	49
Both strangers	70	35	29	15	95	25	33	18
Incomplete data	63		9		35		46	
Total, excluding incomplete entries	199	100	196	100	373	100	181	100

quite a wide area which included the whole of the area within the jurisdiction of the bills of mortality, as Table 7.5 demonstrates. A much smaller proportion travelled from outside London to be married in the capital. Since the evidence about mortality in London shows that the majority of marriage partners must have been migrants to the capital because fewer than half the children born in London survived to a marriageable age, most people must have migrated and settled in London when they were single and married subsequently.

Table 7.5. *Geographical residence of marriage partners where one partner was resident in the parish where the marriage was celebrated*

Residence	Allhallows Bread Street, 1594–1650		St Peter Cornhill, 1592–1615		St Michael Cornhill, 1598–1650		Allhallows London Wall, 1572–98	
	No.	%	No.	%	No.	%	No.	%
97 parishes	56	50	76	57	97	54	46	52
Elsewhere in bills	36	32	38	29	68	37	30	34
Outside London	20	18	18	14	15	8	11	13
Not known	0		0		1	1	1	1
Total	112	100	132	100	181	100	88	100

Although the daughters of Londoners married young, marriage was not universal for all girls living in London. The ages at death given in some of the registers allow the proportion of women in particular age-groups ever married to be shown in Table 7.6. As only two parish registers contain sufficiently good information, the table is not conclusive, but it has the advantage of referring to two parishes at each end of the socio-economic spectrum. There were similarities in the proportions ever married in each age-group in the two parishes, but the main point is that marriage was by no means universal. Fewer than 10 per cent of girls dying up to age 25 were

Table 7.6. *Age of women at death ever married by age-group*

Age-group	St Peter Cornhill, 1579–1605			Allhallows London Wall, 1578–98		
	Total dying	Married/ widowed	% ever married	Total dying	Married/ widowed	% ever married
15–24	56	5	9	30	2	7
25–34	37	26	70	22	16	73
35–44	22	20	91	20	17	85
45–54	19	17	90	10	9	90
55–64	16	15	94	13	13	100
65–74	14	13	93	8	8	100
75–84	13	13	100	3	3	100

married and even at age 35 many women were still single. If the daughters of Londoners married early, the migrant girls must surely have married much later. Doubtless their period in service delayed marriage. It is sometimes argued, especially with reference to French populations, that the process of migration delayed marriage (Perrenoud 1976: 147), and the data for London tend to support this assertion.

Recent work by V. B. Elliott on the London marriage licences confirms many of the comments made here about the marriage pattern. Although her evidence must be treated with caution because only the wealthier minority generally married by licence, the London marriage market was clearly far more complex than can be indicated here. During the period from 1598 till 1619, London bachelors marrying spinsters were on average 27.6 years at marriage. They were significantly older than rural bachelors in Essex, Hertfordshire and Middlesex who married at 27.1 years (Elliott 1978: 254 table 1). The main factor which influenced and was strongly correlated with the age at marriage for men was the length of apprenticeship, men who served a long apprenticeship with companies marrying rather later (*ibid*.: 273 table 9). The licences do confirm that London-born girls married young, at 20.5 years, whereas migrant single women married a little older at 24.2 years (*ibid*.: 325 table 18). The majority of brides would have been migrants. Men from higher status occupations married later and chose brides who were much younger than they were, whilst lower status men married a little younger to girls of about their own age (*ibid*.: 281 table 12). Migration delayed marriage as single women in Essex, Hertfordshire, Kent and Middlesex married at about 22 years (*ibid*.: 341 table 23). However, people in the Home Counties married young compared with the results for a ten-parish national sample between 1600 and 1649 where men married at 28.1 years and women at 26.0 years (Smith 1978: 217 table 8.4). In this context, age at marriage in London was not as high as it appears from comparison with the Home Counties.

One of the main factors influencing the London marriage pattern was

Table 7.7 *Sex ratio at burial before 1650 (males per 100 females)*

Date	Allhallows Bread Street			St Peter Cornhill			St Christopher le Stocks			St Michael Cornhill		
	M	F	SR	M	F	SR	M	F	SR	M	F	SR
1580	58	34	171	51	49	104	48	52	92	51	49	104
1590	53	36	147*	51	49	104*	52	48	108*	66	34	194*
1600	58	42	138*	50	50	100*	54	46	117*	57	43	133*
1610	57	43	133	58	42	138	63	37	170	51	49	104
1620	64	36	178*	57	43	133	53	44	120*	60	40	150
1630	56	44	127	54	46	117	43	35	123	52	48	108
1640	57	43	133	56	44	127	51	49	104	55	45	122
Total	403	278	145	377	323	117	364	311	117	392	308	127

* Sex ratios calculated by including at least some plague deaths.

the sex ratio in the population. The level of apprenticeship meant that there was a surplus of men in the population: about 15 per cent of all Londoners were apprentices (Table 3.7). A shortage of women tended to keep marriage ages reasonably low, even though migration delayed marriage, and encouraged high marital fertility. Tudor and Stuart London differed markedly from the conventional understanding that in the pre-industrial city there would be a surplus of females.[4]

It is not easy to measure the sex ratio before the Civil War because of the absence of census-type data. However, any broad variations in the sex ratio would be shown up by an analysis of the sex of people buried. Between 1629 and 1642, the London bills of mortality tabulated burials by sex. During this period, there were 87,732 males buried compared with only 77,787 females (Graunt 1662: 77), giving a sex ratio of 113 males per hundred females. To confirm this, an analysis of the registers of eight sample parishes was made. The sex ratio was measured for the first hundred individuals in succeeding ten-year periods, beginning in 1580, and is shown in Table 7.8. Cases of indeterminate sex were excluded, as were all stillbirths. This important table shows quite clearly that there were more males and no surplus of females in the London population.[5]

By the end of the seventeenth century, however, there is considerable evidence to suggest that the surplus of males had been turned into a deficit. Using Gregory King's figures, the sex ratio for London in 1695 may be calculated as 77 males per hundred females (1973a: 39), and an analysis of

4. For example, this interpretation is argued in Thompson 1974.
5. In the very large parish of St Margaret Westminster between 1539 and 1660, the sex ratio was 114. This was calculated from the aggregate figures given in Burke 1914: xix.

St Dunstan in the East			St Mary Somerset			Allhallows London Wall			St Botolph Bishopsgate		
M	F	SR	M	F	SR	M	F	SR	M	F	SR
57	43	133	47	53	89	56	44	127	58	42	138
54	46	117*	50	50	100	46	54	85*	60	40	150
49	51	96	61	39	156	50	50	100*	52	48	108
47	53	89	53	47	113	54	46	117	52	48	108
46	54	85	58	42	138	55	45	122	52	48	108
50	50	100	56	44	127	55	45	122	50	50	100
54	46	117	46	54	85	—	—	—	56	44	127
357	343	104	371	329	113	316	284	111	380	320	119

forty London parishes in the same year gave a sex ratio of 87. The sex ratio was 97 in the seven parishes with the greatest percentage of the population assessed at the highest rate of tax (Glass 1972: 280 table 4). Analysis of the sex ratio in other towns at this time and slightly later reveals a shortage of men when compared with country districts (Law 1969: 89; Laslett 1972: 74; Thompson 1974: 162). The sex ratio at burial recorded in the London bills of mortality in Table 7.8 also confirms an increase in the relative proportion of women in the capital. The calculation of sex ratios from the bills of mortality is not affected by their deteriorating quality, provided that male and female burials were not under-recorded by different amounts. This increase in the proportion of women by the end of the seventeenth century reflects the much reduced importance of apprenticeship in London.

The discrepancy between the sex ratio calculated from the bills of mortality given in Table 7.8 and that obtained from the 1695 assessments indicates that the sex ratio at death differs from the sex ratio in the living population. The sex ratio at death must be reduced by a few points to approximate to the ratio in the living population. There are two possible reasons for this: first, a surplus of males at birth, and second, the effect of higher mortality rates for males than for females in the poorer parishes (Table 5.4). Nevertheless, the lower sex ratio at burial in the second half of the seventeenth century given in Table 7.8 both confirms the idea that there was a surplus of men in London before 1650 as shown in Table 7.7 and suggests that the London social structure was changing during the period. This must have reflected a far greater proportion of women migrants to London after 1650. The implications for fertility experience have yet to be discovered, but before the Civil War the shortage of women

Table 7.8. *Sex ratio at burial, 1664–1749 (males per 100 females)*

Dates	Males	Females	Sex ratio
1664–9	91,965	88,928	103*
1670–9	99,295	91,018	109
1680–9	115,693	107,525	108
1690–9	108,163	101,555	107
1700–9	104,754	104,680	100
1710–19	118,609	119,652	99
1720–9	137,222	136,393	101
1730–9	129,207	131,668	98
1740–9	127,475	133,126	96
1664–99	415,116	389,026	107
1700–49	617,267	625,519	99

* Sex ratios calculated by including at least some plague deaths
Sources: Maitland 1756: II, 739–40; and Marshall 1832: 70.

in London meant that the age of marriage would be early, and hence fertility relatively high. Incidentally, the high sex ratio also explains how marital fertility could be high whilst overall fertility may not have been exceptional, as it should not necessarily be assumed that large numbers of children born within marriage means a high birth rate. Migrants and apprentices affected the sex-structure of the population, with a high number of unmarried adults, so that marital fertility could have been high, whilst the birth rate was proportionately lower.

As well as very short mean birth intervals, a second especially distinctive feature of fertility experience in London was the contrast between the wealthy and poorer parishes which we saw in Table 7.1. The causes of this variation in fertility also shed light on the general determinants of fertility in the capital. The shortness of the intervals is particularly striking in the two wealthier parishes, at just 23 months for all intervals between the first and the sixth birth compared with 27 months in the two poor parishes. The distribution of these intervals is shown in Figure 7.1 for the two richer and two poorer parishes combined. For the two Cornhill parishes, the peak is much sharper and there is a smaller proportion of longer intervals between births. A difference of means test applied to the mean of all the intervals between the first and the sixth birth in the richer and poorer parishes respectively was significant at the 1 per cent level, suggesting that the difference in fertility between the two socio-economic areas were of some importance. This parallels the differential mortality between these same areas discussed above. The wealthier districts were characterized by higher fertility and lower mortality than the poorer areas.

The intervals in the two Cornhill parishes are of particular interest because they are very short indeed; in fact, as we have noted, close to the

(a) Wealthier parishes

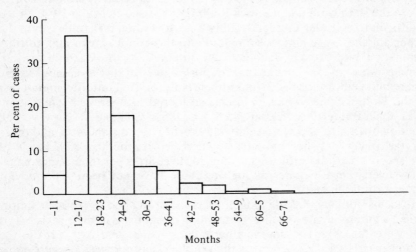

(b) Poorer parishes

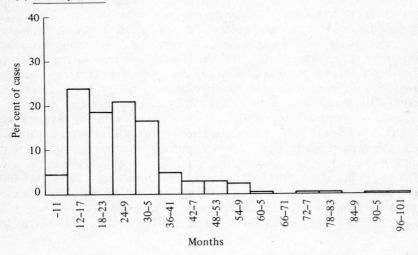

Figure 7.1 The distribution of birth intervals for all births between the first and the sixth for the wealthier parishes (St Peter Cornhill and St Michael Cornhill) and the poorer parishes (St Mary Somerset and St Botolph Bishopsgate).

shortest observed intervals, Table 7.9 shows comparative data from French family reconstitution studies which were characterized by high fertility. The birth intervals in the two Cornhill parishes are close to the 23-month interval for French Canada in the early eighteenth century, although births above the sixth were taken into account in this case (Henripin 1954: 84). It is difficult to consider London fertility to be low when birth intervals in the richer parishes were almost comparable to those in a known high-fertility population like French Canada.[6] The intervals in the Cornhill area of London were not as short as those reported in Brittany, in Geneva in the eighteenth century, or the 21-month intervals for the Hutterite community in the United States which is often considered to approach a maximum level of natural fertility (Eaton and Mayer 1953: 230 table 3). However, all London birth intervals were relatively short by these standards, and those for the richer parishes particularly short, corresponding with levels of age-specific marital fertility exceeding 500 live births per thousand woman-years lived. Fertility rates as high as these have not been reported for English rural parishes.

It seems unlikely that the longer intervals for the poorer parishes simply reflect a greater degree of under-recording of baptisms in their registers. If this were the case, the intervals between marriage and first birth in the poorer parishes would be longer than in the richer parishes because some of the births would not have given rise to a recorded baptism. Since this interval was in fact slightly shorter in the poorer parishes, as Table 7.10 shows, this is obviously not so. Also, Table 7.10 indicates that the mean birth intervals after an infant death are very short, especially when an infant died within a month from birth. Since under-registration of births would have the effect of apparently lengthening birth intervals, such a situation again indicates a good quality of registration, especially as there was no difference between the wealthy and poor parishes.

Thus it is wrong to suggest that fertility in London in the period from 1580 to 1650 was low; in fact, in the wealthier part of the city, the Cornhill area, it was particularly high. It is now possible to consider the determinants of socio-economic variations in fertility levels. The key to this problem lies in a comparison between mean birth intervals (Table 7.1) and infant mortality rates (Table 2.4). It is apparent that the parishes with the shortest birth intervals also had the lowest infant mortality rates, which is the exact opposite of what might be expected. High fertility has been found

6. A pattern of differential fertility between social groups resident in different parts of the city has also been found at Lyons in the eighteenth century. A recent book contrasted the experience of butchers who had at least twelve, and up to twenty children in about the same number of years with the much poorer workers manufacturing silk who had slightly over three children per couple and where it was very rare to have ten children. The birth intervals for the butchers were exceptional and tables showing the mean figures are not presented. Garden 1970: 95–9.

Table 7.9. *Mean birth intervals in eighteenth-century France (months)*

Parish	Dates	0–1st	1st–2nd	2nd–3rd	3rd–4th	4th–5th	5th–6th
				Birth order of children			
French Canada	1700–30	15.8	22.5	21.1	22.6	22.9	25.3
			(154)	(143)	(135)	(117)	(101)
Geneva	1700–4 and	13.3	18.3	20.1	21.5	23.8	
	1770–2	(577)	(132)	(132)	(132)	(132)	
Rumont	1720–90		23.2	22.5	25.6	28.0	
Argenteuil	1720–90		19.9	21.8			
Tonnerrois	1725–1800		20.3	22.0	24.2	25.9	
			(85)	(85)	(85)	(85)	
Villedieu-les-Poëles	1711–90	14.4	15.0	18.1	19.4	19.2	20.8
			(153)	(174)	(175)	(175)	(175)
La Guerche	1733–92		18.6	19.5	21.2	21.0	
St-Aubin d'Aubigné	1740–89		18.2	19.9	21.4	25.0	
St-Méen le Grand	1720–92		20.2	21.6	22.6	25.0	
Saignhin-en-Mélantois	1690–1769	14.8	21.1	21.8	25.0	27.0	
			(39)	(39)	(39)	(39)	
Sotteville-lès-Rouen	1760–90		18.1	18.5	20.8	20.3	22.2
			(40)	(40)	(40)	(40)	(40)
Bleré	1679–1789		21.4	21.8	21.9	22.8	23.0

The figures in brackets refer to the number of intervals from which these means have been calculated. The data for French Canada are based on genealogies, and for Geneva on civil registers.
Sources: Henripin 1954: 85 table 28; Perrenoud 1976: 159 table 10, 160 table 11; Robert 1969: 36; Giachetti and Tyvaert 1969: 46; Dinet 1969: 81; Jouan 1969: 108, 109 table 10; Goubert 1972: 323; Deniel and Henry 1965: 585–8; Girard 1959: 495; Lachiver 1969b: 223.

to be frequently related to high infant mortality in pre-industrial populations. In London, the fact that if the infant died within the first month of life, subsequent birth intervals in all the parishes were very short (Table 7.10), suggests that short birth intervals are related to high infant mortality

Table 7.10. *Mean birth intervals after an infant death (months)*

Parish and dates	Infant dies 0–31 days	Infant dies 32–365 days
St Peter Cornhill, 1580–1650	20.3	20.4
	(38)	(63)
St Michael Cornhill, 1580–1650	17.7	24.1
	(84)	(68)
St Mary Somerset, 1605–53	20.4	22.1
	(163)	(99)
St Botolph Bishopsgate, 1600–50	21.1	26.2
	(76)	(124)

The figures in brackets refer to the number of intervals on which these means have been based.

rates. This was the situation in the poorer parishes where the intervals were still on the shorter side of average. The fact that birth intervals shorten when women are not breast feeding their own infant children has been shown both by observation in the developing countries at the present time and also from written records of child care practices kept in the nineteenth century in England and Germany (Flandrin 1979: 198–203; Knodel and van de Walle 1967; Knodel 1968; Knodel and Kintner 1977). Therefore shorter birth intervals occur after an early infant death, because women would conceive again more quickly since the period of amenorrhoea would be shorter (Ganiage 1963: 96; Gautier and Henry 1958: 149–54; Girand 1959: 497; Henripin 1954: 86; Hyrenius 1958: 128; McLaren 1978).

However, infant mortality rates were particularly low in the wealthier parishes, so it is necessary to find another reason for birth intervals being so short. This was that many women were not breast feeding their infant children themselves but were sending them away to be wet-nursed. They could therefore conceive again more quickly, as if their child had died. This also explains why infant mortality rates appeared to be low in the wealthier parishes, because many infant deaths would have been recorded in outside parishes.

In order to show that the wet-nursing of infants was common and did explain short birth intervals in the wealthier parishes, the parish registers for places outside London can be examined. Three common forms of entry in the burial register were taken as evidence of nursing. The examples given here have been drawn from the parish register of Chesham, Buckinghamshire. The most precise specifically names a nurse-child from London, for example:

xvij December 1619   Henry Skinner a nurse child from London

Another just names a nurse-child without any details of its origins:

1 January 1635   Bedford Stasie a Nursechild

In a third form of entry it was stated that a child was buried whose parents were living in London:

vj September 1615   John soon of Thomas Parrott of London

This latter type was accepted as evidence of nursing only where there were several similar entries. It should also be obvious that there must have been other parishes where nurse-children were not identified in the registers. Some of the places for which evidence is available are marked in Figure 7.2, which shows that some children travelled long distances over an extensive area. The practice of nursing infants was important, with many parishes accepting children from London. In Table 7.11, the percentages of

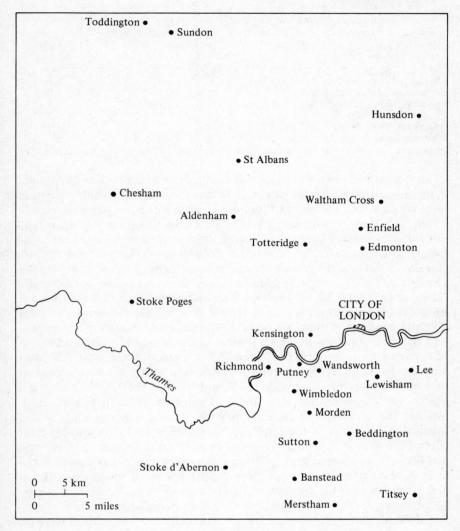

Figure 7.2 Parishes accepting London nurse-children.

nurse-children in the burial registers are shown for six parishes where the registers are quite good. It is a crude measure because it does not take account of the number of women in these parishes able to accept children which had been boarded out, but it does show up the significance of nursing in some parishes. The registers of the receiving parishes hardly ever state the London parishes in which the parents were living and hence

147

Table 7.11. *Percentage of nurse-children in burial registers*

Parish and dates	Nurse-children	Total burials	% nurse-children
Chesham, Bucks., 1581–1636	49	2,128	2.3
Kensington, Middx., 1581–1650	60	1,512	4.0
Hunsdon, Herts., 1594–1650	19	373	5.1
Putney, Surrey, 1620–50	74	1,145	6.5
Aldenham, Herts., 1581–1650	139	1,994	7.0
Waltham Cross, Essex, 1581–1650	379	4,421	8.6

it has not proved possible to link the deaths of children outside London to their baptism in the capital. Some nurse-children were also sent to parishes in other parts of London, and foundlings were often put out to nurses.[7]

The incidence of wet-nursing of children in this period is also demonstrated by literary evidence. What is generally considered to be the first English book on pediatrics, *The boke of chyldren* by Thomas Phaire (1544; 2nd edn 1553), makes this clear, and another early manual, John Jones's *The arte and science of preserving bodie and soule in healthe, wisdome and catholike religion* (1579), devotes a long section to the problem of finding suitable nurses for infants as if this were of great importance to the potential readership of such a book. In the causes of death reported in the bills of mortality, Graunt (1662: pullout table) indicated that in a twenty-year period including years between 1629 and 1658, there were 529 cases included in the category 'Overlayd and starved at nurse', which suggests that nursing was very common. It is well known that the wives of the aristocracy did not look after their own infant children (Stone 1965: 590–3). This pattern of child care may also have existed in some gentry families, for example in the family of Bulstrode Whitelocke who lived for part of the year in London.[8] It would be very unlikely that children who had been nursed would have as great a chance of survival as those looked after by their own mothers, so there is little reason to suggest that infant death rates would be any lower for children born to families of higher social status; indeed they could possibly have been higher.[9]

The discussion up to now has been concerned only with marital fertility; how far would the pattern described be modified by a consideration of non-marital fertility? It is often argued that an urban environment provided the conditions where illegitimacy could exceed the levels recorded in

7. Children admitted to Christ's Hospital between 1563 and 1583 were frequently sent out to nurses both in London and the countryside. Cunningham 1977.
8. Spalding 1975: 27, 43. Also see Stone 1977: 63–6, 426–32; and McLaren 1978: 387–90.
9. It is interesting that infant mortality rates for the British peerage were higher than for ordinary people. See Table 5.5, and Hollingsworth 1977. This may reflect the fact that children of the peerage were nursed.

Table 7.12. *Illegitimacy ratios (percentage of all births)*

Parish and dates	Illegitimate baptisms	Total births	Illegitimacy ratio (%)
Allhallows Bread Street, 1538–1653	34	1,596	2.1
St Peter Cornhill, 1580–1650	79	1,848	4.3
St Christopher le Stocks, 1580–1653	30	1,145	2.6
St Michael Cornhill, 1580–1650	35	2,296	1.5
St Dunstan in the East, 1605–53	49	3,152	1.6
St Mary Somerset, 1605–53	16	2,095	0.8
Allhallows London Wall, 1570–1636	42	1,881	2.2
St Botolph Bishopsgate, 1600–50	75	11,806	0.6
National sample, 1581–1640 (100 parishes)	—	—	2.3

Source: National sample – Laslett 1977: 142 table 3.10.

country districts, and that total fertility in London may have been higher than the study of marital fertility from birth intervals might suggest. Such an idea cannot be justified, however much it might seem that the freedom of city life together with the instability inherent in the degree of mobility in London society would encourage illegitimacy. Table 7.12 shows illegitimacy ratios for the parishes studied, measured as the number of baptisms of illegitimate children expressed as a percentage of total births. It should be noted that illegitimate children here include foundlings and infants deposited in the parish where the name of neither parent is known. The figures are therefore slightly exaggerated because a small proportion of the foundlings would have been orphans. Nevertheless, levels of non-marital fertility were low in London in both the wealthy and the poorer parishes when compared with a national sample for this period. The mean of the illegitimacy ratios for the eight parishes studied was only 2.0 per cent, compared with 2.3 per cent for a hundred-parish national sample assembled by P. Laslett (1977: 142 table 3.10). Pre-marital pregnancy was also low as Table 7.13 demonstrates. An average of only 16 per cent of brides were pregnant at marriage in the four sample parishes, compared with 21 per cent in a national sample of seven rural parishes.[10] Laslett has argued that illegitimacy varied considerably between regions, although he did not include any London parishes in his sample. In the nineteenth century, illegitimacy in the capital reached low levels, and he suggested that this represented a continuation of earlier trends (1977: 146). From this

10. For similar figures of the extent of bridal pregnancy, see Hair 1966; 1970; and Smith and Hindus 1975.

Table 7.13. *Bridal pregnancy (percentage of all marriages with children)*

Parish and dates	Intervals under 9 months	Total intervals 0–1	% pregnant at marriage
St Peter Cornhill, 1580–1650	8	67	11.9
St Michael Cornhill, 1580–1650	9	74	12.2
St Mary Somerset, 1605–53	18	81	22.2
St Botolph Bishopsgate, 1600–50	33	182	18.1
National sample, 1600–49 (7 parishes)	156	733	21.3

Source: National sample – Laslett 1977: 130 table 3.3.

discussion we can infer that rates of non-marital fertility were low, and would not greatly affect the conclusions about overall fertility.

CHAPTER 8

POPULATION AND METROPOLIS

During the late Tudor and early Stuart periods, the most characteristic features of the demographic experience of London was high mortality, due mainly to endemic infections but added to significantly by epidemic plague crises. Diseases spread easily through a large urban population where individuals lived in close proximity to each other. However high fertility may have been, and marital fertility in London was high, the birth rate could not keep pace with the death rate, but migration prevented the population from falling. Economic circumstances in London must have been favourable relative to other places because the capital was growing very rapidly, attracting many more migrants than were necessary to make good the shortfall of births. Because London was so large compared with the country as a whole, accounting for over 5 per cent of the population of England, the connections between the capital and the country through the process of migration were inevitably close. Any interpretation of the population of pre-industrial England must therefore take account of the internal demography of London.

There was a very marked contrast between the pattern of population change in the metropolis and in the remainder of the country. Elsewhere in England, the population was growing, indicating that the birth rate was exceeding the death rate. The chief factor influencing the rate of growth is the incidence of marriage, since marriage controls the formation of new families. The age at first marriage for women and the proportion of women marrying have a strong influence on the birth rate where marital fertility is generally uncontrolled (in the sense that the probability of a couple having a further child is not influenced by the number of children already born), and where fertility outside marriage is low. The incidence of marriage was connected with inheritance practices and local economic circumstances – couples did not normally marry until they had obtained at least a measure of economic independence. It is more difficult to find a mechanism to explain long-term changes in the death rate in country districts.[1]

Relatively little research has been undertaken in urban historical demography, but the distinctiveness of metropolitan demographic characteristics found for London is confirmed to some extent by studies of

1. The most useful studies of population trends in England are Levine 1977; and Smith 1978.

aggregative population trends in Dutch cities (De Vries 1974: 74–118), and by reconstitutions of the population of Geneva, a much smaller city of about 15,000 inhabitants.[2] Many features of the demography of London prove to have had their parallel in Geneva. These include high mortality, a dependence on migration, an imbalanced sex ratio, high marital fertility, low levels of illegitimacy, the use of wet-nurses, and marked contrasts in demographic experience between social groups. Geneva differed from London in that its population declined after the middle of the sixteenth century because of its inability to attract migrants, and this was also why in Spain, Madrid grew at the expense of Toledo in the early seventeenth century (Ringrose 1973). Only Amsterdam matched London's rapid growth through migration.[3]

In reflecting on the arguments presented in this book, several comments are appropriate. Because there have been so few detailed demographic studies of early modern cities there have been difficulties in interpreting the results obtained from the reconstitutions. For example, in evaluating the accuracy of the London parish registers it was not known what levels of endogenous and exogenous infant mortality rates might be expected. It was also difficult to assess whether fertility and mortality rates found for London were high in comparison with the experience of other European metropolitan cities during this period. The reconstitutions are important because they enable demographic rates to be estimated with much greater precision than most other methods of analysis, and they also permit studies of contrasting small areas within the city to be undertaken. However, reconstitution should be regarded as only one of a number of methods of analysis because it is unable to provide all the demographic measures that might be required, and does not deal effectively with the experience of migrants. Other methods which would be appropriate, for example, are to study age at marriage in a metropolitan city by weighting samples of ages drawn from marriage licences according to the way the social composition of individuals married by licence differed from the population as a whole (Elliott 1978).

It has been shown that there were important demographic contrasts between different parts of London. However, the length of time taken to complete reconstitutions means that only a small sample of registers could be studied and so important demographic variations within the city remain to be discovered. Further work is required to establish the extent of these variations and to explain more fully the connections between them and the social structure. Population trends were related to social and economic

2. Comparative demographic measures for Geneva are presented in Tables 5.7, 5.16 and 7.9. Fuller details are given in Henry 1956; Perrenoud 1975, 1976 and 1978; and Monter 1979.
3. In France, the contrasts in rural demographic rates were much greater than have been found for England, so urban population experience may have been comparatively less distinctive. See for example, Bardet 1974; and Smith 1977.

characteristics by selecting parishes typical of contrasting areas for special study. Although very wealthy and very poor areas were the most distinctive, and analysis enables a range of demographic measures to be established, their social composition was more varied than such generalizations might suggest. A more detailed analysis of London social structure would therefore be very valuable and other indicators of social trends could profitably be studied in greater detail. They include occupations (Beier 1978; Elliott 1978), housing (Power 1972), literacy (Cressy 1980), poverty and vagrancy (Beier 1978; Herlan 1979; Pearl 1979), illegitimacy and crime. Some of the main difficulties of developing a coherent viewpoint of the internal structure of London are that there were great differences in the size of London parishes and that the survival of records varies greatly between different parishes. Nevertheless, à better understanding of London social structure would enable the determinants of demographic trends to be studied in greater depth.

Most of the parishes analysed in detail were located within the city walls and were a more convenient size for reconstitution than the parishes outside the walls, many of which were exceptionally large. Size causes problems in analysing data and casts doubt on whether the registers could have been very effectively compiled, because where 2,000 families inhabited a parish rather than 150 families it would be much easier for individual events to be missed. To a certain extent, the choice of especially wealthy and poor parishes for reconstitution studies suggests that the demographic experience of the suburbs lay between the extremes of fertility and mortality levels reported here. However, the role of the suburbs deserves much fuller analysis for several reasons. Because London was growing in size, the changing contribution of the suburbs should be assessed in greater detail. When new migrants came to London, they often settled first in the suburbs and then moved to the centre of the city. The suburbs were poorer that the central part of the city and their inhabitants encountered problems of adaptation and assimilation to metropolitan life. Criminals, vagrants and abandoned children found in the centre of the city could well have come from the suburbs. The growth of the suburbs also enabled the impact of the city on its surrounding area to be traced and this should shed light on the process of urban growth. Aggregative techniques would probably be required to compare population trends in the suburbs with those in the city because many parishes were too large for their registers to be reconstituted.[4]

The substantive findings of this research about the population of London make a contribution to the discussion about the role of the metropolitan city in early modern society. It has been shown how population trends in London differed from the remainder of the country and how migration

---

4. For the suburbs, see Power 1978a; 1978b.

Population and metropolis

connected city and country, but it will be difficult to draw firm conclusions about these changes until more is known about what happened in London itself. Further research on the characteristics of migrants (Elliott 1978, Smith 1973), their background and social position, would help to show what kinds of people became Londoners and to demonstrate more clearly how town and country were inter-related. Since the metropolitan city was a source of new attitudes and changed values (Wrigley 1967; Fisher 1976), it would also be useful to investigate whether the sixfold growth in the population of London between the late sixteenth century and the early eighteenth century affected the demographic factors which accounted for these changing numbers. This book has dealt with only a limited period. After 1650, population trends remained predominantly metropolitan in the sense that the chief factors influencing changes were still mortality and migration. However, a number of important changes occurred towards the end of the seventeenth century – plague disappeared, migrants came from closer to London, there were fewer male migrants – which caused the population structure to change, and there were also changes in fertility. The beginnings of family limitation also require investigation.

APPENDIX 1

THE LONDON BILLS OF MORTALITY

Table A1.1. *The city and Liberties*

Year	Burials (excluding plague)	Plague burials	Total burials	Baptisms	Estimated population[a] (thousands)
1563	3,524	20,136	23,660	—	—
1578	4,262	3,568	7,830	3,150	95–110
1579	2,777	629	3,406	3,430	103–120
1580	2,745	128	2,873	3,568	107–125
1581	3,403	1,140	4,543	3,407	102–119
1582	3,860	3,034	6,894	3,500	105–123
1593	7,182	10,662	17,844	4,277	128–150
1597	5,536	48	5,584	4,256	128–149
1598	3,780	18	3,798	4,236	127–148
1599	4,261	16	4,277	4,674	140–164
1600	3,272	4	3,276	4,760	143–167
1603	7,683	30,561	38,244	4,784	144–167

Note: a. Low and high estimates of the population have been made from the number of baptisms, plus 5 per cent to allow for under-recording, on the assumption of birth rates of 30 and 35 per thousand.

Sources: 1563 Sutherland 1972: 303 table 4.

1578–82 Creighton 1891a: 490. Adjustments have been made so that each total refers to a 52-week year.

1593 Graunt 1662: 33. Figures from March to December only.

1597–1600 Hull 1899: II, 432–5.

1603 As 1593, but the Out-Parishes have been included in the totals from 14 July.

Table A1.2. *The city, Liberties and out-parishes*

Year	Burials (excluding plague)	Plague burials	Total burials	Baptisms	Estimated population[a] (thousands)
1604	4,323	896	5,219	5,458	164–191
1605	5,948	444	6,392	6,504	195–228
1606	5,796	2,124	7,920	6,614	198–232
1607	5,670	2,352	8,022	6,582	197–230
1608	6,758	2,262	9,020	6,845	205–240
1609	7,545	4,240	11,785	6,388	192–224
1610	7,486	1,803	9,289	6,785	204–237
1611	6,716	627	7,343	7,014	210–246
1612	7,778	64	7,842	6,986	210–245
1613	7,503	16	7,519	6,846	205–240
1614	7,367	22	7,389	7,208	216–252
1615	7,850	37	7,887	7,682	230–269
1616	8,063	9	8,072	7,985	240–279
1617	8,280	6	8,286	7,747	232–271
1618	9,596	18	9,614	7,735	232–271
1619	8,000	9	8,009	8,127	244–284
1620	9,691	21	9,712	7,845	235–275
1621	8,112	11	8,123	8,039	241–281
1622	9,420	16	9,436	7,894	237–276
1623	11,095	17	11,112	7,945	238–278
1624	12,199	11	12,210	8,299	249–290
1625	18,848	35,417	54,265	6,983	209–244
1626	7,401	134	7,535	6,701	201–235
1627	7,713	4	7,717	8,408	252–294
1628	7,740	3	7,743	8,564	257–300
1629	8,771	0	8,771	9,901	297–347
1630	9,238	1,317	10,555	9,315	279–326
1631	8,288	274	8,562	8,524	256–298
1632	9,527	8	9,535	9,584	288–335
1633	8,392	0	8,392	9,997	300–350
1634	10,899	1	10,900	8,855	264–310
1635	10,651	0	10,651	10,034	301–351
1636	12,959	10,410	23,369	9,522	286–333
1637	8,641	3,082	11,723	9,160	275–321
1638	13,261	363	13,624	10,311	309–361
1639	9,548	314	9,862	10,150	305–355
1640	11,321	1,450	12,771	10,850	326–380
1641	11,767	3,067	14,834	10,370	311–363
1642	11,999	1,274	13,273	10,670	320–373
1643	12,216	996	13,212	9,440	283–330
1644	9,441	1,492	10,933	8,104	243–284
1645	9,608	1,871	11,479	7,966	239–279
1646	10,415	2,365	12,780	7,163	215–251
1647	10,462	3,597	14,059	7,332	220–257
1648	9,279	611	9,890	6,544	196–229
1649	10,499	67	10,566	5,825	175–204
1650	8,749	15	8,764	5,612	168–196

Note: a. Low and high estimates of the population have been made from the number of baptisms, plus 5 per cent to allow for under-recording, on the assumption of birth rates of 30 and 35 per thousand.
Sources: 1604–42 Graunt 1662: 75–7. Figures checked by Hull 1899: II, 407–8, n. 1; and by Sutherland 1972, against fragmentary surviving manuscripts. There is no original long series.
1643–50 As for 1604–42, but the totals are underenumerated in the bills of mortality.

Table A1.3. *The distant parishes*

Year	Burials (excluding plague)	Plague burials	Total burials	Baptisms	Estimated population[a] (thousands)
1636	2,354	1,702	4,056	1,924	58–67
1637	1,986	521	2,507	1,836	55–64
1638	2,852	145	2,997	1,953	59–68
1639	2,142	9	2,151	1,948	58–68
1640	2,270	189	2,459	2,169	65–76
1641	2,400	128	2,528	2,149	64–75
1642	2,390	99	2,489	2,262	68–79
1643	2,218	244	2,462	2,038	61–71
1644	1,796	384	2,180	1,750	53–61
1645	2,037	247	2,284	1,733	52–61
1646	2,210	211	2,421	1,868	56–65
1647	2,039	354	2,393	1,694	58–68
1748	1,573	82	1,655	1,355	41–47
1649	1,703	4	1,707	1,106	33–39
1650	1,560	0	1,560	1,264	38–44

Note: a. Low and high estimates of the population have been made from the number of baptisms, plus 5 per cent to allow for under-recording, on the assumption of birth rates of 30 and 35 per thousand.
Sources: Graunt 1662: pull-out table at end; and Graunt 1676; II, 410.

APPENDIX 2

BAPTISMS AND BURIALS IN SAMPLE LONDON PARISHES

Number

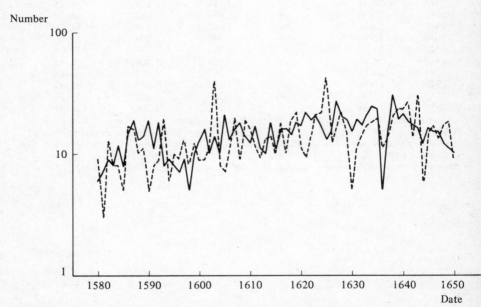

Figure A2.1 Baptisms (solid line) and burials (broken line) in Allhallows Bread Street.

Number

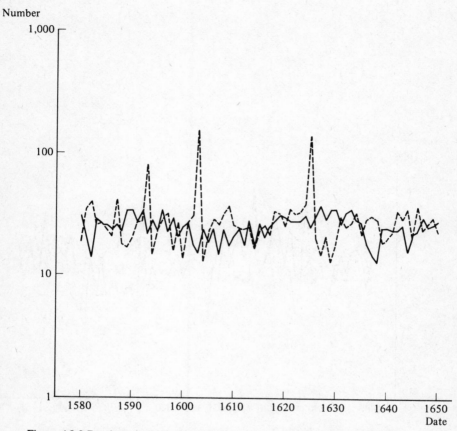

Figure A2.2 Baptisms (solid line) and burials (broken line) in St Peter Cornhill.

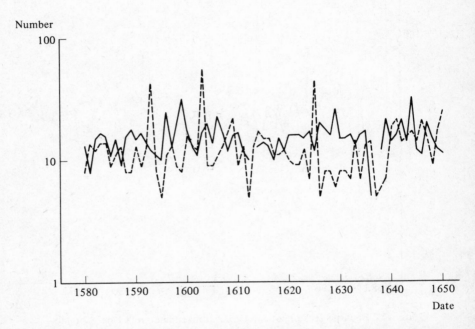

Figure A2.3 Baptisms (solid line) and burials (broken line) in St Christopher le Stocks.

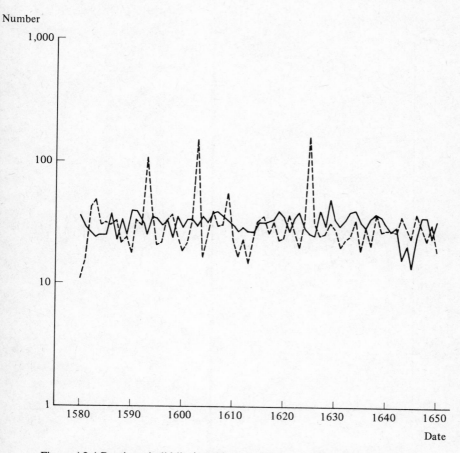

Figure A2.4 Baptisms (solid line) and burials (broken line) in St Michael Cornhill.

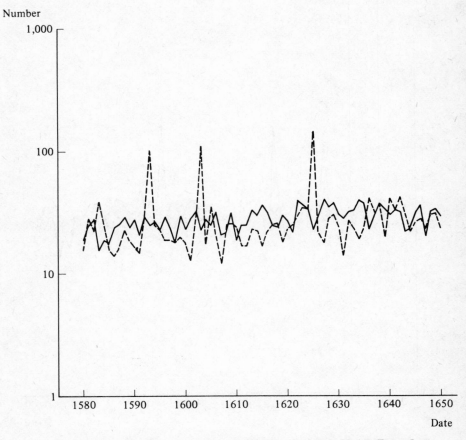

Figure A2.5 Baptisms (solid line) and burials (broken line) in St Vedast Foster Lane.

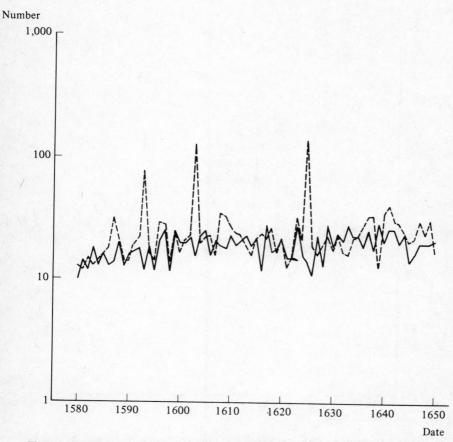

Figure A2.6 Baptisms (solid line) and burials (broken line) in St Helen Bishopsgate.

Number

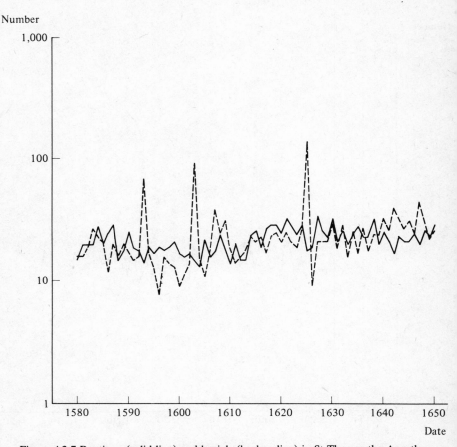

Figure A2.7 Baptisms (solid line) and burials (broken line) in St Thomas the Apostle.

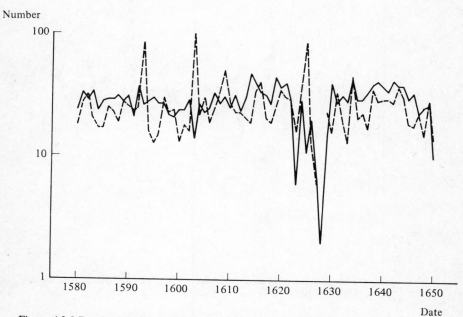

Figure A2.8 Baptisms (solid line) and burials (broken line) in St Lawrence Jewry.

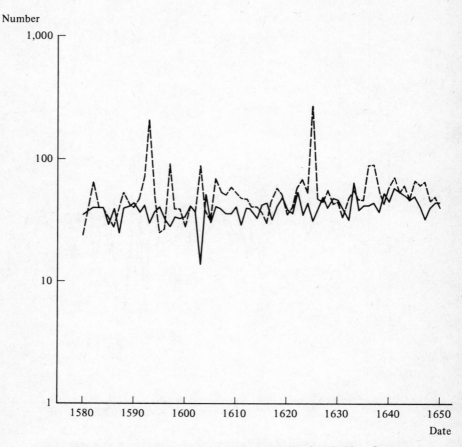

Figure A2.9 Baptisms (solid line) and burials (broken line) in St Mary Somerset.

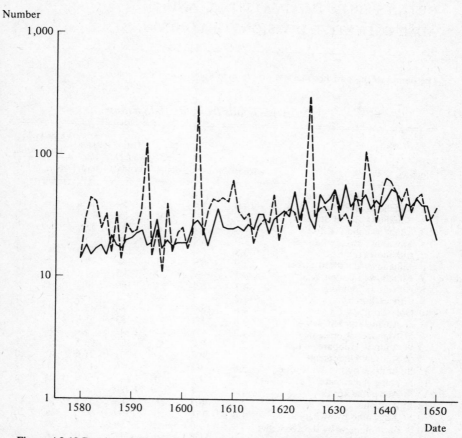

Figure A2.10 Baptisms (solid line) and burials (broken line) in Allhallows London Wall.

APPENDIX 3

DETAILS FROM THE 1638 LISTING AND ADMINISTRATIVE DIVISIONS OF LONDON

The names of the parishes marked on the map are given in the table.

Table A3.1. *Details from the 1638 listing*

No.[a]	Parish	Acres[b]	Houses	Tene-ments	Total house-holds	Houses per acre	Substantial households No.	%
	Parishes within the walls							
1	Allhallows Barking	10.9	449	10	459	42.1	48	11
2	Allhallows Bread Street	2.5	75	0	75	30.0	—	—
3	Allhallows the Great	7.4	248	0	248	33.5	8	3
4	Allhallows Honey Lane	1.0	36	0	36	36.0	20	56
5	Allhallows the Less	3.3	104	0	104	31.5	21	20
6	Allhallows Lombard Street	2.9	67	75	142	49.0	63	44
7	Allhallows London Wall	8.5	196	0	196	23.1	5	3
8	Allhallows Staining	4.1	162	3	165	40.2	14	9
9	Christ Church	12.2	—	—	E411	—	—	—
10	Holy Trinity the Less	1.8	88	0	88	48.9	14	16
11	St Alban Wood Street	3.4	133	50	183	53.8	8	4
12	St Alphage Cripplegate	4.2	—	—	E173	—	—	—
13	St Andrew Hubbard	2.0	92	35	127	63.5	27	21
14	St Andrew Undershaft	9.3	201	0	201	21.6	40	20
15	St Andrew by the Wardrobe	5.6	246	0	246	43.9	11	5
16	St Anne Aldersgate	2.7	142	0	142	52.6	9	6
17	St Anne Blackfriars	11.8	—	—	E429	—	—	—
18	St Antholin	2.6	61	25	86	33.1	36	42
19	St Augustine by St Paul's	1.8	109	0	109	60.6	28	26
20	St Bartholomew by the Exchange	4.1	99	0	99[c]	24.1	24	24
21	St Benet Fink	2.9	113	0	113	39.0	8	7
22	St Benet Gracechurch	1.9	56	0	56	29.5	37	66
23	St Benet Paul's Wharf	5.4	—	—	E138	—	—	—
24	St Benet Sherehog	1.1	30	0	30	27.3	12	40
25	St Botolph Billingsgate	2.6	96	0	96	36.9	28	29
26	St Christopher le Stocks	2.8	63	0	63[d]	22.5	25	40
27	St Clement Eastcheap	1.8	50	0	50	27.8	26	52
28	St Dionis Backchurch	4.8	242	0	242[e]	50.4	55	39
29	St Dunstan in the East	11.8	265	20	285	24.2	65	23
30	St Edmund Lombard Street	2.4	90	0	90	37.5	37	41
31	St Ethelburga	3.3	108	31	139	42.1	11	8
32	St Faith's under St Paul's	5.6	183	0	183	32.7	41	22
33	St Gabriel Fenchurch Street	2.8	76	0	76	27.1	13	17
34	St George Botolph Lane	1.3	43	0	43	33.1	18	42
35	St Gregory by St Paul's	11.4	206	0	206	18.1	69	34
36	St Helen Bishopsgate	7.1	94	0	94	13.2	26	28

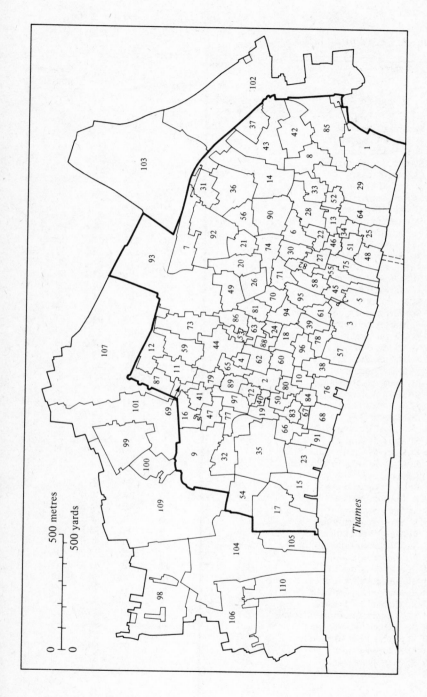

Figure A3.1 London parish boundaries.

Table A3.1. (*continued*)

No.[a]	Parish	Acres[b]	Houses	Tene-ments	Total house-holds	Houses per acre	Substantial households No.	Substantial households %
37	St James Duke Place	3.2	164	0	164	51.3	9	6
38	St James Garlickhithe	3.4	122	18	140	41.2	23	16
39	St John the Baptist	1.9	115	0	115	60.5	5	4
40	St John the Evangelist	0.8	23	0	23	28.8	17	74
41	St John Zachary	2.2	117	0	117	53.2	6	5
42	St Katharine Coleman	6.2	165	64	229	36.9	16	7
43	St Katharine Cree	9.2	—	—	E368	—	—	—
44	St Lawrence Jewry	5.6	144	0	144	25.7	18	13
45	St Lawrence Pountney	2.9	111	11	122	42.1	10	8
46	St Leonard Eastcheap	1.4	73	0	73	52.1	22	30
47	St Leonard Foster Lane	2.5	257	0	257	102.8	48	19
48	St Magnus the Martyr	3.3	100	66	166	50.3	47	28
49	St Margaret Lothbury	3.9	102	15	117	30.0	20	17
50	St Margaret Moses	1.6	61	40	101	63.1	38	38
51	St Margaret New Fish Street	2.0	99	0	99	49.5	16	16
52	St Margaret Pattens	1.6	61	0	61	38.1	9	15
53	St Martin Ironmonger Lane	1.1	41	0	41	37.3	15	37
54	St Martin Ludgate	4.8	228	0	228	47.5	63	28
55	St Martin Orgar	2.7	101	0	101	37.4	33	33
56	St Martin Outwich	3.2	55	0	55	17.2	19	35
57	St Martin Vintry	4.4	263	0	263	59.8	22	8
58	St Mary Abchurch	2.6	112	0	112	43.1	30	27
59	St Mary Aldermanbury	4.4	—	—	E143	—	—	—
60	St Mary Aldermary	2.4	91	0	91	37.9	27	30
61	St Mary Bothaw	1.9	47	0	47	24.7	20	43
62	St Mary le Bow	2.7	93	0	93	34.4	43	46
63	St Mary Colechurch	1.6	46	0	46	28.8	20	44
64	St Mary at Hill	4.4	124	0	124	28.2	23	19
65	St Mary Magdalen Milk Street	1.7	45	0	45	26.5	31	69
66	St Mary Magdalen Old Fish Street	2.4	142	86	228	95.0	17	8
67	St Mary Mounthaw	1.0	55	0	55	55.0	3	6
68	St Mary Somerset	3.6	144	0	144	40.0	12	8
69	St Mary Staining	1.3	45	0	45	34.6	1	2
70	St Mary Woolchurch	2.3	88	0	88	38.3	46	52
71	St Mary Woolnoth	2.6	88	0	88	33.8	52	59
72	St Matthew Friday Street	1.4	54	0	54	38.6	33	61
73	St Michael Bassishaw	5.9	202	0	202	34.2	30	15
74	St Michael Cornhill	3.6	153	12	165[f]	45.8	57	35
75	St Michael Crooked Lane	3.0	115	0	115	38.3	14	12
76	St Michael Queenhithe	3.7	131	200	331	89.5	5	2
77	St Michael Le Querne	1.6	102	0	102	63.8	66	65
78	St Michael Paternoster Royal	2.1	91	0	91	43.3	10	11
79	St Michael Wood Street	2.0	—	—	E101	—	—	—
80	St Michael Bread Street	1.5	77	5	82	54.7	5	6
81	St Mildred Poultry	2.5	99	0	99	39.6	36	36
82	St Nicholas Acon	1.5	56	0	56	37.5	23	41
83	St Nicholas Cole Abbey	1.6	142	0	142	88.8	10	7

No.[a]	Parish	Acres[b]	Houses	Tene-ments	Total house-holds	Houses per acre	Substantial households No.	%
84	St Nicholas Olave	1.4	63	0	63	45.0	16	25
85	St Olave Hart Street	10.3	81	55	136	13.2	33	24
86	St Olave Old Jewry	2.5	60	0	60	24.0	20	33
87	St Olave Silver Street	3.3	124	18	142	43.0	1	1
88	St Pancras Soper Lane	1.2	43	0	43	35.8	24	56
89	St Peter Westcheap	1.6	80	0	80	50.0	32	40
90	St Peter Cornhill	6.0	123	6	129	21.5	77	60
91	St Peter Paul's Wharf	2.5	80	17	97	38.8	26	27
92	St Peter le Poor	9.3	—	—	E126	—	—	—
93	St Stephen Coleman Street	26.7	—	—	E493	—	—	—
94	St Stephen Walbrook	2.8	49	0	49	17.5	30	61
95	St Swithin	3.0	—	—	E126	—	—	—
96	St Thomas the Apostle	2.4	113	0	113	47.1	18	16
97	St Vedast Foster Lane	2.5	128	0	128	51.2	44	34
	Parishes in the Liberties							
98	St Andrew Holborn	20.7	405	0	405	19.6	55	14
99	St Bartholomew the Great	8.9	—	—	E317	—	—	—
100	St Bartholomew the Less	4.2	98	0	98	23.3	14	14
101	St Botolph without Aldersgate	20.0	581	0	581	29.1	—	—
102	St Botolph without Aldgate	38.6	1,248	731	1,979	51.3	13	1
103	St Botolph without Bishopsgate	44.5	336	1,135	1,471	33.1	17	1
104	St Bride Fleet Street	28.7	—	—	E1,413	—	—	—
105	Bridewell Precinct (extra parochial)	5.3	62	14	76	14.3	6	8
106	St Dunstan in the Wast	14.3	518	140	658	46.0	195	30
107	St Giles without Cripplegate	43.7	7	1,196	1,203	27.5	—	—
108	St Olave Southwark (part)	—	—	—	E37	—	—	—
109	St Sepulchre	35.5	—	—	E1,774	—	—	—
110	Whitefriars Precinct	8.5	—	—	E268	—	—	—
111	St George Southwark							
112	St Savour Southwark							
113	St Thomas Southwark							
114	Holy Trinity Minories							

Out-Parishes

115 St Clement Temple Bar
116 St Giles in the Fields
117 St James Clerkenwell
118 St Katharine by the Tower
119 St Leonard Shoreditch
120 St Martin in the Fields
121 St Mary Whitechapel
122 St Magdalen Bermondsey
123 St Mary Savoy

Distant Parishes

124 St Margaret Westminster
125 St Mary Lambeth
126 St Dunstan Stepney
127 St Mary Newington
128 St John Hackney
129 St Mary Redriff (Rotherhithe)
130 St Mary Islington

Notes to Table A3.1 (overleaf)

E – estimated.

Notes:

a. Numbers mainly from Jones and Judges 1935. The parishes are located on Figure A3.1.

b. Acreages from *Index to the Ordnance Survey of the County of Middlesex* (1881).

c. There were 50 shops not included in the total worth £500.

d. There were also shops worth £150.

e. Two or three pages missing. 142 houses enumerated and 100 estimated making 242 on list. Substantial households, 55 out of 142 or 39 per cent.

f. There were also 50 shops not included.

APPENDIX 4

LONDON POPULATION IN 1631 AND HOUSES IN 1638 BY WARDS

Table A4.1. *London population in 1631 and houses in 1638 by wards*

Ward	1631 Population	1638 Houses
Aldersgate	3,595	1,266
Aldgate	4,763	739
Bassishaw	1,006	202
Billingsgate	2,591	451
Bishopsgate	7,688	1,704
Bread Street	2,568	281
Bridge Within	2,392	394
Broad Street	3,503	647
Candlewick	1,696	500
Castle Baynard	4,793	796
Cheap	2,500	439
Coleman Street	2,634	298
Cordwainer	2,238	270
Cornhill	1,439	288
Cripplegate Within	4,231	528
Dowgate	3,516	284
Farringdon Within	8,770	1,589
Langbourn	3,168	839
Lime Street	1,107	—
Queenhithe	3,358	903
Tower	4,248	825
Vintry	2,742	607
Walbrook	2,069	420
St James Duke Place	—	164
Total	76,615	14,434

The names of the parishes contained in each ward are given in Stow 1601.
Sources: 1631 Graunt 1676: II, 405–6. 1638 Table A3.1.

REFERENCES

Full references are given here to all works cited in the notes. A few books and articles of general interest for the history of London have also been included. Abbreviations of journal titles are given in full here.

Abbreviations of journal titles

A.A.G. Bijd.	*A.A.G. Bijdragen*
Ann. Dém. Hist.	*Annales de Démographie Historique*
Annales E.S.C.	*Annales, Economies, Sociétés, Civilisations*
Black. Mag.	*Blackwood's Magazine*
Bull. Centre d'hist. rég. lyon.	*Bulletin du Centre d'historie economique et sociale de la région lyonnaise*
Bull. d'inf.	*Société de Démographie Historique, Bulletin d'information*
Dem.	*Demography*
Econ. Hist. Rev.	*Economic History Review*
Econ. J.	*Economic Journal*
Eug. Qu.	*Eugenics Quarterly*
Guild. Misc.	*Guildhall Miscellany*
Hist. J.	*Historical Journal*
Hum. Biol.	*Human Biology*
J. Brit. Stud.	*Journal of British Studies*
J. Econ. Hist.	*Journal of Economic History*
J. Eur. Econ. Hist.	*Journal of European Economic History*
J. Fam. Hist.	*Journal of Family History*
J. Hist. Med.	*Journal of the History of Medicine*
J. Interdis. Hist.	*Journal of Interdisciplinary History*
J. Roy. Soc. Arts	*Journal of the Royal Society of Arts*
J. Roy. Stat. Soc.	*Journal of the Royal Statistical Society*
L. P. S.	*Local Population Studies*
Lond. J.	*London Journal*
Med. Hist.	*Medical History*
P. & P.	*Past and Present*
Pop.	*Population*
Pop. Bull.	*Population Bulletin of the United Nations*
Pop. Stud.	*Population Studies*
Proc. Hug. Soc.	*Proceedings of the Huguenot Society*
Proc. Roy. Soc.	*Proceedings of the Royal Society*
Proc. Roy. Soc. Med.	*Proceedings of the Royal Society of Medicine*
Trans. Inst. Brit. Geog.	*Transactions of the Institute of British Geographers*
Trans. Roy. Hist. Soc.	*Transactions of the Royal Historical Society*

References

Abrams, P. and Wrigley, E. A. (eds). 1978. *Towns in societies*. Cambridge
Acts of the Privy Council of England, 1630 June–1631 June. London, 1964
Åkerman, S. 1977. 'History and demography: an evaluation of the family reconstitution technique', in Å. E. Andersson and I. Holmberg (eds), *Demographic, economic, and social interaction*, pp. 325–45. Cambridge, Mass.
Andorka, R. 1978. *Determinants of fertility in advanced societies*. London
Appleby, A. B. 1975. 'Nutrition and disease: the case of London, 1550–1750', *J. Interdis. Hist*. vi, 1–22
    1980. 'The disappearance of plague: a continuing puzzle', *Econ. Hist. Rev*. 2nd ser. xxxiii, 161–73
Ashton, R. 1979. *The city and the court 1603–1643*. Cambridge
Baker, D. 1973. *The inhabitants of Cardington in 1782*, Bedfordshire Historical Record Society 1ii
Bardet, J.-P. 1974. 'La démographie des villes de la modernité (XVIe–XVIIIe siècles): mythes et réalités', *Ann. Dém. Hist*., pp. 101–26.
Beier, A. L. 1978. 'Social problems in Elizabethan London', *J. Interdis. Hist*. ix, 203–21
Bell, W. G. 1924. *The great plague in London in 1665*. London
Bennassar, B. 1969. *Valladolid au siècle d'or: une ville de Castille et sa campagne au XVIe siècle*. Paris
Berry, B. M. and Schofield, R. S. 1971. 'Age at baptism in pre-industrial England', *Pop. Stud*. xxv, 453–63
Berthieu, R. 1975. 'Les nourrisons à Cormeilles-en-Parisis (1640–1789)', *Ann. Dém. Hist*., pp. 259–89
Bideau, A. 1973. 'L'envoi des jeunes enfants en nourrice: l'exemple d'une petite ville: Thoissey-en-Dombes 1740–1840', in J. Dupâquier (ed), *Sur la population française au XVIIIe au XIXe siècles: hommage à Marcel Reinhard*, pp. 49–58. Paris
    1976. 'La mortalité des enfants dans la Châtellenie de Thoissey en Dombes – essai de pathologie historique (1670–1840)', *Bull. Centre d'hist. rég. lyon*., pp. 103–42
Biraben, J.-N. 1975–6. *Les hommes et la peste en France et dans les pays européens et mediterranéens*, 2 vols. Paris
Bonar, J. 1931. *Theories of population from Raleigh to Arthur Young*. London
Bourgeois-Pichat, J. 1951. 'La mesure de la mortalité infantile', *Pop*. vi, 233–48, 459–80
    1952. 'An analysis of infant mortality', *Pop. Bull*. ii, 1–14
Bradley, L. 1977a. 'Some medical aspects of plague', in *The plague reconsidered, L. P. S.* Supplement, pp. 11–23
    1977b. 'The geographical spread of plague', in *The plague reconsidered, L. P. S.* Supplement, pp. 127–32
Brenner, R. 1973. 'The civil war politics of London's merchant community', *P. & P.* lviii, 53–107
Brett-James, N. G. 1935. *The growth of Stuart London*. London
Brooke, C. N. L. and Keir, G. 1975. *London 800–1216: the shaping of a city*. London
Brownlee, J. 1925. 'The health of London in the eighteenth century', *Proc. Roy. Soc. Med.* xviii, 73–85, epidemiology section
Burke, A. M. (ed). 1914. *Memorials of St Margaret's church Westminster: the parish registers 1539–1660*. London
Burke, P. 1977. 'Popular culture in seventeenth-century London', *Lond. J*. iii, 143–62
Burn, J. S. 1846. *The history of the French, Walloon, Dutch and other foreign and protestant refugees settled in England from the reign of Henry VIII to the revocation of the Edict of Nantes*. London
Cantrelle, P. 1975. 'Mortality: levels, patterns, and trends', in J. C. Caldwell (ed), *Population growth and socioeconomic change in West Africa*, pp. 98–118. New York
Chambers, J. D. 1972. *Population, economy, and society in pre-industrial England*. London
Charbonneau, H. 1970. *Tourouvre-au-Perche aux XVIIe et XVIIIe siècles*. Paris
    1975. *Vie et mort des nos ancêtres*. Montreal
Clarkson, L. A. 1975. *Death, disease and famine in pre-industrial England*. Dublin

References

Coale, A. J. and Demeny, P. 1966. *Regional model life tables and stable populations*. Princeton, N.J.

Corfield, P. 1976. 'Urban development in England and Wales in the sixteenth and seventeenth centuries', in D. C. Coleman and A. H. John (eds), *Trade, government and economy in pre-industrial England: essays presented to F. J. Fisher*, pp. 214–47. London

1977. 'Economic growth and change in seventeenth-century English towns', in P. Clark (ed), *The traditional community under stress*, pp. 31–71. Milton Keynes

Cox, J. C. 1910. *The parish registers of England*. London

1913. *Churchwardens' Accounts*. London

Creighton, C. 1891a. 'The population of old London', *Black. Mag.* cxlix, 477–96

1891b. *History of epidemics in Britain*, vol. I. Cambridge. Reprinted ed D. E. C. Eversley (London, 1965)

Cressy, D. 1980. *Literacy and the social order: reading and writing in Tudor and Stuart England*. Cambridge

Cullen, M. J. 1975. *The statistical movement in early Victorian Britain*. Hassocks, Sussex

Cunningham, C. 1977. 'Christ's Hospital: infant and child mortality in the sixteenth century', *L. P. S.* xviii, 37–42

Dale, T. C. (ed). 1931. *The inhabitants of London in 1638*, 2 vols. London

Darby, H. C. 1973. 'The age of the improver: 1600–1800', in H. C. Darby (ed), *A new historical geography of England*, pp. 302–88. Cambridge

Davis, E. J. 1924. 'The transformation of London', in R. W. Seton-Watson (ed), *Tudor studies presented to Albert Frederick Pollard*, pp 287–314. London

Deniel, R. and Henry, L. 1965. 'La population d'un vilage du Nord de la France: Saignhin-en-Mélantois, de 1665 à 1851', *Pop.* xx, 563–602

De Vries, J. 1974. *The Dutch rural economy in the golden age, 1500–1700*. New Haven

1978. 'Barges and capitalism: passenger transportation in the Dutch economy, 1632–1839', *A.A.G. Bijd.* xxi, 33–398

Deyon, P. 1967. *Amiens, capitale provinciale*. Paris

Dinet, D. 1969. 'Quatre paroisses du Tonnerrois', *Ann. Dém. Hist.*, pp. 62–84

Eaton, J. W. and Mayer, A. J. 1953. 'The social biology of very high fertility among the Hutterites: the demography of a unique population', *Hum. Biol.* xxv, 206–64

Elliott, V. B. 1978. 'Mobility and marriage in pre-industrial England', Cambridge University Ph.D. thesis

Eversley, D. E. C. 1959. *Social theories of fertility and the Malthusian debate*. Oxford

Farr, W. 1885. *Vital statistics*, ed N. A. Humphreys. London

Finlay, R. A. P. 1978a. 'The accuracy of the London parish registers, 1580–1653', *Pop. Stud.* xxxii, 95–112

1978b. 'Gateways to death? London child mortality experience, 1570–1653', *Ann. Dém. Hist.*, pp. 105–34

1979. 'Population and fertility in London, 1580–1650', *J. Fam. Hist.* iv, 26–38

1981. 'The early modern city: further comments', *P. & P.*, forthcoming

Firth, C. H. and Rait. R. S. (eds). 1911. *Acts and ordinances of the Interregnum 1642–1660*, 3 vols. London

Fisher, F. J. 1935. 'The development of the London food market, 1540–1640', *Econ. Hist. Rev.* v, no. 2, 46–64

1962. 'The development of London as a centre of conspicuous consumption in the sixteenth and seventeenth centuries', in E. M. Carus-Wilson (ed), *Essays in economic history*, vol. II, pp. 197–207. London

1968. 'The growth of London', in E. W. Ives (ed), *The English revolution, 1600–1660*, pp. 76–86. London

1976. 'London as an "engine of economic growth"', in P. Clark (ed), *The early modern town*, pp. 205–15. London

Flandrin, J.-L. 1979. *Families in former times: kinship, household and sexuality*. Cambridge

Fleury, M. and Henry, L. 1956. *Des registres paroissiaux à l'histoire de la population: manuel de dépouillement et d'exploitation de l'état civil ancien*. Paris

References

Flinn, M. W. 1974. 'The stabilization of mortality in pre-industrial Western Europe', *J. Eur. Econ. Hist.* iii, 285–318

Foord, A. S. 1910. *Springs, streams, and spas of London.* London

Forbes, T. R. 1971. *Chronicle from Aldgate: life and death in Shakespeare's London.* New Haven

1976. 'By what disease or casualty: the changing face of death in London', *J. Hist. Med.*, xxxi, 395–420

Foster, C. W. 1926. *The state of the church*, Lincoln Record Society xxiii

François, E. 1975. 'La population de Coblence au XVIIIe siècle: déficit démographique et immigration dans une ville de résidence', *Ann. Dém. Hist.*, pp. 291–341

Freshfield, E. (ed). 1885. *Accomptes of the churchwardens of the paryshe of St Christopher's in London 1575 to 1662.* Privately printed

1887a. *Some remarks upon the book of records and history of the parish of St Stephen Coleman Street, in the City of London.* Westminster

1887b. *The vestry minute books of the parish of St Margaret Lothbury in the City of London 1571 to 1677.* Privately printed

1890. *The vestry minute book of the parish of St Bartholomew Exchange in the City of London 1567–1676.* Privately printed

Galliano, P. 1966. 'La mortalité infantile (indigènes et nourrissons) dans la banlieue sud de Paris à la fin du XVIIIe siècle (1774–1794), *Ann. Dém. Hist.*, pp. 137–77

Ganiage, J. 1963. *Trois villages d'Ile-de-France au XVIIIe siècle.* Paris

1973. 'Nourrissons parisiens en Beauvaisis', in J. Dupâquier (ed), *Sur la population française au XVIIIe et au XIXe siècles: hommage à Marcel Reinhard*, pp. 271–90. Paris

Garden, M. 1970. *Lyon et les Lyonnais au XVIIIe siècle.* Paris

Gautier, E. and Henry, L. 1958. *La population de Crulai paroisse normand.* Paris

George, M. D. 1965. *London life in the eighteenth century*, 2nd edn. Harmondsworth, Middx.

Giachetti, J.-C. and Tyvaert, M. 1969. Argenteuil (1740–1790)', *Ann. Dém. Hist.*, pp. 40–61

Gibson, E. 1713. *Codex iuris ecclesiastici anglicani.* London

Girard, P. 1959. 'Aperçus de la démographie de Sotteville-lès-Rouen vers la fin du XVIIIe siècle', *Pop.* xiv, 485–508

Glass, D. V. 1956. 'Some aspects of the development of demography', *J. Roy. Soc. Arts* civ, 854–69

1963. 'John Graunt and his *Natural and political observations*', *Proc. Roy. Soc.* ser. B clix, 2–37

1965. 'Two papers on Gregory King', in D. V. Glass and D. E. C. Eversley (eds), *Population in history*, pp. 159–220. London

(ed) 1966. *London inhabitants within the walls 1695*, London Record Society ii

1972. 'Notes on the demography of London at the end of the seventeenth century', in D. V. Glass and R. Revelle (eds), *Population and social change*, pp. 275–85. London

1973. *Numbering the people.* Farnborough, Hants.

1976. 'Socio-economic status and occupations in the City of London at the end of the seventeenth century', in P. Clark (ed), *The early modern town*, pp. 216–32. London

Goubert, P. 1972. 'Legitimate fertility and infant mortality in France during the eighteenth century: a comparison', in D. V. Glass and R. Revelle (eds), *Population and social change*, pp. 321–30. London

Graunt, J. 1662. *Natural and political observations made upon the bills of mortality.* London. Reprinted in P. Laslett (ed), *The earliest classics: John Graunt and Gregory King* (Farnborough, Hants., 1973)

1676. *Natural and political observations made upon the bills of mortality*, 5th edn. London. Reprinted in C. H. Hull (ed), *The economic writings of Sir William Petty*, 2 vols. (Cambridge, 1899)

Greenwood, M. 1948. *Medical statistics from Graunt to Farr.* Cambridge

Griffith, G. T. 1929. 'Rickman's second series of eighteenth century population figures', *J. Roy. Stat. Soc.* xcii, 256–63

Guildhall Library. 1967–72. *Parish registers: a handlist*, 3 parts. London

Hair, P. E. H. 1966. 'Bridal pregnancy in rural England in earlier centuries', *Pop. Stud.* xx, 233–43
 1970. 'Bridal pregnancy in earlier rural England further examined', *Pop. Stud.* xxiv, 59–70
Hajnal, J. 1965. 'European marriage patterns in perspective', in D. V. Glass and D. E. C. Eversley (eds), *Population in history*, pp. 101–43. London
Hélin, E. 1963. *La démographie de Liège au XVIIe et au XVIIIe siècle.* Brussels
Helleiner, K. F. 1965. 'The vital revolution reconsidered', in D. V. Glass and D. E. C. Eversley (eds), *Population in history*, pp. 79–86. London
Henripin, J. 1954. *La population canadienne au debut du XVIIIe siècle.* Paris
Henry, L. 1956. *Anciennes familles genevoises.* Paris
 1961. 'Some data on natural fertility', *Eug. Qu.* viii, 81–91
 1967. *Manuel de démographie historique.* Geneva
 1968. 'The verification of data in historical demography', *Pop. Stud.* xxii, 61–81
 1976. 'Étude de la mortalité à partir de la reconstitution des familles', *Bull. d'inf.* xviii, 4–20
Herlan, R. W. 1979. 'Poor relief in London during the English revolution', *J. Brit. Stud.* xviii, 30–51
Hill, C. 1956. *Economic problems of the church from Archbishop Whitgift to the Long Parliament.* Oxford
Hofsten, E. and Lundström, H. 1976. *Swedish population history: main trends from 1750 to 1970.* Stockholm
Hollingsworth, M. F. and T. H. 1971. 'Plague mortality rates by age and sex in the parish of St Botolph's without Bishopsgate, London, 1603', *Pop. Stud.* xxv, 131–46
Hollingsworth, T. H. 1977. 'Mortality in the British peerage families since 1600', *Pop.* xxxii, numéro spécial, 323–52
Holmes, G. S. 1977. 'Gregory King and the social structure of pre-industrial England', *Trans. Roy. Hist. Soc.* 5th ser. xxvii, 41–68
Houdaille, J. 1967. 'La population de Boulay (Moselle) avant 1850', *Pop.* xxii, 1055–84
Hull, C. H. (ed). 1899. *The economic writings of Sir William Petty*, 2 vols. Cambridge
Hutchins, B. L. 1899. 'Notes towards the history of London wages', *Econ. J.* ix, 599–605
Hyrenius, H. 1958. 'Fertility and reproduction in a Swedish population group without family limitation', *Pop. Stud.* xii, 121–30
Imhof, A. E. and Lindskog, B. J. 1974. 'Les causes de mortalité en Suède et en Finlande entre 1749 et 1773', *Annales E.S.C.* xxix, 915–33
Jones, A. T. 1887. *Notes on the early days of Stepney meeting (1664 to 1689).* London
Jones, E. 1980. 'London in the early seventeenth century: an ecological approach', *Lond. J.* vi, 123–33
Jones, J. 1579. *The arte and science of preserving bodie and soule in healthe, wisdome and catholike religion.* London
Jones, P. E. and Judges, A. V. 1935. 'London population in the late seventeenth century', *Econ. Hist. Rev.* vi, 45–63
Jones, R. E. 1976. 'Infant mortality in rural north Shropshire, 1561–1810', *Pop. Stud.* xxx, 305–17
Jouan, M.-H. 1969. 'Les originalités démographiques d'un bourg artisanal normand au XVIIIe siècle: Villedieu-les-Poëles (1711–1790)', *Ann. Dém. Hist.*, pp. 87–124
Kennedy, W. P. M. 1924. *Elizabethan episcopal administration*, Alcuin Club Collections xxvi, xxvii and xxviii
Ketton-Cremer, R. W. 1957. *Norfolk assembly.* London
King, G. 1972. 'Kashnor Manuscript', in J. Thirsk and J. P. Cooper (eds), *Seventeenth century economic documents*, pp. 790–8. Oxford
 1973a. *Natural and political observations and conclusions upon the state and condition of England 1696.* London, 1802, reprinted in P. Laslett (ed), *The earliest classics: John Graunt and Gregory King.* Farnborough, Hants
 1973b. 'L. C. C. Burns Journal', in P. Laslett (ed), *The earliest classics: John Graunt and Gregory King.* Farnborough, Hants
Kirk, R. E. G. and E. F. (eds). 1900–7. *Returns of aliens in the city and suburbs of London from Henry VIII to James I*, Huguenot Society Publications x, 4 vols.

References

Knodel, J. 1968. 'Infant mortality and fertility in three Bavarian villages: an analysis of family histories from the 19th century', *Pop. Stud.* xxii, 197–218

Knodel, J. and Kintner, H. 1977. 'The impact of breast feeding patterns on the biometric analysis of infant mortality', *Dem.* xiv, 391–409

Knodel, J. and Shorter, E. 1976. 'The reliability of family reconstitution data in German village genealogies (ortssippenbücher)', *Ann. Dém. Hist.*, pp. 115–54

Knodel, J. and van de Walle, E. 1967. 'Breast feeding, fertility and infant mortality: an analysis of some early German data', *Pop. Stud.* xxi, 109–31

Krause, J. T. 1965. 'The changing adequacy of English registration, 1690–1837', in D. V. Glass and D. E. C. Eversley (eds), *Population in history*, pp. 379–92. London

Kuczynski, R. R. 1938. 'British demographers' opinions on fertility, 1660–1760', in L. Hogben (ed), *Political arithmetic*, pp. 283–327. London

Lachiver, M. 1969a. *La population de Meulan du XVIIe au XIXe siècle*. Paris

1969b. 'Une étude et quelques esquisses', *Ann. Dém. Hist.*, pp. 215–40

Langton, J. 1975. 'Residential patterns in pre-industrial cities: some case studies from seventeenth-century Britain', *Trans. Inst. Brit. Geog.* lxv, 1–27

Larkin, J. F. and Hughes, P. L. (eds). 1973. *Stuart Royal Proclamations*, vol. I. Oxford

Laslett, P. 1972. 'Introduction: the history of the family', in P. Laslett and R. Wall (eds), *Household and family in past time*, pp. 1–89. Cambridge

1977. *Family life and illicit love in earlier generations*. Cambridge

Law, C. M. 1969. 'Local censuses in the 18th century', *Pop. Stud.* xxviii, 87–100

Lee, R. D. 1974. 'Estimating series of vital rates and age structures from baptisms and burials: a new technique with applications to pre-industrial England', *Pop. Stud.* xxviii, 495–512

Leonard, E. M. 1900. *The early history of English poor relief.* Cambridge

Levine, D. 1977. *Family formation in an age of nascent capitalism*. New York

Macfarlane, A. D. J. 1970. *The family life of Ralph Josselin.* Cambridge

McKeown, T. 1976. *The modern rise of population.* London

McLaren, D. 1974. 'The Marriage Act of 1653: its influence on the parish registers', *Pop. Stud.* xxviii, 319–27

1978. 'Fertility, infant mortality breast feeding in the seventeenth century', *Med. Hist.* xxii, 378–96

McNeill, W. H. 1977. *Plagues and peoples.* Oxford

Maitland, W. 1756. *The history and survey of London*, 2 vols. London

Marsh, J. B. 1871. *The story of Harecourt.* London

Marshall, J. 1832. *Mortality of the metropolis.* London

Moens, W. J. C. 1884. *The marriage, baptismal and burial registers, 1571 to 1874, of the Dutch Reformed Church, Austin Friars, London.* Privately printed

1896–9. *The registers of the French Church, Threadneedle Street, London*, Huguenot Society Publications ix and xiii

Monter, E. W. 1979. 'Historical demography and religious history in sixteenth-century Geneva', *J. Interdis. Hist.* ix, 399–422

Morris, C. 1971. 'The plague in Britain', *Hist. J.* xiv, 205–24

New, J. F. H. 1964. *Anglican and puritan: the basis of their opposition 1558–1640.* London

Nuttall, G. F. 1957. *Visible Saints: the congregational way 1640–1660.* Oxford

Overall, W. H. and H. C. (eds). 1878. *Analytical index to the series of records known as the Remembrancia A.D. 1579–1664.* London

Patten, J. 1978. *English towns 1500–1700.* Folkestone, Kent

Pearl, V. 1961. *London and the outbreak of the puritan revolution.* London

1979. 'Change and stability in seventeenth-century London', *Lond. J.* v, 3–34

Perrenoud, A. 1975. 'L'inégalité sociale devant la mort à Genève au XVIIe siècle', *Pop.* xxx, numéro spécial, 221–43

1976. 'Variables sociales en démographie urbaine: l'exemple de Genève au XVIIIe siècle', in M. Garden (ed), *Démographie urbaine XVe–XXe siècle*, pp. 143–72. Lyons

1978. 'La mortalité à Genève de 1625 à 1825', *Ann. Dém. Hist.*, pp. 209–33

Perrot, J.-C. 1970. *Genèse d'une ville moderne: Caen au XVIIIe siècle*, 2 vols. Paris

Peter, J.-P. 1975. 'Disease and the sick at the end of the eighteenth century', in R. Forster and O. Ranum (eds), *Biology of man in history*, pp. 81–124. Baltimore

Petraccone, C. 1974. *Napoli dal cinquento all' ottocento: problemi di storia demografica e sociale*. Naples

Phaire, T. 1553. *The boke of chyldren*. Ed A. V. Neale and H. R. E. Wallis (Edinburgh, 1955)

Polton, J.-C. 1969. 'Coulommiers et Chailly-en-Brie (1557–1715)', *Ann. Dém. Hist.*, pp. 14–32

Potter, R. G., Jr. 1963. 'Birth intervals: structure and change', *Pop. Stud.* xvii, 155–66

Power, M. J. 1972. 'East London housing in the seventeenth century', in P. Clark and P. Slack (eds), *Crisis and order in English towns 1500–1700*, pp. 237–62. London

1978a. 'The east and west in early-modern London', in E. W. Ives, R. J. Knecht and J. J. Scarisbrick (eds), *Wealth and power in Tudor England: essays presented to S. T. Bindoff*, pp. 167–85. London

1978b. 'Shadwell: the development of a London suburban community in the seventeenth century', *Lond. J.* iv, 29–46

Prest, W. R. 1972. *The Inns of Court under Elizabeth I and the early Stuarts*. London

1976. 'Stability and change in Old and New England: Clayworth and Dedham', *J. Interdis. Hist.* vi, 359–74

Privy Council Registers, vol. III, 1 March–9 August 1638 (facsimile reprint, London, 1967)

Ramsay, G. D. 1975. *The City of London in international politics at the accession of Elizabeth Tudor*. Manchester

1978. 'The recruitment and fortunes of some London freemen in the mid-sixteenth century', *Econ. Hist. Rev.* 2nd ser. xxxi, 526–40

Rapp, R. T. 1976. *Industry and economic decline in seventeenth-century Venice*. Cambridge, Mass.

Razzell, P. E. 1972. 'The evaluation of baptism as a form of birth registration through cross-matching census and parish register data', *Pop. Stud.* xxvi, 121–46

1977. *The conquest of smallpox*. Firle, Sussex

Ringrose, D. 1973. 'The impact of a new capital city: Madrid, Toledo and New Castile, 1560–1660', *J. Econ. Hist.* xxxiii, 761–91

Robert, P. 1969. 'Rumont (1720–1790)', *Ann. Dém. Hist.*, pp. 32–40

Russell, J. C. 1948. *British medieval population*. Albuquerque, N.M.

Schofield, R. S. 1977. 'An anatomy of an epidemic: Colyton, November 1645 to November 1646', in *The plague reconsidered, L. P. S.* Supplement, pp. 95–126

Schofield, R. S. and Wrigley, E. A. 1979. 'Infant and child mortality in England in the late Tudor and early Stuart period', in C. Webster (ed), *Health, medicine and mortality in the sixteenth century*, pp. 61–95. Cambridge

Scouloudi, I. 1938. 'Alien immigration into and alien communities in London, 1558–1640', *Proc. Hug. Soc.* xvi, 27–49

Seaver, P. S. 1970. *The puritan lectureships: the politics of religious dissent 1560–1662*. Stanford, Calif.

Sharlin, A. 1978. 'Natural decrease in early modern cities: a reconsideration', *P. & P.* lxxix, 126–38

Shaw, W. A. 1900. *A history of the English church during the civil wars and under the Commonwealth 1640–1660*, 2 vols. London

Shrewsbury, J. F. D. 1970. *A history of bubonic plague in the British Isles*. Cambridge

Sjoberg, G. 1960. *The preindustrial city*. New York

Slack, P. 1977. 'The local incidence of epidemic disease: the case of Bristol 1540–1650', in *The plague reconsidered, L. P. S.* Supplement, pp. 49–62

Smith, D. S. 1977. 'A homeostatic demographic regime: patterns in West European family reconstitution studies', in R. D. Lee (ed), *Population patterns in the past*, pp. 19–51. New York

Smith, D. S. and Hindus, M. S. 1975. 'Premarital pregnancy in America 1640–1971: an overview and interpretation', *J. Interdis. Hist.* v, 537–70

181

References

Smith, R. M. 1978. 'Population and its geography in England 1500–1730', in R. A. Dodgshon and R. A. Butlin (eds), *An historical geography of England and Wales*, pp. 199–237. London

Smith, S. R. 1973. 'The social and geographical origins of the London apprentices, 1630–1660', *Guild. Misc.* iv, 195–206

Smith, T. L. and Zopf, P. E., Jr. 1970. *Demography: principles and methods*. Philadelphia

Soliday, G. L. 1974. *A community in conflict: Frankfurt society in the seventeenth and early eighteenth centuries*. Hanover, N. H.

Spalding, R. 1975. *The improbable puritan: a life of Bulstrode Whitelocke 1605–1675*. London

Steel, D. J. 1968/73. *National index of parish registers*, vols. I and II. London

Stone, L. 1965. *The crisis of the aristocracy 1558–1641*. Oxford

1977. *The family, sex and marriage in England 1500–1800*. London

Stow, J. 1601. *A survey of London*. London. Ed C. L. Kingsford, 2 vols. (Oxford, 1908)

Sunderland, S. 1915. *Old London's spas, baths, and wells*. London

Supple, B. E. 1959. *Commercial crisis and change in England 1600–1642*. Cambridge

Sutherland, I. 1963. 'John Graunt: a tercentenary tribute', *J. Roy. Stat. Soc.* Ser. A cxxvi, 537–56

1972. 'When was the great plague? Mortality in London 1563 to 1665', in D. V. Glass and R. Revelle (eds), *Population and social change*, pp. 287–320. London

Tate, W. E. 1969. *The parish chest*, 3rd edn. Cambridge

Terrisse, M. 1961. 'Un faubourg du Havre: Ingouville', *Pop.* xvi, 285–300

Thomas, K. V. 1971. *Religion and the decline of magic*. London

Thompson, R. 1974. 'Seventeenth century English and colonial sex ratios: a postscript', *Pop. Stud.* xxviii, 153–65

Tolmie, M. 1977. *The triumph of the saints: the separate churches of London 1616–1649*. Cambridge

Valmary, P. 1965. *Familles paysannes au XVIIIe siècle en Bas-Quercy*. Paris

Van de Walle, E. and Preston, S. H. 1974. 'Mortalité de l'enfance au XIXe siècle à Paris et dans le département de la Seine', *Pop.* xxix, 89–107

Van der Woude, A. M. and Mentink, G. J. 1966. 'La population de Rotterdam au XVIIe et au XVIIIe siècle', *Pop.* xxi, 1165–90

Wagner, A. R. 1960. *English genealogy*. Oxford

Wall, R. 1978. 'The age at leaving home', *J. Fam. Hist.* iii, 181–202

Weber, A. F. 1899. *The growth of cities in the nineteenth century*. New York

West, F. 1974. 'Infant mortality in the East Fen parishes of Leake and Wrangle', *L. P. S.* xiii, 41–4

Westergaard, H. 1932. *Contributions to the history of statistics*. London

Widen, L. 1975. 'Mortality and causes of death in Sweden during the 18th century', *Stat. Tids.* 3rd ser. xiii, 93–104

Willcox, W. F. 1940. *Studies in American demography*. Ithaca, N.Y.

Wilson, F. P. 1927. *The plague in Shakespeare's London*. Oxford

Wrigley, E. A. 1961. *Industrial growth and population change*. Cambridge

1966a. 'Family limitation in pre-industrial England', *Econ. Hist. Rev.* 2nd ser. xix, 82–109

(ed) 1966b, *An introduction to English historical demography*. London

1966c. 'Family reconstitution', in E. A. Wrigley (ed), *An introduction to English historical demography*, pp. 96–159. London

1967. 'A simple model of London's importance in changing English society and economy 1650–1750', *P. & P.* xxxvii, 44–70

1969. *Population and history*. London

1972a. Mortality in pre-industrial England: the example of Colyton, Devon, over three centuries', in D. V. Glass and R. Revelle (eds), *Population and social change*, pp. 243–73. London

1972b. 'Some problems of family reconstitution using English parish register material: the example of Colyton', *Third International Conference of Economic History, Munich 1965*, pp. 199–221. Paris

182

1977. 'Births and baptisms: the use of Anglican baptism registers as a source of information about numbers of births in England before the beginning of civil registration', *Pop. Stud.* xxxi, 281–311

INDEX

Figures in *italic type* indicate graphs, maps or statistical tables. Modern authors are only included where their opinions are quoted as part of the argument in the text or footnotes.